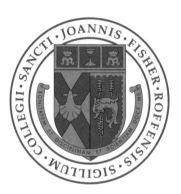

Lavery Library

St. John Fisher College

Rochester, New York

Three Faces of Love

Three Faces of Love

Rolf M. Johnson

NORTHERN ILLINOIS UNIVERSITY PRESS   DeKalb

Library of Congress Cataloging-in-Publication Data

Johnson, Rolf M.

Three faces of love / Rolf M. Johnson.

p. cm.

Includes bibliographical references and index.

ISBN 0-87580-270-2 (alk. paper)

1. Love. I. Title.

BD436.J64 2000

128'.46—dc21   00-037996

Chapter 1 of this book is an expanded version of Johnson's "The Meaning of 'Love'" article that was published in 1988 as a disk supplement to *Philosophy & Theology* (Disk Supplement #1: "Issues in the Philosophy of Sex & Love," pp. 22–29). Used with permission. "A Third Body", from *Loving a Woman in Two Worlds* by Robert Bly, copyright © 1985 by Robert Bly is used by permission of Doubleday, a division of Random House, Inc. "A Marriage" and "The Wife" by Robert Creeley from *Collected Poems of Robert Creeley, 1945–1975*, pp. 170, 252 (copyright © 1983 The Regents of the University of California) are reprinted with permission of the University of California Press. Excerpts from "The Holy Longing" by Goethe, translated by Robert Bly in *News of the Universe: Poems of Twofold Consciousness* (copyright © by Robert Bly 1980) are reprinted with permission of Sierra Club Books. A portion of "Please Call Me By My True Names" is reprinted from *Call Me By My True Names: The Collected Poems of Thich Nhat Hanh* (1999) by Thich Nhat Hanh with permission of Parallax Press, Berkeley, California. Excerpts from *Teachings on Love* (1998) by Thich Nhat Hanh are reprinted with permission of Parallax Press, Berkeley, California (510/525–0101). John Myne's and Coleman Barks's translation of Maulana Jalal al-Din Rumi's Quatrain 1246 from *Open Secrets: Versions of Rumi* is reprinted with permission of its publisher: it was originally published by Threshold Books, 139 Main Street, Brattleboro, Vt. 05301. John Knoepfle's translation of Cesar Vallejo's "Agape" from *Neruda and Vallejo: Selected Poems*, edited by Robert Bly (1971, pp. 194–95) is reprinted with permission of Robert Bly and Beacon Press, Boston, Mass.

Dedicated to the memory of Donna Datko Johnson

Contents

Acknowledgments

❖ A work so long in the writing has acquired many debts. I would like to express my appreciation, first, to three of my colleagues in the Department of Philosophy and Humanistic Studies at Western Connecticut State University: Kristin Aronson, Terry Flynn, and James Munz. Each has read my manuscript at least three times in various incarnations, offering innumerable suggestions and criticism. In the fall of 1997 our philosophy reading group at Western devoted several weeks to my work in progress. As I recall, the members who attended regularly were once again Terry Flynn and James Munz, together with Thomas Doyle, Robert Krause, Frank McClusky, and William Spontak. A similar thank you is due fellow members of the Connecticut Society for Asian and Comparative Philosophy—Helen Browne, Robert Browne, Hope Fitz, Kristin Forbath, and Joseph Mckeon—for listening and reflecting upon my presentation of several portions of this work. I owe a special debt to Irving Singer for reading and commenting upon much earlier versions of Chapter 1 and the section devoted to his work now in Chapter 5. I have benefited also from the comments of Rita DeBruyne, Joel Marks, and Margaret Evans, who all read the entire manuscript and shared their reactions.

The students in my Philosophy of Love course over the past several years have read versions of this work, offering their insights and providing me the opportunity to find how it works as an undergraduate text. I have benefited as well from the hundreds of students over the years who have taken my freshman humanities course, Love in Western Civilization. I would especially like to thank the otherwise forgotten student who asked the question that gave rise to this project.

Less directly, I wish to express my gratitude to my three favorite psychotherapists—Jean Getoff, Diane Feinberg, and John Pierrakos—from whom I have learned much concerning the nature of love (and the nature of me). A similar acknowledgment, and for the same reasons, must be extended to numerous anonymous friends at various twelve-step meetings in and around Danbury, Connecticut. The wisdom and honesty of these people has added significantly to my understanding of love.

A special appreciation goes to all those friends and acquaintances, present and past, with whom I have discussed matters relating to the subject of this book, even if they are too numerous to name. Paramount among them are Kristin Aronson, Rita DeBruyne, Terry Flynn, together with Lewis Camp, Bill Quinnell, Ingrid Pruss, and Wallace Wold. I thank them all for years of fruitful sharing, both personal and philosophic. Without these friends of heart and word, I cannot imagine how I might have thought of love (or even who I would now be).

My editor at NIU Press, Martin Johnson, has made many helpful and perceptive suggestions, as have the several anonymous readers to whom my manuscript was sent by NIU and other publishers. Thanks are due for their praise, criticism, and numerable suggestions. I suspect I learned the most from the one who praised the least, but I have benefited from the comments of all of them.

Finally, I wish to express my deepest gratitude and appreciation to my wife, Beverly Dumonski, for being herself and for providing me the best opportunity ever to practice all three loves.

Three Faces of Love

Introduction

❖   Some twenty years ago, near the end of a course I was teaching on the history of the idea of love, a student asked: "I know we've studied all these theories, but what is love, really?" At a loss and stalling for time, I reminded him of Plato's theory, answers found in the Bible, and Freud's view of the matter. But the student was not going to let me off. He wanted to know what love really is. Finally I told him I would think the matter over and respond to his question the following night. I spent the next day sketching an outline of a theory of love, quite different, as it happens, from the one contained in this book. Evidently I enjoyed the task, because I have been working on it ever since.

Not that I am going to tell you what love *really* is. Rather, the central concern of the present study is the less ambitious matter of what the word "love" means. Although not opposed in principle to what Medieval philosophers called realism (the belief that there are real meanings to concepts independent of the history and conventions of natural languages), the approach taken here will be more nominalistic, almost Wittgensteinian. The goal is to express in words, as clearly and systematically as I can, what the concept "love" means, in all its varied senses, taking as a guide its use both in everyday speech and in the history of theoretical reflections on the subject. The approach will not be strictly Wittgensteinian, however, because it seems there is more than just a family resemblance between the senses of "love" that we shall be examining. Nor am I committed to the theory of those Wittgensteinians who hold that the meaning of a word simply is its use in the language. Indeed, I do not subscribe to any particular theory of meaning; but I will be following the common philosophical and lexicographical principle that one of the clearest indicators of the meaning of a word or concept is how it is used.

Throughout most of this work I will ignore the distinction sometimes made between words and concepts—that words are specific to the languages in which they occur whereas concepts are more universal and common to different languages—and will sometimes speak of the word "love," sometimes of the concept. Only near the end of our journey will the question be addressed as to whether the analysis in which we have been engaged applies to the English word alone or is of more universal significance. Every effort will be made, however, to make clear when we are considering the meaning of the word or concept "love" and when our subject is love itself. We shall be concerned with both throughout, moving back and forth between them on nearly every page; for if "love" has more than one primary sense (as I shall maintain), these different senses must correspond to distinguishable forms of loving. Thus, while conceptual clarification is this work's central objective, frequent excursions will be made along the way into matters psychological, ethical, metaphysical, and theological, as we attempt to uncover the phenomena to which the concept points.

Often, when theorists undertake an investigation of this subject, they limit their inquiry to a specific kind of love such as romance, friendship, or neighbor love or to some more encompassing category such as personal love. This, decidedly, is not the intent here. I wish to investigate the full range of "love's" meanings. In my view, it is more profitable to scrutinize specific types of love after the generic concept has been clarified. Particularly troubling is the tendency to use the word "love" as if it meant simply "romantic love," or to treat this complex and rather peculiar form of love as a kind of paradigm for love in general.

What follows is a new typology of love, a proposal for classifying both the ways in which we love and the range of meanings of the concept. The most familiar ways of dividing love into types are those based on major historical notions such as "eros," "*philia*," "agape," "*caritas*," "courtly love," and "Romantic love" (love as conceived by the Romantics) and those based on ordinary language distinctions such as "friendship," "neighbor love," "romantic love," "mother love," "filial love," and so on. Both these approaches are useful, the first especially when the investigation is historical in nature. The second provides insights into distinctions that already are part of our language, thereby enabling us to use it with greater intelligence and precision.

My own intention in offering a typology is more analytic than historical and springs from the wish to dig deeper than the distinctions already embedded in language. The Greek concepts mentioned above have sometimes been used with this intention as well but with less comprehensive results and without penetrating as deeply as will be attempted here into the underlying structure of love. My aim is to create a system of classification that embraces all that we call "love"—from simple attractions to exalted passions, from self-sacrificial giving to all-consuming obsession, and much else besides. Historical concerns, however, will never be far away, since any analysis of the concept that does not embrace within its range of meaning all of the major historical ideals mentioned above must be considered inadequate.

There are those who are opposed to philosophical or scientific investigations of love on the grounds that the subject is so personal and subjective neither reason nor research can shed much light on it—or even that love itself, or our ability to practice and enjoy it, may be harmed by rational inquiry. Both of these concerns have merit. Our experience of love is highly personal. Yet writings on love across the ages and from a wide variety of cultures demonstrate how similarly lovers express the feelings and experiences they consider so unique. Still, it is wise to recognize that our ways of thinking and feeling about love have been shaped by personal experience and that any systematic reflections on the subject are bound to be influenced by the theorist's personal history. One may attempt to disguise the fact by using objective-sounding language or references to scholarly works or by citing empirical research, but regardless of attempts to conceal it we all see love through the filter of our own life experience, however much expanded by imagination, reflection, and vicarious experience.

There is merit as well to the charge that love's nature is not adequately revealed through empirical generalizations and conceptual analysis, which are necessarily external to love itself. The heart does have reasons of which the mind knows not, but then mind and heart are not natural enemies, nor are they inherently closed to each other's territory. It is only when the intellect insists on explaining away what is to be understood, or reducing it to something simpler and less, that it violates what it investigates. Rather than riding roughshod over the subtleties of its subject, however, philosophical analysis ought to peel away confusion, ambiguity, and vagueness, allowing genuine mystery to stand forth. Such at least is the goal of this inquiry.

Chapter 1 begins by considering whether any coherence can be found in the multiplicity of uses of the word "love." It will be argued that the concept is coherent and has three primary senses: (1) care for or about the love object, (2) the desire to unite or merge with it, and (3) appreciation or delight in the love object as an end. These will be called respectively, "care-love," "union-love," and "appreciation-love." Chapters 2 through 4 and also Chapter 6 investigate in detail these three primary senses of "love" and the ways of loving to which they correspond. We will explore the objectives of each form of love, its affective character, the nature of the relationship between lover and object, and the sorts of objects most appropriate to each. These chapters begin with purely conceptual considerations but proceed to matters ranging from ethical and psychological to metaphysical and spiritual. In covering such wide territory the style of writing may vary as well, for I do not believe that it is an intellectual or scholarly virtue to make the affective or the sacred sound academic. A comprehensive philosophy of love should speak to heart and spirit as well as to the intellect.

Chapter 5 is concerned with the important question of valuation in loving and how subjective, objective, and/or realistic those valuations are. Irving Singer's views on these matters will be analyzed at length. Chapter 7 will present a brief but more philosophically technical discussion of the interrelations between the three forms of love. We shall consider how the three loves (or their concepts) presuppose, imply, give rise to, or even conflict with one another. It is here where we consider whether the argument contained in this book concerns only the English word, or applies more universally. In Chapter 8 we turn our attention to the intriguing matter of love's darker side, showing how the typology developed in the preceding chapters can be used to analyze and classify some of love's less wholesome possibilities.

The epilogue will show how this same tripartite typology enables us to see how there are three distinguishable spiritual ideals of love. Having given much attention throughout to the differences between care-love, union-love, and appreciation-love, to their logical independence from one another, and to the potential for conflict between them, the focus now will be on how interconnected they usually are—and how and under what conditions they harmoniously blend. As an example of such an integration, we shall look especially at the Buddhist vision of love.

CHAPTER

WHAT LOVE IS

❖   The word "love" is used to refer to such a bewildering diversity of phenomena that it is difficult to know where to begin in attempting to say what love is.[1] So let us start with the diversity itself by considering the following list of sentences in which the word "love" occurs:

> I love my mother.
> I love my wife.
> I love my mistress.
> I love blondes.
> I love chocolate cake.
> I love God.
> God loves me.
> I love my two-year-old child.
> My two-year-old loves me.
> "Love your neighbor as yourself."
> I love my country.
> I love life.
> I love truth.
> I love gin.[2]

There are also sentences such as "I treat you so well because I love you" and "I treat you so badly because I love you," both of which, unfortunately, also make sense.

Anyone fluent in English knows roughly what the speaker in each of the above sentences might mean, yet "love" clearly does not have the same sense in each of them. "I love my mother," when spoken by mature adults, probably conveys a feeling of gratitude toward the person

who took care of them during infancy and childhood, together with affection and a strong sense of caring. "I love my wife" or "I love my husband" might also express affection and caring, along with sexual and
romantic feelings, friendship, and a commitment to the marriage. On
the other hand, "I love my mistress" may indicate little more than sexual desire, joined perhaps with a peculiar sense of property rights. Although it could as well express a tender romantic passion. And this passion, which we also call "love," refers among other things to an
experience of or desire for emotional union with the beloved.

The man who says "I love blondes" may not intend anything more
than that he finds women with blonde hair especially beguiling,
whereas "I love chocolate cake" probably indicates the speaker's urge
to devour the object of his or her passion, deriving as much pleasure
as possible in the process. "I love God" suggests devotion, worship,
and obedience, attitudes not usually involved in our love for other
people. For the mystic, however, love of God implies a longing for
union somewhat akin to that sought by romantic lovers. "God loves
me," on the other hand, is frequently taken to refer to a fatherly stew-
ardship but certainly does not suggest that God worships or obeys me,
and may or may not, depending on the speaker's theology, suggest
personal intimacy.

We speak of parents' love for their children and of children's love
for their parents. Yet how different these loves are. Parental love involves a long-range commitment to protect and care for the love object throughout the long years of childhood—while, according to the
standards of the modern Western world, gradually letting go of control
over the child's life and welfare. Children's love for their parents has a
different set of associations (gratitude, respect, honor, and obedience,
for example) and has as its basis the children's dependence on, rather
than responsibility for, the love object.

The practitioner of neighbor love loves quite differently from the
way a parent loves a child or a wife her husband. Both of the latter involve a strong preference for the loved one over others, who do not
stand in a similar special relationship to the lover. Neighbor love, on
the other hand, is often construed to be completely without preference
and embraces that most unnatural of love objects—one's enemy. And
what are we to say of the lover of life or the lover of truth? The first
may simply be an enthusiast, one who enjoys life; the second is inclined
to pursue the love object wherever it leads, regardless of the consequences. Finally, a man who loves gin might be an addict, obsessed
with the object of his passion to the point of personal destruction.

It is tempting to conclude from this brief survey that the word "love" is a beast of many and varied burdens. In some contexts it connotes caring and commitment, in others desire and possession, in others devotion and obedience. Sometimes, liking or admiration may be all that is meant. It takes only a little imagination to supply the contexts in which "I love you" might be used to mean "I am concerned for your welfare," "I want to possess you," "I want to take care of you," "I need you to take care of me," "I am totally obsessed with you," "I cannot live without you," "I feel that you and I are one," or "I wish that you and I were one." These little words, it seems, convey such a multitude of blessings and afflictions that we may begin to doubt whether any commonality at all can be found. Perhaps it is impossible to say what "love" means.

Actually, the situation is not as chaotic as it appears. Though we do use the word in all the above ways, we recognize that some of these uses are not as proper or as central as others. We can imagine, for example, someone saying, "that's not love," to the man who professes to love blondes but means only that he finds women with blonde hair sexually alluring. When such a protest is made, we know what is meant. We recognize that, although the word "love" is sometimes used to denote mere sexual attraction, there is at the same time something amiss with this usage, and the man who only desires a woman does not really love her.

It seems that, according to the conventions of our language, some uses of "love" are central and others peripheral, some literal and others metaphoric, some more and some less legitimate. Thus, when we read "Love Murder" in a tabloid headline we not only understand what is being said but know at the same time that murder is not likely to be motivated by love in any of the deeper, more central senses of the concept. In theorizing about the nature of love, it is to these more central meanings that we must attend, without, however, neglecting the secondary or tertiary senses of the term. The first step in the process of seeking the more central meanings of "love" is to uncover some ways in which the word is misused, and some ways in which its range of meaning is extended beyond primary to more peripheral applications.

"Love" is often used as a synonym or near synonym for "like" or "like very much" (as in "I love chocolate cake") or for "desire" or "attracted to" so that every object one desires or is drawn to is said to be loved. It would be odd to call these misuses of the word since they are so well established, but it is safe to say that they are not central to what makes "love" a distinct and philosophically interesting concept.

The declaration "I love chocolate cake," however, can also be hyperbolic, indicating not merely that the speaker likes or desires chocolate cake but has a passion for it akin to the romantic lover's passion for the beloved. This hyperbolic usage implies another, more fundamental meaning—that of romantic love, which is in itself a special case. In order to understand such hyperboles we must first address the form of love to which comparison is being made.

As the expression is generally used, "romantic love" refers to a form of love that is passionate, typically but perhaps not essentially sexual, and concerned with both reciprocation and union with the beloved. For many it is also accompanied by a sense of the sacred, the feeling that there is something blessed about the love for or the relationship with the beloved. It is this phenomenon that we usually have in mind when we use the locution "in love," as in "fall in love." "In love" is also used in a different and perhaps deeper sense, however, to refer not to romantic passion but to the feeling of dwelling in, or being encompassed by, love. It is likely that lovers who speak of being "in love" usually have the first meaning in mind in the early months or years of their relationship, but intend the latter meaning after they have been together for a longer time.

Although most call the phenomenon in question "romantic love," those who have written about it often refer to it by other names such as "passion," "passionate love," "sexual love," or "erotic love." I prefer "romantic love," however, not only because it is the expression most widely used but because it is the least misleading. The word "passion" is too broad, covering many things having nothing to do with love, such as passionate hatred or envy. "Passionate love" is better, and I will sometimes employ this phrase when discussing an author who prefers this usage, but this expression is also too broad—a mother may passionately love her child or a mystic his God.[3] The locution "sexual love," in my judgment, gives undue emphasis to the role of sex. Although romantic love is normally intensely sexual, sometimes sex in the ordinary, conscious, adult, genital sense of the term plays no part in it. Children long before the age of puberty may fall in love in ways that strike me as sufficiently akin to the adult sexual version as to warrant the use of the same label. Moreover, "sexual love" may be misleading because it sometimes means simply "sexual desire" or "sexual obsession," without any of those accoutrements we usually think of as romantic. Finally, the expression "erotic love" has the dual difficulty of being, in ordinary English, virtually synonymous with "sexual love" while, to the philosopher, it takes on Platonic or Neoplatonic connotations ranging far beyond the kind of love we are considering—love for the Good, the One, or God.

Perhaps the strongest objection to the expression "romantic love" comes from those who find the adjective "romantic" pejorative, as if it implied "illusory," "immature," or even "diseased." Although romantic love may be all three, it is not so, inherently. For others "romantic love" suggests a historical connection with Romanticism. This is not my intention. I have in mind a more generic and universal phenomenon. In accordance with my usage, therefore, courtly love is romantic love under a particular historical configuration.

Romantic love is not a simple phenomenon: it is, one might say, both more and less than love. It can be more, in that it often involves elements such as obsession, the desire to possess or be possessed, intense sexual attraction, or an urgent demand for reciprocation—ingredients not generally present in other forms of love. It may also be judged less than love, in that it is sometimes wanting in the caring and respect for otherness often associated with love. If romantic love is something of a special case, we would be ill advised to treat it as a paradigm for love in general and to base a general theory of love upon it. Nonetheless, it is from romantic love that expressions such as "love murder" or "I treat you badly because I love you" receive their meaning. In pathological cases of this love the desire to possess may be so extreme that a demented lover might prefer to see the "beloved" destroyed rather than lost to another.

Another example of hyperbolic uses of the word "love" would be a statement such as "she sure loves her booze," when the person in question is an alcoholic. Here "love" means something like "obsessed with," "possessed by," or "cannot do without." Again, the hyperbole seems to be based on romantic love.[4]

The word "love" can also be used euphemistically as a polite or socially acceptable way of referring to sex. Anyone who searches through secondhand bookstores for works on love will find that many of the books with the word "love" in their titles are actually about sex. Yet even though we sometimes use "love" as a synonym for "sex," nearly everyone would agree that love and sex are not the same thing—there can be loveless sex and sexless love.

Closely related to the euphemistic use of "love" is what might be termed the deceptive use, where the word serves as a cover for something else, which the speaker wishes to keep hidden. Because we think of love as good, we sometimes use the word to conceal other motives. Abusive parents, for example, who beat or are excessively critical of their children—"because they love them"—may be employing the approved word to conceal their cruelty, even from themselves.

Other questionable uses of the word occur through a process of overgeneralization—as when people attribute to love everything that ensues between lovers. For example, if a man becomes inordinately jealous when his wife talks to another man, his jealousy might be attributed to the fact that he loves her. However, even if it is true that the man loves his wife, it does not follow that the jealousy is a consequence of his love. When the man himself blames his jealousy on love, it is probably an instance of the deceptive strategy just discussed; if someone else makes the attribution it is more probably overgeneralization. Perhaps the man is chronically insecure or incapable of believing that anyone could love him. Factors such as these are more apt to be causes of extreme jealousy than love itself. It is not that love can never give rise to jealousy, just that we cannot automatically attribute to love everything that transpires between people who love each other. Love relationships are complex; they consist of many not always harmonious elements, not all of which should be labeled "love."

A familiar instance of this phenomenon of overgeneralization is the tendency to confuse love *for* someone with the desire to be loved *by* that person. Most often when we love someone, we wish to be loved in return. This is typically, and perhaps essentially, the case with romantic love. Other notions of love, however, such as Judeo-Christian neighbor love, are said to be indifferent to reciprocation. In any case, it is clear that "Frankie loves Johnny" neither means nor implies "Frankie wishes to be loved by Johnny." Yet because these two phenomena so often occur together, they are frequently confused. Thus someone may say "I love you" when what he or she means is "I want you to love me." Indeed, the former utterance may be offered with the hope of eliciting the response "I love you too." While there is a natural psychological connection between the two phenomena, the concepts are distinct.

Universal Features of Love

Having identified some of the ways the word "love" is misused, or used in secondary or peripheral senses, let us explore what is implied or presupposed by the more legitimate, central uses of the concept. The results of this investigation should not be startling since we are attempting only to make explicit what is generally understood. The first universal feature of love, on which nearly everyone would agree, is that love involves a relationship between a subject (the one who loves) and an object (that which is loved). The subject we will call the lover; the object will be referred to variously as the love object, the loved one, the beloved, or more simply, the loved.[5] The loved may be another person, or even the lover himself or herself.

In some spiritual notions of love, it might be argued, love has no subject; it is simply a transcendent power or energy. Even transcendental theories of love, to the best of my knowledge, are not wholly subjectless, however. Love is either identified with or grounded in some supernatural lover. Another apparent exception to the requirement that love have a subject is suggested by certain noun uses of "love" such as, "love seeketh not its own" or "love conquers all." Here again love seems to operate without a subject. Such expressions are best construed as figures of speech, personifications of love, not to be taken literally. Thus read, Saint Paul's "love seeketh not its own" means something like: "Those who love in the Christian manner, seeks not their own good but the good of the loved." (Should it turn out that there are spiritual theories of love as yet unknown to me that are devoid of a subject as source of the love, the principle under discussion will have to be modified to accommodate them.)

A second noncontroversial feature of love is that love has something to do with value or the process of valuation. What one loves, one necessarily values. According to one tradition, exemplified by Plato, we love something because it is, or is judged to be, valuable. Here, loving is preceded by the judgment that the loved is appropriately deserving. According to another tradition, exemplified by Martin Luther and his twentieth-century champion Anders Nygren, the relationship between love (in this case agape) and value is quite the reverse of that supposed by Plato. God, the ultimate source of agape, does not love something because it is valuable; rather, He bestows value through His love. Irving Singer has labeled these two forms of valuation "appraisal" and "bestowal."[6]

The value that is inseparable from love need not be objectively demonstrable. I may love a friend for his brilliance and wit even if he possesses neither. All that matters, if these are the reasons for my love, is that I think him brilliant and witty. I love him none the less if I am mistaken. Not that love is blind, rather it can be either clear-sighted or blind or anywhere between. Love that is clear-sighted, and grounded in an assessment of the loved's value that is objective, may be more rational, mature, or stable than blind love, but both qualify as love. Perhaps the most critical question regarding the relationship between love and value is whether it is sufficient that the loved be valued instrumentally, or whether the loved must be valued as an end.

A third universal characteristic of love is that the lover is drawn or inclined toward the love object. The exact nature of this inclination—whether elicited by benevolence, compassion, concern, or desire, for example—is a matter that not only differentiates kinds of love from one another but also divides love theorists. Much of the following work will be a sustained analysis of the principal ways that lovers are inclined toward their love objects.

This is not to deny that one may sometimes withdraw from what one loves, only that one withdraws *because* of love. For example, a woman may run away from the man she loves because she feels smothered by him, or because she is frightened by intimacy. Here she both loves him and flees from him, but love is not the reason for her flight. Love draws her toward him, whereas the other, conflicting motives—not intrinsic to love but features, perhaps, of her particular psychology of loving—push her away. Another possible counterexample to the thesis that love inclines the lover toward the loved would be a lover withdrawing from the loved because the latter demands it. Here, in a sense, the lover withdraws because of love; but the lover's inclination is still toward the loved, both in the desire for closeness with the loved and in that the intention remains focused on him or her. The lover is withdrawing for the loved's sake.

The inclinations inherent in love are also action tendencies. To love is not merely to undergo some internal state of consciousness, it is a tendency to act in roughly specifiable ways. As we shall see, love inclines us to actions that serve the welfare of the loved, moves us toward union with the loved, or leads us to admire or contemplate the love object or its qualities. It is tempting to make this tendency to act a separate feature of love, but I have included it within our discussion of inclination because there seems to be no clear way of separating tendencies to act from inclinations. This is especially evident in appreciation-love where the action tendency may be nothing more than to contemplate the love object. In such cases inclination and action tendency coincide.

A fourth widely agreed upon, if not absolutely noncontroversial characteristic of love, is that love must have an affective component; the lover must feel something for or with the loved. (This is quite different, as we shall see, from the contention, often taken for granted in discussions of the topic, that love simply is a feeling.) In the New Testament we find a strong tendency to associate love for the neighbor with action. This emphasis is most evident in the First Epistle of John—"love must not be a matter of words or talk; it must be genuine, and show itself in action."[7] John's concern, however, was with the reduction of love to intentions or words, not with repudiating the role of feeling. In seeking to avoid the danger of reducing love to action alone, Saint Paul proclaims, "I may dole out all that I possess, or even give my body to be burnt, but if I have not love, I am none the better."[8] Unfortunately, Paul does not tell us explicitly what the missing element is. We cannot be certain that feeling was what he had in mind. A few centuries later, Augustine, perhaps the most influential of all Christian love theorists, assigns a central role to feeling in all forms of love. John Burnaby sums up his position: "It is important to observe that both *amor* and *caritas* involve feeling as well as striving or conation: indeed it is the affective element in love that supplies its dynamic."[9]

One important Christian philosopher of love, however, does deny that feeling is essential to neighbor love. Immanuel Kant sees love in general, what we might call human or natural love, as nothing but feeling: "*Love* is a matter of *feeling*, not of *will*, and I cannot love because I *will* to, still less because I *ought* to (i.e., I cannot be necessitated to love). So a *duty to love* is logically impossible."[10] Yet if this is so, if love as pure feeling cannot be a duty, what are we to make of the Biblical love commandments? Kant offers the answer:

> It is in this way, undoubtedly, that we should understand those passages of Scripture which command us to love our neighbor and even our enemy, for love as an inclination cannot be commanded. But beneficence from duty, when no inclination impels it and even when it is opposed by a natural and unconquerable aversion, is *practical* love, not *pathological* love; it resides in the will and not in the propensities of feeling, in principles of action and not in tender sympathy; and it alone can be commanded.[11]

So love for the neighbor is "practical love," a matter of will and duty, as distinct from ordinary human love, which Kant denominates "pathological" (because it proceeds from *pathos*, or feeling). Kant stops just short of concluding that neighbor love is not love at all. Instead, as we have seen, he dichotomizes love into two different forms, one affective and the other volitional. It comes as a surprise, then, to learn that even Kant's practical lover often does feel for the one he loves:

Helping others to achieve their ends is a duty. If a man practices it often and succeeds in realizing his purpose, he eventually comes to feel
love for those he has helped. Hence the saying: you *ought* to *love* your
neighbour as yourself, does not mean: you should immediately (first)
love him and (afterwards) through the medium of this love do good to
him. It means, rather: *do good* to your fellow-man, and this will give
rise to love of man in you (as an aptitude of the inclination to benefi-
cence in general).[12]

A major difference then, between Augustine's and Kant's understanding of neighbor love concerns where the impetus to action lies.
For Augustine, love of the neighbor proceeds from feeling for the
neighbor (or, more accurately, feeling for God in the neighbor),
whereas Kant's ideal Christian is propelled to action by the sense of
duty. Nonetheless, for both, feeling for the neighbor is typically and
also ideally present. Yet, Kant insists, feeling is not the motivating
force and could be altogether absent.

Turning from the second to the first of Jesus' love commandments, the command to love God, Kant argues that feeling can have
no place at all because "He is not an object of the senses."[13] Kant's
view is that inclination or feeling belongs solely to the sensory side
of human nature. Objects of sensory perception such as our fellow
humans can be loved pathologically whereas God can be loved only
practically. And this practical love for God, it turns out, is nothing
other than obedience to the divine law. It follows that, on Kant's
reading, the first of Christ's love commandments is little more than
an admonition to follow the second—to love our neighbors as ourselves. Thus, whereas the Augustinian tradition subordinates the
love of neighbor to the love of God, a Kantian theology has exactly
the opposite effect.

Finally, theologians in the Aristotelian tradition such as Saint
Thomas Aquinas sometimes deny that feelings or emotions can have
any role in God's love of us. God, as an infinite and purely active being, is simply not subject to any alterations analogous to human feeling. Affect presupposes being acted upon, and a being who is Pure
Act can never be passive. In Aquinas's succinct formulation: "He
loves without passion,"[14] that is, without anything that we would call
feelings or emotions. God's love is not without appetite but His appetite, Aquinas assures us, is purely intellectual—a matter of will.
The sensitive appetite that is linked to the body and the passions
plays no role at all in divine love.

As the preceding counterexamples demonstrate, there are a few exceptions to the thesis that love always involves feeling something for or with the loved. If, as will soon be argued, analysis of ordinary language requires that feeling is inherent in love, we may have encountered a place where our two criteria of "love's" meaning—the linguistic and the historic—yield slightly different results. To the degree that this is so, we simply have to live with the inconsistency. Yet it is worthwhile to consider further some of the reasons why love theorists have sometimes denied the presence of feeling in specific kinds of love.

Part of the inconsistency arises simply because we use the same word to embrace both natural love and love that is, or is taken to be, divine. When gods are conceived according to the propensities of the mythic imagination, divine love and human love are not far apart. Aquinas, however, built his Christian theology upon Aristotelian metaphysics. In consequence his account of how God loves may reveal more about the pitfalls of the marriage between biblical anthropomorphic religion and Aristotelian philosophy than it does about the nature of love, human or divine. Aristotle was more consistent than Saint Thomas in holding that the God required by his metaphysics loves nothing at all unless it be His own thoughts. Aquinas's position, however, stems as well from his attitude toward the body, the home of the sensitive appetite, and from the preference he gave to intellect and will over sensation and emotion.

These latter biases no doubt influenced Kant as well. He objects to an affective impetus to neighbor love because, as an ethical love, love of the neighbor must be a matter of duty. Kant is convinced that feelings—as nonvoluntary—can never be obligatory. Similarly, love for God must have nothing to do with feeling because, he reasons, feelings arise solely from sensory objects. Were Kant right about this, the entire eros tradition would have to be rejected, for the Platonist sees desire for the divine as fundamental to human nature.

Setting aside the question of whether Kant's understanding of neighbor love is good theology or sound biblical exegesis, few today would be comfortable with its implications. Were someone, for example, to help you in some significant way, but do it solely from a sense of duty without feeling anything whatever for you (no compassion, no affection, no benevolence), I doubt that you would describe the action as one of love or, more emphatically, that you would *feel* loved. The reason for your reluctance would be that the sensibility we associate with love, its affective dimension, was absent. Most of Western love theory conforms to this intuition. If a few theories do not, perhaps they should be judged eccentric or even suspect, especially by those who regard the traditional hostility of Western intellectuals toward the corporeal and emotional aspects of human nature as a prejudice or even a cultural disorder.

Love's having a feeling component does not imply that love presupposes any particular feeling or that there is any single feeling we label "love." In the example just presented of helping another, sympathy or the pleasure of helping could be the affective qualities accompanying the action. On other occasions, the feeling component might be some kind of desire, admiration, or affection. Obviously not all feelings mark the presence of love, any more than all actions do. Feelings that often accompany love include compassion, sympathy, affection, admiration, concern, benevolence, attraction, the feeling of being one with or extremely close to the loved, and many kinds of desire, including the desire to touch, caress, be close to, help, make love to, and merge with.

Some feelings, though they do not mark the presence of love, are perfectly compatible with it, whereas others may conflict with or even exclude love. It is easy, for example, to experience anger and love simultaneously for the same individual. Fear (in the sense of fear *of*, rather than *for*) is less compatible with love because it closes down the heart and places us in a protective mode. It produces an action tendency opposite to that of love: rather than drawing the lover toward the loved object, fear gives rise to aversion. Thus, as we come to fear a loved object, love diminishes—although our need to be loved, which we sometimes misleadingly call "love," might increase.[15] Although it is certainly not impossible to both love and fear the same object, doing so creates a complex and conflicted state in which one simultaneously seeks and avoids the same object.

If love and fear are psychologically conflicting tendencies, indifference is logically incompatible with love. The very concepts exclude one another, for it is impossible to love something and simultaneously be indifferent to it. Love entails a positive valuation of the loved and an inclination toward it; indifference suggests the absence of both.

The relation between love and hatred is more complex. There is no doubt that we can alternate quickly between hating and loving the same person, but can we simultaneously love and hate the same individual or object? By confusing loving and wanting to be loved, it might seem that we can. If I need you to love me, but you do not, I may hate you for frustrating my desire. Then, owing to the confusion between loving and wanting to be loved, I might conclude that I hate you precisely because I love you. Nonetheless, since one may both love and need to be loved by the same individual at the same time, it is certainly possible to simultaneously love and hate the same object when that object is a person from whom one needs to be loved.[16] And this can happen even without confusion between love and the need to be loved. Hatred, however, is incompatible with those forms of love that seek the well-being of the loved because such loves strive to protect or preserve their object, while hatred seeks its harm or destruction.

To return to the general thesis that love must be accompanied by feelings, the point is not that a lover must experience the appropriate feelings at every moment throughout the duration of a love relationship, that a mother, say, must continuously undergo certain feelings for her daughter for the twenty years she has known and loved her. Rather, appropriate feelings will almost certainly appear on specifiable occasions. If the woman feels nothing when her daughter is seriously ill, we would be justified in doubting whether she loves her after all, unless some extraordinary circumstance were blocking the mother's normal emotional response.

It may be useful to distinguish between an act of love and a love relationship.[17] Love relationships differ from acts of love at least in that they are of considerably longer duration. Acts are relatively short events while relationships may last a lifetime. Thus an act could be accompanied by a particular feeling throughout its duration, but feelings will vary considerably over the course of a relationship. When we identify a relationship as one of love, therefore, we cannot mean that it is accompanied by a particular feeling throughout its entire history. Rather, when "love" is used to modify "relationship," the modifier indicates among other things the presence of certain kinds of feelings in the course of the relationship and the probability of their occurring on specifiable occasions. If the feelings that are the marks of love were never to occur, it would be inappropriate to describe the relationship as one of love.

Given this distinction it would even make sense to say, "I love you, but I am not *feeling* love for you at this moment"—if, for example, the speaker were too angry, resentful, sick, depressed, or preoccupied. In such a case the expression "I love you" would probably signify the speaker's belief that the love relationship still exists even though his or her feelings are momentarily out of kilter. It probably signifies as well the belief that the feelings will return once the difficulty is over.

Let us now consider more carefully the position that love is simply a particular feeling and the word "love" is thus nothing more than the name of that feeling. This is a standard commonsense position uncritically assumed by many. Were it correct, our task of saying what love is would be much easier; we would only have to identify and describe the feeling.

Perhaps people assume that love is a feeling because of the simple fact that we can feel it. This, however, would be like concluding that heat is a feeling because we can feel it. Feeling love, like feeling heat, is but one of the ways in which we detect its presence. In my view, the belief that love is a feeling is mistaken on at least three counts. First, there is not any one particular feeling associated with love but several quite different feelings, many of which already have names of their own. If we are to equate love with feeling, then the equation would have to be made, disjunctively, to several distinct feelings.

A second, more serious objection is that, if feelings are understood as subjective states (the usual understanding of their nature), then love cannot be equated with them, for, as we have seen, love has also to do with the relationship between a subject and an object, with positive valuation of the object, and more crucially, with inclinations and tendencies to act regarding the object. It is this subjectivist reduction of love that I find particularly objectionable. Love has its existence not merely in the minds or hearts of lovers but in what Martin Buber called "the between."[18]

Closely related to this objection is a third: that love (some forms of it, at least) can to a significant degree be willed. Love can be practiced; we can, within limits, discipline ourselves to be more loving. Feelings as internal states, on the other hand, are less subject to our control. Here it might be objected that feelings such as anger are amenable to will and discipline too. This objection, however, confuses feelings with the more complex conditions we call emotions. So let us consider instead the view that love is an emotion, not just something felt. This thesis has greater plausibility, for emotions are clearly more than internal states. They typically, some would argue essentially, involve beliefs and dispositions to act in roughly predictable ways.[19]

That love is an emotion is virtually an axiom of psychologically oriented love theorists. On psychologist, for example, begins his book on love with the words, "Love is one of the most intense and desirable of human emotions." Yet he also describes love "as the interaction of three components—intimacy, passion, and commitment."[20] When these two statements are combined, we get the following result: that the interaction of three multifaceted and diverse phenomena—intimacy, passion, and commitment—is an emotion, one single emotion. Herein lies the difficulty with the "love is an emotion" theory. Love cannot be any single emotion for, just as the affective states that accompany love vary greatly, so do the belief and action tendencies associated with it. If love is emotion, it has to be more than one. Even this variation on the theory loses some of its plausibility when it is noticed that not every form of love is emotional. Romantic love surely is, but few would so characterize love for one's neighbor. If some forms of love are not emotional, shall we nonetheless say that love consists entirely of emotions? I propose the following conclusions regarding the relation between love and both feelings and emotions:

1. The presence of love can be felt.
2. It includes feelings on the part of the lover for the loved as a central, and arguably essential, component.
3. It is not itself a feeling.
4. It sometimes is, and sometimes is not, emotional.
5. It certainly is not a single emotion.
6. In reply to those who wish to insist that love consists entirely of some disjunctive set of emotions—on the grounds that, when properly analyzed, emotions consist of precisely those elements enumerated above (relationship between subject and object, valuation, inclination and action tendency, and feeling)—I would have no grounds to disagree, except to underscore the awkwardness of saying that something not necessarily emotional consists entirely of emotions.

LOVE, LIKING, DESIRE, AND ATTRACTION

It might be argued that the four characteristics shared by all forms of love (relationship between subject and object, positive valuation, inclination and action tendency, and feeling) are not peculiar to love, but are universal features of the emotions. An obvious difficulty with this view is that not all emotions involve a positive valuation of the object toward which they are directed. Liking, desire, and attraction, however, do seem to share all of these universal features of love, including positive valuation. Shall we conclude, then, that liking, desiring, and attraction are simply forms of love or, more radically, that "liking," "desire," and "attraction" are synonyms for "love"? Previously, when it was acknowledged that each of these relations is sometimes called "love," the suggestion was made that such uses be ignored as not "central to what makes love a distinct and philosophically interesting concept." If this is so, it should be possible to explain how love differs from liking, attraction, and desire.

Even though "love" is sometimes used to refer to each of these relations, we must admit we also frequently distinguish them from love, as in "I like [desire, am attracted to] you, but I don't *love* you." What difference might be indicated by such a declaration? With regard to liking, which surely is the closest to love, I can think of three possible answers. First, the speaker might be distinguishing liking from some specific kind of love, such as romantic love. In this case, "I like you, but I don't love you" means "I like you, but I'm not in love with you." This leaves open the possibility, however, that "liking" still denotes some other nonromantic form of love.

Philosophically more interesting is a second possibility: we sometimes make a distinction between liking and loving on normative grounds. Liking is more compatible with means-ends relations. Perhaps I could like you without having to view you as an end in yourself, whereas loving you (it might be argued) requires valuing you as an end. If this difference were to hold there would then be a difference between liking and loving based upon one of the universal features of love—positive valuation—such that, although both involve positive valuation, the nature of the valuation differs. Love values its object (at least partly) as an end, whereas liking involves only instrumental value. As appealing as this solution to the problem is, however, it does not work. Although the connection between loving and valuing as an end is strong, valuing as an end is not a necessary condition of all love. As we shall see, both care-love and appreciation-love presuppose end-value, but union-love does not.

Moreover, "liking," especially "liking very much," is not entirely free of the same normative implication. It would be odd to say "I like you very much," for example, if I liked you only as a means to the gratification of my own needs and would cease liking you as soon as you failed me in this regard. Were this the case I might be judged a fickle liker. Yet if all that were meant in declaring liking for someone is that one likes one of the individual's qualities (as when someone says, for example, "I like Pavarotti very much," and means only liking his singing), then liking may be purely instrumental. Liking a person, however, seems to move in the direction of love by sharing some of its normative character. This constitutes further evidence that loving and liking overlap through at least one dimension of "love's" meaning. Nonetheless, it is true that the suggestion that the object be valued more than instrumentally is stronger with "love."

A third interpretation of "I like you, but I don't love you" undermines the very existence of a qualitative distinction between the concepts. The declaration might mean simply, "I like you, but not enough to call it love." Here, "love" simply means "like a great deal" or "like very much"—the difference between them being one only of degree. Even a quantitative difference is a difference, however, albeit a rather vague one. On this interpretation, liking and loving form a continuum with no clear boundary between them.

But is it reasonable to suppose that "loving" always means "liking very much"? Surely not. "Loving" has a vast number of implications involving feelings, inclinations, action tendencies, and ways of valuing that are not well expressed by "liking very much." No one, for instance, has ever tried to found an ethic on "liking very much." "Like your enemies as yourself" simply does not work; there are no spiritual ideals of liking. Consider the theological potential of the proposition "God is liking." Nor is anyone likely to hold forth on the dark side of liking. Finally, just as it makes sense to say, "I like you, but I don't love you," so it makes sense to say, "I like you very much, but I don't love you," and even, "I love you, but I don't really like you at all." "Love" evidently has meanings that are utterly foreign to "like very much." If "like" overlaps with "love," as it surely does, it manages to capture only a portion of the latter. There are vast territories of love—sublime, tragic, and ridiculous possibilities—that lie utterly beyond the range of "liking very much."

"Desire" and "attraction" are easier to distinguish from "love." Neither carries any suggestion that the object is valued as an end. The action tendencies for desire and attraction are more limited; they typically encourage us to take possession or make use of their objects; and they lack the respectful attitude so often found in love. When "love" is used as a synonym for either word (and to a lesser degree for "liking"), hyperbole is often involved—it is a way of giving emphasis to the strength of the inclination.

THREE CENTRAL MEANINGS OF "LOVE"

It has been argued thus far that love is a relation between a subject and an object that inclines the lover toward the object. A major source of disagreement among theorists concerns the exact nature of this relation—how the lover is inclined toward the object, what the lover's interest in it is, how he or she is apt to behave toward it, and the nature of the lover's feelings regarding it. If we are to analyze "love" honoring the full range of its meanings the question we must now ask is what kinds of relation between a subject and an object, and what kinds of inclinations or action tendencies regarding it, enable us to identify a relation as love.

A central thesis of the present work is that, if we allow ourselves to be guided by ordinary English usage and also by the history of love theory, there is no single correct answer to this question. Instead there are three different answers and, thus, three distinguishable phenomena we call "love." The names we will use for these phenomena are "care-love," "union-love," and "appreciation-love." They differ from each other principally in how the lover is inclined toward the loved and, thus, in their respective action tendencies. Each love has a different objective, though not necessarily a different object. By "object" I mean the one or the thing that is loved, whereas "objective" refers to the goal the lover has in loving. Thus, if Jack has care-love for Jill, Jill's well-being is his objective. With union-love, his objective is some kind of union with her and appreciation-love has the appreciation of Jill as its objective. All three loves have the same object—Jill. Along with their differing objectives, the three loves vary in affective character, in what and how the lover feels with regard to the loved. Moreover, each love tends to be directed toward a somewhat different range of objects.

One mode of relating to an object we love is simply to care for or about it. This is the form of love found in ethical ideals such as biblical neighbor love, but "care-love" is a more inclusive concept. Where neighbor love is a fairly radical ideal, commonly characterized as self-less, self-sacrificial, universal, and impartial, care-love embraces all forms of concern for the well-being of the loved. Its objective is simply the good of the love object. The lover seeks to benefit the object, serving its interests or welfare in whatever way he or she can. Its affective component includes feelings of care, concern, or compassion for the loved. Care-love is most apt to be directed toward objects that can benefit from, respond to, or even reciprocate the lover's care. But it is also possible to experience care-love for valued inanimate objects such as personal possessions. Effective care-love presupposes a degree of distance or detachment from its object because caring well requires seeing clearly who or what the love object is, and discerning what contributes to its welfare. Any confusion of the loved's good with that of the lover will serve to undermine the objective of the caring.

A second notion of love, equally familiar, has union with the loved as its objective. Rather than having the relatively detached attitude of care-lovers, union-lovers seek to diminish the distance between themselves and what they love; they wish to merge or unite themselves with it. "Union" may be understood in diverse ways, making for a vast spectrum of union-loves. What they all have in common, however, is that union of some sort is the objective. Union-love's action tendencies have to do with efforts to effect, preserve, or deepen the valued union. Affectively, union-love tends to be more passionate than either of the other loves, but it has a wide emotional range because of the diversity of unions it may seek. Romantic love and mystical love are both examples of this form of love. Its most obvious objects are persons, both human and divine, but we can also experience union-love for pets, places or regions, personal possessions, or nature as a whole.

In our third form of love, appreciation-love, the response to the loved is less active.[21] Instead of reaching out to care for or striving to unite with, these lovers merely behold what they love, appreciating it for being what it is (or is taken to be). The lover's response is admiration, affirmation, appreciation, or simply acceptance. The object may be cherished, even revered, but with no need for the lover to act in its behalf or attempt to get closer to it. This love tends to be even more detached than care-love but leans more toward the aesthetic than the ethical. Its emotional character is varied, ranging from cool to hot, but in its purer forms it merely contemplates its object without asking anything from it or needing to do anything to or for it.

It has been difficult to find a suitable name for this love. There is no single response or objective (like caring for or seeking union with) whereby it might be identified. Thus "appreciation" may be taken as a technical term covering a wide range of phenomena, including admiration, affirmation, appreciation, reverence, cherishing, or respectful acceptance. Here we have the purest response to the value of the loved. Like the title of an old song, it declares simply, "I'm glad there is you." The most obvious objects of appreciation-love are not persons but rather entities that are difficult or even impossible to care for or merge with such as ideals, principles, or abstract qualities. Appreciation for persons is usually mixed with either or both of the other loves.

Each of these three loves is logically independent, in that none can be reduced to either or both of the others. It might appear that both care-love and union-love presuppose appreciation-love on the grounds that the impulse to care for or unite with could only arise for an object already appreciated. This, however, is to confuse appreciation-love with the universal feature of love, positive valuation. Appreciation-love, we shall see, involves more than valuing the loved; the love must be valued as an end in itself.

That these three ways of loving can be distinguished one from another does not mean they usually, or even ever, occur in isolation. Indeed, pure instances of each type, if they exist at all, are quite rare. Just as there might be logical links between the three concepts, so may there be psychological or causal links between the three ways of loving. For example, if what I love appreciatively is in danger, and there is something I can do to protect it, care-love for it might be psychologically inevitable. While this is probably true when the loved is the kind of thing that can be cared for, there are also circumstances under which caring for an appreciation-love object is impossible or inappropriate. For example, I may love a sunset appreciatively without any impulse to care for it, because I recognize that caring could have no effect and is therefore pointless.

In addition to logical and causal links between the three loves, there is also the possibility of conflicts. Clashes arise because the objectives of the three loves are so different. While appreciation-love stands back and beholds its object, union-love rushes in. A man's union-love for a woman, for example, might be occasioned by his appreciation-love of her independence. Then, through union with her, he might endeavor to undermine the very quality that originally elicited his passion. Similarly, although both union-love and care-love are frequently experienced for the same object (as they are in most intimate human relationships), they do not always blend easily and may sometimes conflict. This can happen because some forms of union undermine the distance, detachment, or respect for otherness that is necessary for effective caring. As you and I become closer, I may lose the ability to see that your well-being does not always coincide with mine.

Even from this preliminary investigation, it is apparent that love is a complex and rather awkward concept.[22] This complexity accounts partially at least for the widespread confusion about what love is and for the common belief that it is irrational. One of the objectives of the present study is to show that, however complex and mysterious love may be, the concept is coherent and open to philosophical analysis. Moreover, any theory of love that does not take account of the three principal forms of love, and the linkages between them, will be seriously incomplete.

NORMATIVE AND NONNORMATIVE APPROACHES

Before we proceed to analyzing these three senses of "love" and the phenomena they denote, it is necessary to take note of the distinction philosophers often make between normative or prescriptive and non-normative or descriptive definitions of a concept (and the difference between normative and nonnormative interpretations of the phenomena the concept denotes). A descriptive definition, like those offered by lexicographers, tells us how a word is actually used by those who speak or write the language. A prescriptive definition, on the other hand, informs us of how the definer thinks it ought to be used.

It is not always easy to determine which kind of definition is intended, nor are their authors necessarily aware of the distinction. Nonetheless, it is usually possible to discern when a prescription or a norm is present. Consider, for example, the definition: "'love' means placing another's interest above one's own." This cannot, plausibly, be interpreted as a description of how the concept is used, for the simple reason that we are generally willing to call less altruistic tendencies "love." It is more probable that one who proposes such a definition is telling us that this is how the word ought to be used, proposing a change in ordinary usage rather than following it. Or the definer might be telling us how he or she intends to use it. In this case it is called a stipulative definition.

There is nothing wrong with prescriptive definitions so long as they are recognized as such by both their authors and their audience. Confusion is generated, however, when prescriptive definitions are treated as if they were descriptions, or when a writer wanders back and forth between normative and descriptive uses of a word, unmindful of the difference. Ashley Montagu is guilty of such wandering in his essay "A Scientist Looks at Love." Using the parent-child relationship as a paradigm, Montagu defines "love" as "the relationship between persons in which they confer mutual benefits upon each other." Or as he later puts it: "love is the relationship between persons which contributes to the welfare and development of each."[23] These are not very satisfactory definitions (indeed, they are not definitions of "love" at all, but of "interpersonal love relationship"), but they certainly sound more descriptive than normative.

Later in the same essay, Montagu tells us that love "is sacrificial, it is self-abnegative. It always puts the other first." To this he adds: "Love is unconditional." It "promises that you will always be present to support the other, no matter what the conditions you will never fail him."[24] Clearly these remarks do not describe what we ordinarily mean by "love" (or "interpersonal love relationship"). Indeed, it seems that Montagu is now telling us not merely how the word ought to be used but how we ought to love. Yet he tells us this in the guise of saying what "love" means. To assert that agape is unconditional or puts the other first would not be prescriptive, because these are widely held to be inherent features of this normative notion of "love." But to say that the love intrinsic to human nature (which seemed originally to have been Montagu's topic) is unconditional and always puts the other first is to go far beyond description.

⟨What Montagu has done, is to define "love," first, by identifying it with purely natural phenomena (relationships that confer mutual benefits) and then tack onto this apparently descriptive definition some highly normative requirements (that love is self-abnegative, unconditional, and never fails the loved). It is apparent that his two ways of characterizing love are quite different. Indeed, they conjure up profoundly conflicting associations. The first (conferring mutual benefits) would fit well into a tract on laissez-faire economics; the second (that love is self-abnegative and so on) would be more at home in the biography of a saint.

It is my perception that many of those who have written about romantic love in particular use their definitions of the concept (or their fundamental descriptions of the phenomenon) as weapons in defending their own normative point of view. These authors tend to be either strongly for or strongly against this form of love. To bolster their thesis they build the normative conclusions they wish to reach, implicitly and probably unconsciously, into their fundamental definitions or descriptions. One such author, not especially fond of the phenomenon, characterizes falling in love as a "partial and temporary collapse" of one's ego boundaries.[25] With this beginning, it is not difficult to construct a compelling argument that romantic love is regressive and tinged with psychopathology since for most psychotherapists having strong well-defined ego boundaries is the sine qua non of mental health. Consider what would happen to this author's argument if he began by describing romantic love not as a collapse but as an expansion or transcendence of the ego boundaries? It is the choice of the word "collapse" that makes his argument appear convincing.

Another author, whose announced goal is to demonstrate that romantic love is for grown-ups, regularly differentiates between romantic and immature love, thereby suggesting that the very concept excludes immaturity. Interestingly his formal definition does not make this exclusion explicit: "Romantic love is *a passionate spiritual-emotional-sexual attachment between a man and a woman that reflects a high regard for the value of each other's person.*" It is evident, however, from his frequent dichotomizing of romantic and immature love that the latter is barred from the former by his actual but unstated working definition. Notice, for example, that the formal definition rules out romantic love between homosexuals. Only much later do we learn the reason: homosexuality reflects "a detour or blockage on the pathway to full maturity as an adult human being." Leaving aside the dubious judgment regarding the maturity of homosexual love, it is evident the author requires love to be fully mature in order to qualify as romantic.[26] We can now see how he establishes his thesis that romantic love is for grown-ups: the conclusion is already there in his working definition. Throughout the book, whenever the author encounters pathology, immaturity, or irrationality in what others might classify as romantic love, he is able to dismiss the cases as irrelevant to his thesis on the grounds that the love involved belongs to that other species, immature love. He apparently thinks he has proved that romantic love is mature, realistic, and rational when in fact he has merely assumed it.

Praising or condemning love or some particular kind of love by concealing the desired normative conclusion in definitions or basic descriptions is little more than a linguist trick, a sleight-of-word, as it were (of which the authors themselves, together with most of their unsuspecting audience, are probably unaware). A contribution philosophers can make to the investigation of love is to identify such errors in others' work and endeavor to avoid them in their own. Accordingly, the intention here is to analyze the concept "love" nonnormatively, so that foolish and wise, effective and ineffective, mature and childish, healthy and neurotic, even divine and demonic loves are all possible. After the concept has been analyzed and the phenomena falling under it have been described, norms can and will be invoked in order to delineate between more and less desirable forms of loving.

It might be argued that even when analyzed descriptively some uses of "love"—as in expressions such as "neighbor love," for example—simply are normative. While this is quite true, neither love in general nor any one of its principal subvarieties (care-love, union-love, or appreciation-love) is inherently normative. It is only when we get down to subdivisions of these that norms become intrinsic; and here the normative character of the concept is usually apparent. Whenever norms are inherent to the form of love under discussion, every effort will be made to take them into account. At the risk of being repetitive, let me clarify that I have no objection to making normative judgments about love—many will be offered in what follows. My objection is to concealing those norms in what are ostensibly neutral definitions or descriptions.

CHAPTER

Care-Love

2

❖   Care-love can be described simply as concern for the good or the welfare of someone or something. To love, in this sense, is to care for or to care about the object. The lover is concerned with the loved and is disposed to act on its behalf. If the object of care-love is in danger, our impulse is to protect it. If it is the kind of thing that can grow and develop (the most appropriate objects of care-love), the lover is inclined to assist in this realization. He or she is bound to the loved by concern, experiencing a kind of union with it. However, to the extent that the love in question is care-love rather than union-love, the objective is not union with but rather the welfare of the loved. Some degree of felt union or identification with the loved, though, would seem to be a precondition of care-love, since it is doubtful we can care for something we consider completely other.

Care-love may be characterized as either caring *for* or caring *about* the love object. Although these two expressions are often used interchangeably, "caring for" suggests the activity of caring more strongly than does "caring about" which in comparison seems more abstract or merely intentional. North Americans who are concerned with the destruction of the tropical rain forests of South and Central America are more apt to say they care about the rain forests than that they care for them, on the grounds that they are not directly engaged in any activity contributing to the rain forests' well-being.

In most cases, "care-love" can simply be equated with "caring-for" or "caring-about," although both of the latter expressions are sometimes used in ways that extend beyond the bounds of what could reasonably be considered love. For example, "he cares for my car," when spoken of a mechanic simply doing his job, denotes the activity of taking-care-of more than any felt concern for the automobile's welfare. This sort of caring-for would not qualify as love because it lacks the affective component associated with the latter concept. Similarly, caring-about, as in the example of the rain forest, may be so abstract that it too lacks the affective component associated with love, and may lack as well the disposition to act in behalf of the cared-for that is a part of care-love. These marginal uses of "care-for" and "care-about," then, may be taken as irrelevant to an analysis of care-love.

Aside from a few extreme cases, such as those just described, there seems no reason to distinguish care-love from the ordinary phenomenon of caring. Just as the word "love" has uses that are more or less central and those that are more or less peripheral, so it is with "care." Both terms denote a natural human disposition and yet, in some contexts, have ethical or other normative significance. In general, then, anything we love in the care-love sense, we care for or about. And anything we care for or about, we love to that degree and for that reason. Of course, loving does not always imply caring, but this is because there are other kinds of love besides care-love.[1]

If there is any difference at all between care-love and caring, it is that the word "love" may suggest somewhat greater intimacy or emotional involvement. Perhaps, "I love you, but only a little," stretches the limits of language a bit more than "I care for you, but only a little." Yet it does not seem there is any great difference here. What is apparent is that both caring and loving admit of degrees. It might be thought that we do sometimes make a distinction between caring and loving—as when, for example, a woman says about her husband of many years, "I really care about him, but I no longer love him." Yet here, it is something other than care-love the woman has in mind. Most probably what she means is that she is no longer *in* love with him, and being in love involves more than caring.

Some might argue that calling all concern for another's welfare "love" pushes the concept a bit far, on the grounds that the word "love" should be reserved solely for more personal relations. Judged exclusively by the standard of contemporary English usage, this argument has merit, even if it is not fully convincing. However, since the present analysis is guided by standards set by the history of love theory as well as by ordinary usage, the objection fails. Theologically oriented love theorists have long referred to concern for the well-being of one's neighbor as love, without necessarily regarding this concern as personal in the sense that romantic love, friendship, or even liking are. So even though contemporary English usage may sometimes balk at extending the concept this far, the historical criterion requires it.

The modern classic on the subject of care-love is the eloquent essay *On Caring* by Milton Mayeroff. While the present work is largely in agreement with Mayeroff's, there is one major difference between our two approaches: Mayeroff employs the concept "caring" in a normative manner. What I might consider poor, ineffectual, or ignorant caring does not qualify as caring at all on Mayeroff's analysis because it fails to meet the normative standards he sets. For example, Mayeroff says caring must contribute to the growth of the cared-for; when it falls short of this objective it simply is not caring. Similarly, ignorant caring is for Mayeroff a contradiction in terms, for caring he tells us requires knowledge.[2] Rather than identify caring in its entirety with a particular ideal (no matter how laudable) of how one should care, my preference is to say that caring aims at the growth of the cared-for (though it may fail in this), and that caring well requires knowledge (though caring may also be blind or foolish). Following this nonnormative approach, lack of success or knowledge indicates a deficiency in the quality of care but does not constitute evidence of its absence.

The objection could be raised that caring simply is a normative concept, because to care foolishly is to be careless. Caring must, as a matter of necessity, be careful. This objection rests on a simple equivocation, however. The word "care" not only means "caring for" or "about" in the sense of being concerned for the well-being of something, it can also mean watching out for errors as in the injunction "take care!" Here we have two distinct concepts for which we happen to use the same word. When this is understood, even a bizarre locution such as "careless caring" makes sense, for one may care for someone but do it with insufficient attention, actually harming the person one intends to benefit.

Directionality, Action, and Proximity

An important feature of caring is its directionality, or what logicians call its nonsymmetricality: "Jill cares for Jack" does not entail "Jack cares for Jill." Indeed, not only may Jill care for Jack without Jack caring for Jill, she may do so without even wanting him to care for her or without him knowing that she cares. The last two cases may be psychologically improbable but they are not logically impossible. Caring is a one-way directional relationship. It does not presuppose the mutuality of Buber's I-Thou, nor the reciprocity inherent in friendship: "Jill is the friend of Jack" entails "Jack is the friend of Jill."

Caring is likely to be facilitated by both the response and reciprocation of the cared-for, but neither is required by the logic of the concept. Jill may care for her geraniums without their appreciation or
even knowledge of the fact. Their responding to her care with lots of
gorgeous red blossoms may motivate and increase the probability of
her continued caring, but she might continue to care even if she gets
no blossoms and the plants just wither away.

Directionality is not peculiar to care-love. It may, however, be ob-
scured in more complicated forms of love, such as romantic love,
which normally involves care for the beloved. For if I love you romantically I not only care for you, I also desire union with you; and I
want you to care for and want union with me. We even use the words
"I love you" to mean all these things: "I care for you," "I want to be
one with you," "I want you to care for me," and "I want you to want
to be one with me." Amid this complexity of desires and feelings, the
directionality of love may be hard to discern. Yet the person who says
"I love you" (in any sense of the words) and means "I want you to
love me" is using language loosely. If we are to theorize coherently
about this subject, we must insist on there being a distinction between "Jack loves Jill" and "Jack wishes to be loved by Jill," even
though we may sometimes overlook this difference in daily speech.
Even union-love is directional: "I want to be one with you" is logically distinct from "you want to be one with me." However, "I want
to be one with you" may strongly suggest that I want you to want to
be one with me, on the grounds that if we were one, as I wish, you
would want the same as I do.

Nel Noddings apparently disagrees with some of what has just been
said regarding the directionality of caring. She writes:

> Caring involves two parties: the one-caring and the cared-for. It is com-
> plete when it is fulfilled in both. We are tempted to say that the caring
> attitude is characteristic of caring, that when one cares, she characteris-
> tically exhibits an attitude. But, then, it could be missed by the cared-
> for. Suppose I claim to care for X, but X does not believe that I care for
> him. If I meet the first-person requirements of caring for X, I am
> tempted to insist that I do care—that there is something wrong with X
> that he does not appreciate my caring. But if you are looking at this re-
> lationship, you would have to report, however reluctantly, that some-
> thing is missing. X does not feel that I care. Therefore, sadly, I must ad-
> mit that, while I feel that I care, X does not perceive that I care and,
> hence, the relationship cannot be characterized as one of caring. This

result does not necessarily signify a negligence on my part. There may be no way for my caring to reach him. But, then, caring has been only partly actualized.[3]

As an ethicist, Noddings is less interested in the ordinary meaning of the concept than in articulating an ideal of how to care, and in what she calls "the full care relationship." She is right that there is something incomplete when caring is not received, but it is also true that as we ordinarily use the concept, caring has taken place even when the cared-for does not realize or appreciate it. The fact of caring is not altered by the ignorance or incapacity of the cared-for. Noddings's approach is different but not contradictory to the nonnormative one taken here. Rather than formulating an ideal of the full care relationship, the aim of the present study is to analyze the ordinary concept in a way that embraces not only interpersonal care but also caring for inanimate things, which, though possibly affected by our caring, do not receive it in Noddings's sense.

Another feature of caring is its link to action or, more accurately, to the tendency to act. Caring is never a matter of sentiment or thought alone and is not, therefore, merely an internal, mental, or affective state. It is a disposition to act on behalf of the cared-for. If I profess to care for you but do nothing to assist you when you are in trouble, it would be reasonable for you to doubt I care at all. Yet it is still possible that I do care. Many factors may keep me from acting in accordance with my disposition. I may have other conflicting commitments or cares making a greater claim on my time and energy. Or I may have decided it would be better for you if I did nothing to help you. In this case, doing nothing may be more caring than taking positive action.

We must remember that caring admits of degrees and is not necessarily all absorbing. I may care for someone or something just slightly. When I hear about people starving on the other side of the world I may feel for their suffering and, in some sense, care about them, yet I may do nothing simply because I find involvement inconvenient or upsetting. In this case, it would be tempting to conclude that I do not care at all. This conclusion is sound if a normative notion of "caring" is intended. However, it is equally correct to say that I do care, but not very much. Perhaps I am more concerned about the inconvenience to my life that would arise from getting involved. Still, it might be objected that in these minimal cases one does not *really* care. My response to this criticism is that the introduction of the qualifier "really" signals a switch to a normative sense of the concept.

To say "really care" or "really love" is usually to point to an ideal of how one ought to care or love.

Caring is a tendency to act on behalf of the cared-for. Sometimes the tendency is overwhelming, as when a mother sees her child in danger. Under these circumstances the mother may risk or even knowingly sacrifice her own life to save the child. On other occasions the tendency to act may be slight and easily overridden by other considerations. This may happen not because the individual is uncaring but because his or her life is already filled with cares.

Another interesting feature of natural (as opposed to ethical or divinity-assisted) caring is the fact just alluded to that caring tends to diminish with distance. We usually care more for those who are closest to us, not only geographically but in race, nationality, age, social class, religion, or species. As has been noted, natural caring presupposes some element of union or identification with the care object.[4] We care most readily for what is most like ourselves or what is closest to us. If an eighteen-year-old boy were to hear about the death of another eighteen-year-old, for example, he will be more apt to care than if the dead person were sixty. In this case he might think, "Well, he'd lived most of his life anyway." By the time the young man reaches his fifties, however, things look different. Now he thinks it terrible that anyone should die so early. The point is not that it is impossible for caring to reach beyond the narrow boundaries created by proximity but simply that caring normally does diminish with distance.

Individuals differ considerably in how wide the range of their caring is. The stereotypical Mafioso cares deeply for the members of his own extended family but little if at all for the rest of humankind. A saint, on the other hand, may care equally for all human beings without regard to nationality, geography, or any other boundary and may even be prepared to sacrifice his or her life for any of them should the need arise (though here we may be outside the domain of purely natural caring). Most of us fall somewhere between these two extremes. Some care profoundly for other species of animals or for rivers or mountains whereas others value such things only instrumentally. Some would willingly sacrifice a human life for a principle, others would not do so under any circumstance. Today there is considerable disagreement among morally sensitive people over how much we should care about a human fetus. Disagreements such as these are probably not entirely rational but result from what we happen to identify with and the intensity of those identifications.

One of the great frustrations of human life is that we lack the time, energy, or resources to act on all of our impulses to care. Moreover, caring can cost us dearly and may even place us at risk. We sometimes find ourselves escaping from caring by ignoring the most troubling aspects of what is happening in the world around us because we fear that if we paid more attention to these problems we might begin to care deeply and would then have to change our lives. Each significant care relationship alters how we live, even who we are. It costs less to care about the lawn or the Yankees making it to the World Series than to care about the homeless. I suspect we sometimes use relatively trivial cares to keep from facing the more life-altering ones.

One of the more puzzling features of caring is how it seems to involve both union with and separation from what we care for. Mayeroff writes: "I experience what I care for . . . as an extension of myself and at the same time as something separate from me that I respect in its own right." Noddings apparently holds the same view. She maintains that caring is other-regarding, which clearly presupposes separation from the cared-for, yet notes as well how the care-giver and care-receiver are united through the activity of caring: "Caring involves, for the one-caring, a 'feeling with' the other. . . . I receive the other into myself." Thus for both authors, caring requires a subtle interaction of separation and union.[5]

The first side of this duality, separation, while important is theoretically unproblematic. Caring for another requires serving his or her welfare. One cannot do this effectively without knowing what that welfare is, independent of one's own. Moreover, caring well demands respect for the otherness of the cared-for. Although this matter is clear and noncontroversial in theory, it can be treacherously difficult in practice. To raise a child, for example, without ever confusing the child's good with one's own is probably humanly impossible. I will leave to others the practical question of just how the separation requisite for ideal caring is to be achieved, except to note that appreciation-love helps us see and value the separateness of the loved while union-love, in some of its forms, obscures it. It is in our union-love relationships where healthy caring will be most challenging. Even here, however, the detachment necessary for effective caring is possible when the love is grounded in genuine appreciation of the cared-for.

It is not only union-love that makes the separation critical to healthy caring difficult to effect. The problem exists within care-love itself because of its own dual nature. So let us turn our attention to the other side of this duality: the union with the cared-for that both

Mayeroff and Noddings believe is present in caring. First, there is an intriguing difference in how Mayeroff and Noddings describe this union. Mayeroff characterizes it as a movement toward whereas Noddings sees it as an opening up to receive the cared-for. First Mayeroff:

> To care for another person, I must be able to understand him and his world as if I were inside it. I must be able to see, as it were, with his eyes what his world is like to him and how he sees himself. Instead of merely looking at him in a detached way from outside, as if he were a specimen, I must be able to be with him in his world, "going" into his world in order to sense from "inside" what life is like for him, what he is striving to be, and what he requires to grow.

For Mayeroff the carer reaches out beyond himself to enter the world of the cared-for. Noddings describes the union side of caring as "feeling with" the cared-for. This she sharply differentiates from empathy, which she views as a merely mental projecting of oneself into the other's world by asking, hypothetically, how I would feel if I were in the other's place. Her analysis continues:

> This is, perhaps, a peculiarly rational, western, masculine way of looking at "feeling with." The notion of "feeling with" that I have outlined does not involve projection but reception. I have called it "engrossment." I do not "put myself in the other's shoes," so to speak, by analyzing his reality as objective data and then asking, "How would I feel in such a situation?" On the contrary, I set aside my temptation to analyze and to plan. I do not project; I receive the other into myself, and I see and feel with the other. I become a duality.

The last phrase, "I become a duality," is particularly intriguing. Rather than emphasizing the union of the one who gives and the one who receives care, Noddings stresses the duality of the carer who remains within the self while simultaneously opening to receive the other. Just as the care relation is one of unity and difference so, for Noddings, both of these conditions are realized within the one who cares. In caring, one simultaneously remains oneself while also receiving and joining with the other—thus becoming "a duality."[6]

Despite this subtle difference in emphasis between Noddings and Mayeroff, their positions are fundamentally alike. They agree that the carer must participate in the reality of the cared-for. Whether we describe this participation as "entering into" or "receiving" seems a secondary matter, affecting the style more than the substance of the caring. Perhaps what separates the two authors is only the choice of a masculine or a feminine metaphor for what is essentially the same experience, but their metaphors may also reflect a subtle difference in how men and women typically care. In any case, both agree that caring is not merely an objective, mental phenomenon (what Noddings calls "empathy") but requires an affective participation in the other's reality.

CARING AND END-VALUE

Central to understanding care-love is the problem of whether the cared-for must be loved for its own sake. Do I really care for something if I care for it only for my (or someone or something else's) sake? If I care about something solely because it is useful to me, it might be urged, I do not care about it at all; I care only for myself. This is presumably Mayeroff's point of view when he remarks that caring is the antithesis of using.[7]

Aristotle dealt with a similar problem when he distinguished complete or perfect friendships from friendships of use and friendships of pleasure.[8] He claimed that perfect friends, who must necessarily be good themselves, wish the good of each other for the other's sake; whereas friends of use or pleasure wish each other's good only because it is useful or pleasant to do so. Yet Aristotle does not refuse to call the latter cases friendship; he simply regards them as imperfect forms of friendship. Paralleling Aristotle's approach, then, we might distinguish between end-care-love (caring for the sake of the cared-for) and instrumental-care-love (caring for the sake of the carer, or possibly someone or something else), while maintaining that both are legitimate forms of care-love.[9]

Our question then is, Should only end-care be classified as love, or does instrumental-care also qualify? To find the answer let us first examine care for inanimate things: Is it possible to care for mere things as ends? If they cannot be, and yet are cared for, caring can be purely instrumental. Suppose Bill owns a painting to which he is particularly attached. He values the painting not because of its monetary value (indeed, he would not sell it at any price) but simply "because he loves it." Doubtless the kind of love he has for the painting is principally appreciation-love; he admires it and is drawn to its qualities. Yet insofar as his appreciation inspires him to care for the painting, he has care-love for it as well. He demonstrates this caring by ensuring that the painting is not exposed to conditions of temperature, humidity, and light that might harm it. Let us suppose further that no one knows Bill owns the painting, so it is clear he is not concerned with any prestige that comes his way from possessing it. In this case, his concern is not instrumental in any transparent way. Even so, it may be urged, his concern can hardly be free from all instrumentality, such as interest in the pleasure or satisfaction that the work gives him. This granted, is the painting merely a means to these ends? Not necessarily. He may have made provisions in his will ensuring that it will be cared for after his death. Thus his concern is independent of any benefit that might accrue to him. (It might still be objected that his concern is really for future art lovers rather than the painting itself, but this possibility we shall set aside for the moment.)

Even at this point, some may protest that Bill is not concerned with the painting for the painting's sake because a painting does not have a sake about which he could be concerned. For something to be an object of end-care, it must be the kind of thing that has interests and, therefore, can benefit from another's care. And nonconative things (so the argument runs) cannot have interests. Since interests of the painting itself are not served by his care, as would surely be the case with an animate love object, it cannot be loved for its own sake.

Insofar as Bill's love for the painting is appreciation-love rather than care-love, that the painting does not benefit from his love is not problematic, for appreciation-love has no such requirement. One can appreciate something (an ideal such as virtue or truth, say) without believing that it benefits from one's love. It is sufficient that one value the love object as an end, whether or not it gains from one's doing so. This is because the objective of appreciation-love is merely appreciation itself. But how do matters stand with care-love? Does the cared-for have to have interests? Must it be the kind of thing that could benefit from being cared for?

One might answer this question saying, "No, not necessarily," on the grounds that it is possible to care for something for its own sake even if it does not have interests of its own, so long as one is not aware of the irrationality of doing so. Bill may care for his painting for its own sake, as long as he fails to realize that interests of the painting are not actually served by his care. If he examined the matter more carefully he might realize that the true object of his concern is neither himself nor the painting but future generations of art lovers who will enjoy the painting after he is gone. If he does not think this through, however, he may well continue to care for the painting as if it were for its own sake.

Another example of such "irrational" caring might be the animist's love of nature. (The beliefs characterized here as "animistic" may not actually be irrational, but this question need not concern us.) Believing that everything in the natural world has a soul, an animist may love a river, say, in a way a nonanimist cannot. Following this line of argument, it would seem that virtually anything could be cared for as an end, even if only irrationally. In case this talk of animism seems far-fetched, one does not have to be a "primitive" to be an animist in the required sense. A pet lover may invest a pet with qualities it perhaps does not possess and love it accordingly. A lover of plants may do the same. A poet—Wordsworth and Robinson Jeffers come to mind—may find in a forest or a rock all manner of quasi-human or spiritual qualities that awaken his or her love.

What is clear so far is this: if one regards something as having interests and as therefore benefitable, it makes sense to care for it for its own sake. But must an object be thought to have interests, or to be benefitable, in order to be cared for? Consider how tenderly we care for the dead body of a loved one. Why do we do this? Is it genuine caring for the deceased person? Or is it merely a ritual observance, even a superstition? Perhaps it is respect and not caring at all.

Still searching for an example of care-love that does not presuppose the benefitability of the cared-for, let us imagine the case of an apocalyptic environmentalist who cares for the earth even after concluding that the cause is hopeless. Our environmentalist is convinced it is too late, that nothing can be done to save the planet, yet continues to work as if something could be done. (This case too may be judged irrational—but not, as before, because the carer irrationally believes the cared-for can be helped. Rather, the carer's action might be judged irrational because he or she continues the effort even while believing that the cared-for cannot be helped.) Such hopeless caring might be improbable but hardly seems impossible. We might find ourselves wondering how long the environmentalist can keep it up, and whether he or she truly believes the effort is useless. But let us suppose that the environmentalist has taken to heart the spiritual teaching found in The Bhagavad-Gita, that one must do what is right without attachment to the fruits or consequences of doing so. Since the consequences of our actions can never be known with certainty, and since worrying about them often keeps us from acting altogether, we should do our duty regardless of the consequences. Here, we seem to have an instance of caring without expectation of benefit to the cared-for.

It is significant, nonetheless, that the kinds of actions in which our apocalyptic environmentalist is engaged are precisely those that would be beneficial if benefit were possible. Benefit of the cared-for remains the intention of the action, even if in this peculiar case the carer does not believe the intended benefit can be realized. This, incidentally, is quite consistent with Krishna's teaching in the *Gita*. His point was not to prohibit intentions, merely the attachment to particular outcomes—nonattachment, not indifference.

To sum up, care-love as a matter of logic must intend benefit to the loved; this after all is the objective of caring. But the intended benefit need not be achieved. Results mark off successful from failed caring, but not caring from noncaring. Finally, although benefit to the cared-for must be intended, it is not absolutely necessary that the carer believe even in the possibility of success.

Thus far the phrases "the benefit of the cared-for" and "serving the interests of the cared-for" have been used interchangeably, but clearly they do not have the same meaning, at least when "benefit" is broadly construed. An object need not be sentient and have interests of its own in order to benefit in some fashion from caring. A coffee table, for example, will benefit from its owner's care in that it will not crack, fade, or get scratched if it is cared for properly. We can conclude then that the notions of "benefit" and "benefitability" required by caring are highly extended ones. That the object itself has interests is not essential; all that is necessary is that caring can impinge on the object so that its condition is affected. It is this possibility that motivates care-love. Recall as well that it is necessary neither that the object know nor that it approve of the effects of the caring (although, to be sure, caring is fuller and more complete when these conditions pertain).

Given that the benefit of the cared-for is the intended result of caring (not that the object has interests of its own), we now return to our original question: Must the cared-for be loved as an end, or is instrumental care-love also possible? In answering, we will use another example involving care-love for an inanimate object. If I approach the purchase of a house, say, knowing that it is a means to some clearly specifiable end (as an investment, for example, which I intend to sell as soon as the price is right), we would be reluctant to say that I have care-love for the house, though I might indeed take care of it as an investment. On the other hand if I buy a house to live in, choosing it because I find it beautiful and peaceful, we might well be prepared to say that I love it (in the care-love sense). What is the difference here? Even in the latter case, the house could be a means to an end: I need a place to live, the house is peaceful and beautiful (qualities I love as ends), it is a good investment, it is in the right location, my family is fond of it, and so on. Without the convergence of ends such as these, presumably I would not purchase the house at all.

Is the house, then, merely a means to these ends? In situations such as these the use of means-ends thinking may be inappropriate because the sharp distinction we make analytically between means and ends does not coincide very well with the way we actually experience matters. The means to a desired end have a way of becoming imbued with the value of the end. While means-ends analysis may be analytically useful, it can be phenomenologically misleading. As a thinker engaged in philosophical analysis I may conclude that my house is only a means and has no end-value but as a homeowner, family man, and sentimental human being this is not how I actually experience it.

We are especially apt to imbue a means with end value if we regard it not merely as *a* means, but as *the* means. To the degree that I believe (rightly or wrongly) that there is no other possible or available means, the path itself becomes infused with the value of the end, and the means-ends distinction effectively collapses or at least loses its relevance. Since this is or seems to be my only means, it acquires, experientially, the value of the end for which it is pursued. It is my only avenue to the desired goal.

The problem goes deeper than this, however. It is sometimes argued that loving an object because of the qualities it possesses is to love that object as a means to the enjoyment of those qualities. Looked at this way, loving a house because it is beautiful and peaceful is understood as using the house as a means to the ends of beauty and peacefulness. But, once again this is phenomenologically misleading. We do not experience the beauty of the house as something separate from the house; we experience it as a property of the house. And this, I submit, is how it should be regarded. The house is beautiful, not merely a means to the experience of beauty. Moreover, it is the specific beauty of this particular house that I love, not beauty as an abstract quality that just happens to be instantiated in this house. Since this beauty is not something separate from the house, I love the beautiful house itself as an end. It follows that material objects can have end-value; they have the end-value of the qualities they possess.[10]

Once more the objection may be raised that the house is not loved for its own sake, because it does not have a sake of its own. Until now we have been using the expressions "cared for as an end" and "cared for for its own sake" as if they were synonyms. Clearly, however, they are not, at least not in all contexts. To see how they may differ, we need to distinguish between something being an end-*in*-itself and its being an end-*for*-itself. The second presupposes that the object is, in some sense, capable of regarding itself as an end. Sidestepping the issue as to just which beings this might apply, we can be sure that nearly all humans can be ends-for-themselves, in the sense of having goals they strive to achieve. The same, presumably, cannot be said of a house. Still, a house may be an end-in-itself in that it can be loved for being just the particular house it is, with its own specific qualities and associations.

Now that we have distinguished between "end-in-itself" and "end-for-itself," we can return to the question of whether loving something for its own sake means the same as loving it as an end-in-itself. The answer I propose is this: to speak of loving something for its own sake is ambiguous. It may mean either loving it as an end-in-itself or loving it as an end-for-itself. Both constitute loving as an end. With this distinction understood, both conative and nonconative objects can be cared for as ends, but in somewhat different ways. What has to be recognized is that, in caring well, we must take into account what sort of being the care object is and then care accordingly. A person who is an end-for-himself or -for-herself ought to be cared for in a way that acknowledges this fact of his or her nature. To attempt to care for a person while failing to see what the person's own ends are would be a violation. Thus, a father who loves his pretty little girl as if she were simply a pretty-little-girl-thing, and who fails to notice how she does not always fit this perception of her, does not love his daughter appropriately. Indeed, he is not seeing his daughter clearly but projecting on to her his own idea of who or what she is. Such a father may still be said to care for his daughter, but he does not care for her appropriately.

So what, finally, is the answer to our original question concerning whether the cared-for must be loved for its own sake? If "for its own sake" means "as an end-for-itself," the answer is No, because things that cannot be ends-for-themselves can still be cared for as ends by others. If, on the other hand, "for its own sake" means "as an end-in-itself," the answer is Yes. Things can be objects of care-love only to the degree that they are valued as ends by the one who cares. It is not necessary that they have intrinsic value in any objective sense; nor is it necessary that the object be loved *only* as an end. Most of the things we care for as ends are also useful as means.

Having gone through this lengthy argument the reader may be chagrin to learn that there is a much simpler way of seeing that there is something wrong with the notion of instrumental-care. If an object were cared for purely as a means, the care would not be directed toward the putative care object but through and beyond it to something else. To care for X only as a means to Y is to care for Y rather than for X. Under these circumstances, it is misleading to describe the caring as caring for X. Caring to be sure exists, but its object has been misidentified.

This rather abstract way of presenting the matter, however, conceals the fact that convincing examples of purely instrumental-care, at least in the domain of interpersonal love, are hard to come by, even if the concept made sense. What may we use to replace the X and Y in the above formula? Is it likely that any woman, for example, cares for her husband simply as a means to her own happiness? In this case she would "love" him only insofar as he meets her needs. Should he ever cease to do so, she would stop caring immediately and without a qualm since he is, by hypothesis, only a means to an end. There is something peculiar in this scenario. Not only is it morally disturbing, it is empirically improbable. I do not think I have ever known anyone whose "caring" for another human being was instrumental to this degree (although I might be able to come up with a case or two that come distressingly close). Moreover, if we were to encounter such a person, we would think his or her "caring" seriously abnormal.

Having argued at length that care-love cannot be instrumental, it is necessary to consider what appears to be a serious historically based counter example. Augustine insists that the Christian does not love his or her neighbor for the neighbor's sake—or oneself for one's own sake—but both for the sake of God:

> I call "charity" the motion of the soul toward the enjoyment of God for His own sake, and of the enjoyment of one's self and one's neighbor for the sake of God; but "cupidity" is a motion of the soul toward the enjoyment of one's self, one's neighbor, or any corporeal thing for the sake of something other than God.[11]

For Augustine the neighbor is used as a means to an end—the love or enjoyment of God. "Through his love of the Creator, every one can make a good *use* even of created things." He presents his position at greater length:

> [T]here is a profound question as to whether men should enjoy themselves, use themselves, or do both. For it is commanded to us that we should love one another, but it is to be asked whether man is to be loved

by man for his own sake or for the sake of something else. If for his own sake, we enjoy him; if for the sake of something else, we use him. But I think that man is to be loved for the sake of something else.[12]

Augustine's point of view was presumably influenced by his understanding of the double commandment—the commandment to love God and to love one's neighbor as one's self. The version contained in Matthew (22:37–39) gives priority to love of God over love of neighbor. It reads: "'Love the Lord your God with all your heart, with all your soul, with all your mind.' That is the greatest commandment. It comes first. And the second is like it: 'Love your neighbor as yourself.'" (The versions found in Mark and Luke do not identify either commandment as greater.) But probably Augustine is influenced more by his Neoplatonic heritage, according to which all love must be directed ultimately toward the Absolute. Only God should be loved as an end. All else, including self and neighbor, is to be used as a means to this end.

Are we to conclude then that there is, after all, a care-love that is purely instrumental? I think not, for when Augustine speaks of loving one's neighbor for the sake of God, what he has in mind is not caring for the neighbor so much as it is enjoying him or her; Augustine instructs us to enjoy ourselves and our neighbor for the sake of enjoying God. This enjoyment is not care-love but appreciation-love, since it has as its objective not the welfare but the appreciation or enjoyment of the loved. Augustine's Neoplatonism, it seems, has lead him to construe the biblical commandment to love our neighbors in accordance with an appreciation-love model. Is Augustinian love of the neighbor, then, to be understood as pure appreciation-love, and what exactly does Augustine mean by loving or enjoying one's neighbor for God's sake?

> Whoever, therefore, justly loves his neighbor should so act toward him that he also loves God with his whole heart, with his whole soul, and with his whole mind. Thus, loving his neighbor as himself, he refers the love of both to that love of God which suffers no stream to be led away from it by which it might be diminished.

John Burnaby sums up Augustine's position: "The true love of neighbor is the will 'that he too may love God with a perfect love: you do not love him as yourself, unless you do all you can to bring him to that good which is your own.'"[13]

These passages make it apparent that love of the neighbor is not merely appreciation-love but is also care-love for the neighbor, in that we seek to bring to the neighbor the good that we ourselves have found. Neighbor love is care for the neighbor's spiritual well-being. But notice that it is not in the care element of Augustinian neighbor love that the instrumentality lies. To care for the neighbor instrumentally— as a means to caring for God—could make sense only if caring for God made sense, that is, only if God's welfare could be our goal. This Augustine denies: "He wills not that we do good to Him, because He has done good to us. He has need of nothing." From this passage it is clear that Augustine does not hold an instrumental notion of care-love.[14]

In the ordered love that Augustine advocates, all love must be directed toward the highest good. Love of self, love of neighbor, and love of God all converge in one stream. "The Delight which the lover cannot help taking in the beloved is in this earthly life a lodging, a refreshment for the pilgrim. A rightly ordered love will 'pass through' such delight, not 'remaining at rest in it,' but 'referring' it to God." Christian love for God is delight in and enjoyment of God. Love for self is none other than this same love, mediated through the self but leading to the enjoyment of God. "The love wherewith a man truly loves himself is none other than the love of God." And love of the neighbor is the same love once again, seeking "to instill in the neighbor a self-love similar to his own." It is clear, then, that while the appreciation element in Augustine's theory of love is instrumental, the care element is not.[15]

THE OBJECTS OF CARE-LOVE

If the proceeding analysis of care-love and end value is correct, there are two classes of objects that cannot, in principle, be recipients of care-love: (1) objects that can never be ends but only means; and (2) objects whose benefit cannot possibly be intended. An obvious candidate for the first class is money. Allowing for the possible exception of numismatologists, in loving money we presumably are not seeking its good. Nonetheless, that money can be an object of love, even for those utterly lacking in numismatological tendencies, is only too evident. Such love is not care-love, however. A consideration of the language used to express pecuniary love—"obsession," "intoxication," devotion," "slave"—provides the clue to what is involved. The expression "love of money" is a hyperbole, which no doubt derives its meaning from obsessive forms of romantic love. Candidates for the second class of excluded objects—those whose benefit cannot be intended—are even harder to find because the benefit of anything could be intended under some circumstances, if irrational intentions are not ruled out. So it seems this line of inquiry, of looking for those things that could not be recipients of care-love, is not particularly fruitful. Let us consider instead what kinds of objects are the most suitable recipients of caring?

One answer has already been given: we tend to care for those kinds of things that are likely to benefit from our attention; caring is encouraged by the prospect of results. We are also influenced by the perception of a need for care, especially when we think we are capable of meeting that need. Thus it is that children and pets make especially attractive candidates for human caring. It seems natural as well to care for those who have the capacity and inclination to reciprocate by caring for us in return, or who at least show appreciation for our efforts. Allowing for the diversity of individual love psychologies, however, it must be admitted there are some who prefer to bestow their caring on those who do not or cannot reciprocate.

Another factor influencing care-love is our ability to identify with the potential care object. Interpersonal caring is especially affected by this factor. Someone with whom one cannot identify at all is unlikely to elicit the sorts of feelings that give rise to love. An obvious corollary is that we are apt to care more when identification is strong: the greater the identification, the greater the caring. Identification plays a significant role in our caring for other living things such as pets, or animals closely resembling ourselves such as chimpanzees. Most of us can squash an insect without a qualm, even when it is not thought to be harmful; but the human capacity for identification is highly plastic so that a devout Buddhist or a Jain may experience kinship even with the least inviting of creatures.

In care for inanimate things, identification plays a lesser role. Most of us identify, in some sense of the word, with personal possessions such as our home or a favorite sweater. To a considerable extent, though, we Westerners tend to experience the inanimate world as beyond the range of what can be identified with; but this is by no means universally the case. Consider the following passage written by the environmental philosopher J. Baird Callicott after revisiting the Mississippi River of his childhood:

> As I gazed at the brown silt-choked waters absorbing a black plume of industrial and municipal sewage from Memphis, and, as my eye traced bits of some unknown beige froth floating continually down from Cincinnati, Louisville, or St. Louis, I experienced a palpable pain. It

was not distinctly locatable in any of my extremities, nor was it like a headache or nausea. Still, it was very real. I had no plans to swim in the river, no need to drink from it, no intention of buying real estate on its shores. My narrowly personal interests were not affected, and yet somehow I was personally injured. It occurred to me then, in a flash of self-discovery, that the river was a part of me.[16]

Another factor that influences caring is the esteem with which an object is held; we tend to care more for objects we respond to with appreciation-love. A physically attractive person (the beautiful heroine of a melodrama, say) is apt to elicit a stronger care response than a homely one in the same situation. It is also possible, however, for esteemed qualities to count against a potential care object's appeal. This could happen because the individual seems too remote, so independent that our caring cannot touch him, or so endowed with talent and good fortune as to elicit envy. Especially interesting is the question of care-love for God. If God is conceived of as absolutely perfect, nothing we do could possibly benefit Him. As was noted above, Augustine acknowledges this and in consequence rejects all possibility of caring for God. Yet, since most theists also believe that God is a person they probably do care for Him without noticing the logical difficulty. While most monotheists (influenced by a theology that derives from Greek metaphysics) say that God is infinite and perfect, they act and feel (under the influence of the more mythopoetic language of the Bible) as if He were a grand but quite finite person. If so, when the nontheologian calls God infinite or perfect, probably the appellations function more as honorifics than as literal descriptions.

Inanimate things in general are less compelling objects of care-love. When we do love them in this way, it is often their beauty or other admired quality that motivates our response. Yet our understanding of the history of an object and our association with it also plays a role. For example, the only possession I have from my father's family is a long narrow bread board that belonged to my grandmother, which I like to think she brought with her from Norway. It disquiets me if someone cuts into the soft wood while slicing a loaf of bread. In my view, it should be better cared for.

ALTRUISM, NORMS, AND SELF-LOVE

Reflecting upon the centrality of caring to human life one begins to see the implausibility of the view that we are completely egocentric, that we are looking out always and only for ourselves. Rather, we are connected to one another and to much else besides by an elaborate web of care relations, in which many things are valued as ends. Were this not the case, the world outside us would consist of nothing but objects of use. The thoroughgoing ethical egoist, if there is such a creature, must conceive of himself or herself as the sole and solitary inhabitant of the kingdom of ends. Such a condition would be lonely to the point of desperation. When we deny intrinsic value to the rest of reality, we isolate ourselves and diminish the world in which we live. How can one possibly value living in a universe where nothing but oneself has value?

To be human is to care for and about the people, other living beings, and inanimate things that surround us. These linkages of caring determine our place in the world and define our values. Although caring can burden us, it also gives meaning to our lives. We are not, as philosophers have sometimes supposed, detached spectators of an external world; we are participants engaged with and disposed toward a wide and diverse community of beings. If all our care linkages with the members of this wider community were suddenly broken, I doubt we would know who we are. Mayeroff remarks: "In the sense in which a man can ever be said to be at home in the world, he is at home not through dominating, or explaining, or appreciating, but through caring and being cared for."[17] This is not a rosy picture of human nature but a description of it as it is. Although we are not often—possibly, not ever—selfless, we are not often completely selfish either. Most of what we do is done from mixed motives.

No thoroughgoing defense of altruism will be attempted here, but there are two errors in reasoning often made by those who would deny its existence that must be pointed out.[18] One error is to deduce from the fact that a self-interested motive for a particular action exists that this must be the only motive, or the overriding one. When one is pleased with oneself for helping an old man across the street, for example, it is sometimes inferred that the feeling of self-congratulation must be *the* motive of the action. In fact, however, there is nothing problematic in self-regarding motives operating together with other-regarding ones. An individual merely acts from different, but complementary, motives. To suppose that self-regarding motives somehow override or obliterate other-regarding ones, far from being self-evident, requires considerable defense.

A second and more subtle error arises from the confusion between the locus of the motive and its objective. It does not follow from the fact that a motive is *in* me that it must be *for* me. A self-interested motive is one that has my welfare as its objective, not me as its place of origin. Opponents of altruism often reach a point in their argument where, after the presentation of much evidence that a particular motive is other-regarding, they say, "Yes, but it is the agent's motive so it is his need that is being satisfied." This is to beg the question. Precisely what needs proving is that all motives are self-interested. The conclusion cannot merely be assumed; nor can it be inferred from the fact that all motives are self-located, located, that is, in the agent. Psychological egoists tend to assume either that the proposition "all of my motives are self-interested" is true a priori or that it is deducible from "all of my motives are mine." Neither is the case.

The benevolence of a motive is determined by its objective, not its location. If we ignore this distinction, a desire to help one's neighbor is indistinguishable from a desire to help oneself at one's neighbor's expense. If all acts were completely and therefore equally selfish (which would be the case if selfishness could be inferred from the locus of the motive), the word "selfish" could never be used as a term of moral disapprobation, which, to say the least, would require a considerable revision of moral discourse.

Yet it does not follow from the fact that care-love is other-regarding, that it is intrinsically moral, or that "care-love" is inherently an ethical concept. Caring is a natural phenomenon upon which ethical and other normative ideals can be built. Although we sometimes have a duty to care, caring itself is not necessarily moral in either its intent or its effects. It is simply, as a Heideggerian would say, constitutive of the human way of being-in-the-world. Not only is caring not intrinsically ethical, caring for friends, family, tribe, nation, race, or species often conflicts with the dictates of morality. Hideous things are done every moment because of the preferences inherent in natural care-love.

This is precisely why we need ethical notions of caring, such as that found in the biblical injunction to love our neighbors, and corresponding ideals from other ethical-religious traditions. These ideals of care-love regulate natural care in the direction of more universal and less preferential concerns, enjoining us to love those we are not by nature disposed to care for. Consider the familiar words of Jesus:

> Love your enemies; do good to those who hate you; bless those who curse you; pray for those who treat you spitefully. When a man hits you on the cheek, offer him the other cheek too; when a man takes your

coat, let him have your shirt as well. Give to everyone who asks you; when a man takes what is yours, do not demand it back. Treat others as you would like them to treat you.

If you love only those who love you, what credit is that to you? Even sinners love those who love them. Again, if you do good only to those who do good to you, what credit is that to you? Even sinners do as much. And if you lend only where you expect to be repaid, what credit is that to you? Even sinners lend to each other if they are to be repaid in full. But you must love your enemies and do good; and lend without expecting any return. (Luke 6:28–35)

There can be no doubt that Jesus is asking for something far beyond the realm of natural human love. Indeed, He sometimes rails against natural love, treating it as an obstacle that must be sacrificed if universal love is to be realized:

You must not think that I have come to bring peace to the earth; I have not come to bring peace, but a sword. I have come to set a man against his father, a daughter against her mother, a young wife against her mother-in-law; and a man will find his enemies under his own roof.

No man is worthy of me who cares more for father or mother than for me; no man is worthy of me who cares more for son or daughter; no man is worthy of me who does not take up his cross and walk in my footsteps. (Matthew 10:34–39)

In addition to ethical norms for caring, we also employ psychological standards according to which the emotional health of care-love relations are evaluated. These normative ideals are much closer to natural caring. They do not constitute moral imperatives but, instead, reflect an understanding of how emotionally healthy people care for themselves and others. A man who has made himself physically ill through overwork, for example, might be charged with not caring for himself properly. He may not be morally condemned for this, but questions may certainly be raised regarding his emotional health. Psychological norms of caring presumably derived from how people normally do care, but they go beyond this and prescribe standards for how we ought to care. Thus, a counselor might inform her client that his caring for his son is overprotective and therefore unhealthy. In expressing psychological norms, we are less likely to use obviously moral concepts such as "duty," "obligation," and "right," yet normative expressions such as "should" and "better" are common. These two realms of normative discourse, however—the psychological and the ethical—overlap and are not always easy to tell apart.

It might seem that the distinction between natural and normative notions of caring covers the territory pretty well, so that no other notion is needed. This is not the case, however. In Christian love theory we encounter an ideal of care-love that can only be described as nonnatural or supernatural. There is, we are told, a love that transcends natural human capacities through participation in divine love. Any theory of care-love that is broad enough to embrace the history of Western love theory must make room for this concept as well.

Given the extremity of the New Testament commandment to love our neighbors one might well wonder how such love is possible. The solution given in the First Epistle of John (4:7–21) is that it is not possible, in strictly human terms, but that we are not limited to our own resources. The love we are commanded to is not—or not only—ours. It is the divine agape operating through us, employing us as its instrument. According to Christian theologians, neighbor love is either God's love pure and simple (the position taken by Luther) or a divinely assisted love (the interpretation more often favored by Roman Catholics). Regardless of whether such a supernatural care-love actually exists, a comprehensive philosophy of love must make room for the concept.

The discussion so far may have created the impression that caring must be other-regarding, but this obviously is not the case. We can care for ourselves as well as for others. What is essential to caring is not that it be altruistic but that the cared-for (who, with the exception of self-care, happens to be other) must be valued as an end. Thus, understood, self-care does not constitute a special case; it fits our general theory because it, too, involves valuing the cared-for as an end. And just as with care for another, doing this well presupposes detachment from the care object, which in this case is oneself. In caring well for ourselves we must have a reasonably objective and clearheaded sense of who we are and what our own welfare is.

It is often said that our ability to love others presupposes love of self. Psychologically this is probably true, but conceptually it is other-love that is primary and serves as a model for our understanding of self-love. As so often, Mayeroff captures the idea perfectly: "To care for myself, I must be able to experience myself as other (I must be able to see myself from the inside as I appear from the outside), and at the same time I must feel at one with myself rather than cut off and estranged from myself." Even when the object of love is oneself, then, the same duality of union with and separation from pertains. Mayeroff also insists there is a great difference between self-love and selfishness, egocentricity, or self-indulgence. In keeping with Mayeroff, I propose we think of selfishness not as self-love but as the failure to love others, the failure to recognize their equal worth. It consists particularly in placing one's own interest before that of others, even when others' needs are greater than one's own:

> Egocentricity is morbid preoccupation with self and opaqueness to the needs of others. But there is nothing egocentric about caring for myself. First, the self-idolatry and the preoccupation with whether or not others admire me that are characteristic of egocentricity have nothing to do with helping myself to grow. In fact, the egocentric person is not fundamentally interested in himself; he avoids looking honestly at himself because he is essentially indifferent to his own needs to actualize himself. The self-complacency that often accompanies egocentricity is the converse of responding to one's own needs to grow.[19]

For Mayeroff, caring for oneself (what I would call caring well or wisely) actually includes within it caring for others. We can fulfill ourselves only by serving something outside. To do so is actually a requirement of our own self-actualization. We become who we are through helping others realize themselves. The Peruvian poet Cesar Vallejo gives expression to this in his poem "Agape":

> Today no one has come to inquire,
> nor have they wanted anything from me this afternoon.

> I have not seen a single cemetery flower
> in so happy a procession of lights.
> Forgive me. Lord! I have died so little!

> This afternoon everyone, everyone goes by
> without asking or begging me anything.

> And I do not know what it is they forget, and it is
> heavy in my hands like something stolen.

> I have come to the door,
> and I want to shout at everyone:
> —If you miss something, here it is!

> Because in all the afternoons of this life,
> I do not know how many doors are slammed on a face,
> and my soul takes something that belongs to another.
>
> Today nobody has come;
> and today I have died so little in the afternoon![20]

What I take to be the central idea of this poem, that it is theft to refuse to take from others what they need to give, calls our attention to how pointless is the attempt to make too sharp a separation between self-regarding and other-regarding interests. The filling and emptying of the self are equally fundamental—and are inseparable. When you take what I need to give, you have given to me; and when you refuse my gift, you take something from me. If I serve only my own interests, I diminish myself by failing to recognize my own need to be of use to others. In this way, I constrict the boundaries of my self by conceiving of it too atomistically.

UNCONDITIONALITY AND UNIVERSALITY

One of the most familiar observations about love is that it is unconditional. This has been said most often by religious love theorists, but authors of popular books on the subject frequently make the same claim. What is discussed far less often is what it means to call love unconditional. There seem to be two obvious but widely divergent ways of construing the claim: (1) that there can be no specific conditions placed upon loving ("I'll love you if you take out the garbage" or "I'll love you if you love me first"); and (2) that love admits of no conditions whatever ("I will love you no matter what you do, no matter who you are, or what you become"). When conditions of the first kind are placed on loving, the promise to love is little more than a badly concealed manipulation, a way of getting others to do what we want. There is nothing especially loving in this strategy, although we do sometimes use it on those we love. Obviously care-love is unconditional in this first sense.

The second formulation, if taken strictly, would require that loving not be conditioned by any of the qualities or behaviors of the loved. This is not how caring usually works. Typically, and some would say always, care is a response to the nature of, and our consequent feelings for, the loved: I care for you "because you are such a nice person," "because you are so responsible," "because you are fun to be with," "because you bring forth the best in me." This is the way caring naturally arises; it arises in response to the conditions that govern our affections. Clearly, natural (personal) caring is not unconditional in this second sense. At the same time, there are nonpersonal forms of care-love arising from our altruistic emotions that are far less conditional than personal care-love. For example, we may learn of the suffering of a complete stranger and respond with care. Here the love is conditioned by the fact of suffering, but presumably not by other qualities of the loved.

Ethical and especially nonnatural caring, however, are less conditional than natural care-love. These loves at least reach toward the ideal of complete unconditionality. Some ethical ideals of caring require that we love all human beings equally, without regard to who they are individually or how they are related to us. It may be doubted that this is actually possible, but this is where the supernatural ideal of love comes to the rescue with its claim that, although such a love is not *humanly* possible, it can occur through grace.

Since there is a considerable gap between the two meanings of "unconditional" examined thus far, it makes sense to search for a middle ground, for a less radical sense of "unconditional love." Love normally arises amid what we might call conditions—"you are my child" (rather than someone else's) or "you have a beautiful voice and a sweet smile"—but once love has been awakened and the heart opened, these conditions tend to soften and become less relevant. As our relationship develops, I come to accept your shortcomings and foibles, much as I have learned to accept my own. So even if your voice changes and your smile is not always so sweet, I continue to love you. Here we have a third construal of "unconditional."

Saying that love is unconditional in this third and intermediate sense does not mean that it is conditioned by nothing at all but, rather, that once the love for a specific individual has come into existence, it is not destroyed merely because the person changes and the qualities that initially attracted the lover alter or disappear—"Love is not love / Which alters when it alteration finds."[21] Actually, love probably will alter when it encounters alterations in the beloved, but it need not vanish, or even diminish. It could deepen, in fact, becoming more human and forbearing. A woman's love for her son may be conditioned by the fact that he was such an adorable baby, but now that the boy is a disgusting adolescent whom the mother finds impossible to like probably will not destroy her love. These changes may have altered the character of the mother's love but almost certainly not the fact that she loves him. Even here, the love is not fully unconditional (in the second sense); it is conditioned by the facts that the boy is the woman's son and that she has invested so many years in their relationship. This third interpretation of "unconditional" is no doubt closer to what is usually meant when love is said to be unconditional. In any case, there is no doubt that this kind of unconditionality plays a considerable role in caring for persons.

It is significant that "unconditional" (in either the second or the third sense of the term) does not generally apply to care-love for inanimate things.[22] The reason, I believe, lies in the different attitude we take toward continuity in our love for things and our love for persons or even pets. My love for my favorite oriental carpet is not challenged by its alterations in the same way as my love for my wife might be. To be sure, the carpet may change with age, and I may love it either more or less as it wears and its colors soften, but the alteration of my love does not have the same significance as would a corresponding change in my love for my aging wife.

This points up an important fact about caring for persons. It has a moral dimension not found in the love of things—to care for someone, especially over a long period of time, is to acquire an obligation to continue caring. Were I to cease caring for my wife merely because she now weighs twenty pounds more than when I married her, I would be judged a shallow and fickle husband. An alteration in my love for my oriental carpet may be viewed merely as a change in taste; my taste in carpets has improved over time. My taste in wives may have improved as well, but any alteration of my love consequent upon this change is morally more problematic.

One reason that caring for persons carries with it moral obligations is that it involves a concern for the other's growth and development. To care well is to make a commitment to the ongoing well-being of the ones we care for. How well we honor these commitments says much about our moral character.

It is interesting to note how the commitment to care, and caring's consequent unconditionality, varies with different kinds of relationships. My caring for a colleague might be conditional upon our formal association, that we teach at the same university, for instance. If either of us moves on to a new job, the care bond between us may very nearly cease. With a personal friend, the bond is stronger and my obligation greater. I make the effort to care even when it is inconvenient, and even if distance separates us. Still, friendships do change and friends move in and out of our lives with comparative ease. The care bonds that hold families together are different again. I may have little in common with my father and realize that if I were to meet him today for the first time I would not choose him as a friend. Yet because he is my father—the only father I will ever have—I care for him deeply, even perhaps if I also dislike him, disapprove of the way he lives, or for that matter sometimes hate him. Thus it is that the child of abusive parents often continues to love them.

Marital bonds usually stand somewhere between the bonds of friendship and those of blood. Like friendships they are (in our culture) voluntary, but like relationships with parents, siblings, and children they cut deeply into who we are. The bond of marriage in Western society has traditionally been regarded as indissoluble. Increasingly, however, we have come to accept the fact that marital love does not always last and that dissolution of the bond may be legitimate. Our increasing tolerance of divorce does not necessarily signify a change in how we love, or that our ancestors loved better or more deeply than we just because they were less likely to divorce. Not divorcing hardly constitutes proof of love. Robert Creeley offers this unforgettable comment on the subject:

> The first retainer
> he gave to her was a golden
> wedding ring.

> The second—late at night
> he woke up,
> leaned over on an elbow,
> and kissed her.

> The third and the last—
> he died with
> and gave up loving
> and lived with her.[23]

It is sometimes said that love simply is a commitment. While acknowledging that we often make a commitment to love, I think it best to regard the kind of love under discussion as a natural phenomenon, to which commitment is sometimes added as a separate intention or act of will. Rather than viewing love itself as a commitment, I would prefer to say that we can and do commit to love.

In conclusion to this analysis of care-love's alleged unconditionality, we may say that when natural care-love is directed toward persons and animals, it is not usually (and possibly not ever) unconditional in the most extreme sense, but tends to be unconditional in the modified sense just delineated. Were we articulating an ideal of caring, we might want to make complete unconditionality (the second sense described above) a part of our conception of care-love, for there is no doubt that ethical and spiritual forms of love tend in this direction even if we never fully reach the ideal in practice.

The concern thus far has been to describe and analyze care-love as a natural phenomenon. There is, however, an ethical ideal of universal love that can be found, with some variation, in the teachings of all of the world's great spiritual traditions. In the West we have usually referred to this phenomenon as "neighbor love,"[24] from the biblical commandment "love your neighbor as yourself." As voluminous as are the attempts to analyze and interpret this apparently simple utterance, no consensus yet exists as to its exact meaning; but there is wide agreement that "neighbor" embraces all human beings. Since neighbor love is principally a form of care-love, loving one's neighbor requires caring for all human beings.

The question may reasonably be asked, "Is it actually possible to care for all?" Noddings is convinced it is not: "I shall reject the notion of universal caring—that is, caring for everyone—on the grounds that it is impossible to actualize and leads us to substitute abstract problem solving and mere talk for genuine caring." It is in some sense possible, she explains, to care *about* everyone but not to care *for* them. The former she views as merely verbal and as "unattainable in any but the most abstract sense and thus a source of distraction [from genuine caring]." She continues:

> Our ethic of caring—which we might have called a "feminine ethic"—begins to look a bit mean in contrast to the masculine ethics of universal love or universal justice. But universal love is an illusion. Under the illusion, some young people retreat to the church to worship that which they cannot actualize; some write lovely poetry extolling universal love; and some, in terrible disillusion, kill to establish the very principles which should have entreated them not to kill. Thus are lost both principles and persons.[25]

Noddings's attack on the ideal of universal love has merit. There is a merely verbal, abstract, and archetypically male ideal of universal love that sometimes has the pernicious consequences she describes. She does well to contrast this with a more feminine and grounded ideal of caring-for.

A wholesale rejection of universal love as merely abstract and verbal will not do, however. Certainly Jesus did not view neighbor love as an abstraction. When asked, "Who is my neighbor?" he responded by relating the well-known parable of the good Samaritan (Luke 10:29–37), which concludes with the admonition, "go and do as he did"—a concrete ending to a concrete story. No mere intentions or abstract theorizing here! To love your neighbor is to love anyone you meet who is in need; and loving him or her requires nothing less than meeting those needs. To live up to this commandment is a formidable task that, in my judgement, few have earnestly undertaken.

Given the enormity of the task, it is understandable that believers have often reduced it to a verbal formula or an abstract intention, even though this was not its original meaning. One of our contemporaries who has taken the original meaning of the biblical commandment seriously is Mother Teresa of Calcutta. She and her followers put it into daily practice. They do not "retreat to the church to worship that which they cannot actualize." Rather, they devote their lives to caring for the poorest of the poor. Mother Teresa's first postulate, Sister Agnes, explains that their ability to do this work rests upon devoting hours each day to prayer, meditation, adoration, and participation in the mass. "It would be impossible to work otherwise. There must be a spiritual motive. You can work only for God. You can never work for any man."[26] This labor is accomplished, they insist, only through the recognition that it is not their human love that is at work but God's love. Such love, according to its practitioners, does not and cannot come from the human will alone. Here we have something quite different from the natural and ethical caring that Noddings celebrates and so eloquently elucidates. Rather it is what the author of the First Epistle of John described as God's agape, which uses us as its vehicle. This kind of love is accomplished through surrender, through the willingness to be used, more than through any assertion of individual will.

It is difficult for the secular mind, even one as sensitive and intelligent as Nodding's, to understand this spiritual love. As philosophers we might, at least on the literal level, question the theology and metaphysics employed by Mother Teresa and her followers in accounting for how they do what they do, but there is no denying these women's work is extraordinary and goes well beyond the limits of the natural and ethical caring familiar to most of us. To anyone acquainted with the remarkable work of Mother Teresa and her order, it is difficult to dismiss universal love as "an illusion" or "merely verbal."[27] Universal care-love does exist, even though most of us may have never encountered it in our personal lives.

CHAPTER 3

Union-Love

❖ That lovers seek to become one, or believe they already are, is a commonplace found in much of the love literature of the world, both romantic and mystical. Yet what exactly do lovers want in this quest for union? And what do they find when they get there? The idea is so familiar we assume we know what is meant. As soon as we attempt to say what union is, however, we encounter formidable difficulties. Eventually we run up against some of the thornier problems of philosophy, psychology, and religion: the nature of personal identity, the symbiotic union of mother and infant and its impact on later life, the baffling claim of the mystics that "all is one." Before bruising our heads on these difficult matters, however, let us explore the simpler conceptual issues that arise in analyzing union-love.

It was noted in the last chapter that care-love presupposes a kind of union between the lover and the loved, the union we call identification. Apparently we care only for that with which we can, in some measure, identify. Caring well, however, demands a degree of separation and detachment so that we distinguish the loved's well-being from our own. No doubt union-love too presupposes identification—would we seek union with someone or something we could not identify with at all?—but its fundamental nature is not this presupposed union of identification so much as it is the desire for union. To the extent that union already exists, union-love is the desire to preserve, perpetuate, or deepen it. Minimally, union-love requires a positive attitude toward the union. This is evident from the following considerations. If I believe that you and I are one, in any understanding of the expression (we have the same interests, we share a common destiny, we are psychically in tune, we are devoted to the same political or religious cause, we complement each other making a perfect whole between us, our ego boundaries are so confused that we can no longer tell each other's thoughts and feelings apart), it hardly follows that I love you. Indeed, although any of these kinds of union might be grounds for my loving you (and may, under many circumstances, make it probable that I would), they are also compatible with my hating you. I might hate you precisely because you are too close, too much like me, a threat to my autonomy. Interpersonal union becomes love only when our attitude toward it is favorable.

Recalling that all forms of love involve a relation between a subject and an object, and that what principally differentiates one form of love from another is the exact character of the relation (that is, the specific tendencies or inclinations on the part of the subject toward the object), we can see that what sets union-love apart from its sister loves is this (frequently passionate) desire for union; (or for preserving, deepening, or extending an existing union). We can say, then, that care-love and union-love have different objectives. The first aims at the welfare of the loved. To the extent that I experience care-love for you, I am concerned with what is in your best interest, even if it should prove contrary to mine. The second, on the other hand, has union itself as its objective, even should it turn out to be good for neither of us. Thus if my beloved feels it is necessary to separate from me, insofar as I love her with union-love alone, I could be said to resist her desire for independence "because I love her." To this, she might protest that, if I really loved her, I would want what was best for her. And she is right, to the extent she is thinking of caring or some normative ideal of caring rather than union-love. Yet my apparently contradictory claim, that I want her to stay because I love her, is also true. My lover and I are using "love" in two different but legitimate, even if in this case conflicting, senses.

Should I love her with both care-love and union-love (a more likely scenario) I will be out of harmony myself, wanting her both to leave and to stay, and wanting both because of love. (This of course assumes that I am able to recognize she would be better off without me, which might be more than many union-lovers could manage.) The objection might still be offered: "You don't really love her at all. What you call 'love' is merely possessiveness. You wish to hang on to her for your own selfish reasons, not because you love her." The objector has a point, but the lover's desire for union is not necessarily the desire to possess the beloved as one possesses an item of clothing. Indeed, it could be quite the opposite: the desire to be possessed by one's

lover. Yet both these desires, to possess and to be possessed, are extreme and arguably perverse forms of union-love. As we shall see,
there are many other forms of love union.

ONE CRITIC AND ONE CHAMPION OF UNION

Rainer Maria Rilke was critical of the ideal of love as union. Rather
than attempt to paraphrase a writer of Rilke's ability, whose persua-
siveness has much to do with how his ideas are expressed, we will let
him speak for himself, with the aid of an English translator:

> I hold this to be the highest task of a bond between two people: that
> each should stand guard over the solitude of the other. For, if it lies in
> the nature of indifference and of the crowd to recognize no solitude,
> then love and friendship are there for the purpose of continually pro-
> viding the opportunity for solitude. And only those are the true shar-
> ings which rhythmically interrupt periods of deep isolation. . . .
>
> It is a question in marriage, to my feeling, not of creating a quick
> community of spirit by tearing down and destroying all boundaries, but
> rather a good marriage is that in which each appoints the other
> guardian of his solitude, and shows him this confidence, the greatest in
> his power to bestow. A *togetherness* between two people is an impossibil-
> ity, and where it seems, nevertheless, to exist it is a narrowing, a recip-
> rocal agreement which robs either one party or both of his fullest free-
> dom and development. But, once the realization is accepted that even
> between the closest human beings infinite distances continue to exist, a
> wonderful living side by side can grow up, if they succeed in loving the
> distance between them which makes it possible for each to see the
> other whole and against a wide sky! . . .
>
> At bottom no one in life can help anyone else in life; this one experi-
> ences over and over in every conflict and every perplexity: that one is
> alone.
>
> All companionship can consist only in the strengthening of two
> neighboring solitudes, whereas everything that one is wont to call giving
> oneself is by nature harmful to companionship: for when a person aban-
> dons himself, he is no longer anything, and when two people both give
> themselves up in order to come close to each other, there is no longer
> any ground beneath them and their being together is a continual falling.[1]

There is wisdom in these words as well as eloquence. For those who
love solitude or who have had the experience of extricating them-

selves from an overly enmeshed love relationship, Rilke's words are likely to have a definite appeal. Especially compelling is the comment that loving the distance between them makes it possible for lovers to see each other "whole and against a wide sky!" However, to my ears, there is a ring of bitterness in some of these words as well. One wonders if he would have written in this manner had Lou Salome, the great love of his life, not finally rejected him, or indeed if he had been raised by a less invasive mother.[2]

In any case, Rilke makes two distinct claims in these passages. He asserts first that union is impossible. Consider his rather chilling words: "this one experiences over and over in every conflict and every perplexity: that one is alone." There is truth here: human existence is individual in that we each have our unique histories, our own feelings and thoughts (accessing them in a way that others cannot), we make our own decisions for which we are responsible, and as Heidegger reminds us, each of us must die alone.[3] But is human existence so solitary that all union is impossible? Is it true that, "even between the closest human beings infinite distances continue to exist"? *Infinite* distances?

Rilke's second point emerges when, after remarking again that "a *togetherness* between two people is an impossibility," he adds, "and where it seems, nevertheless, to exist it is a narrowing, a reciprocal agreement which robs either one party or both of his fullest freedom and development." So in addition to claiming that union is impossible, Rilke is convinced that even where it seems to exist it diminishes either one or both of the lovers. Rather than responding to this critique—the task really of the remainder of this and all of the next chapter—we will go on to consider a diametrically opposed point of view.

Robert C. Solomon has written two engaging and insightful (if sometimes exasperating) books on love, in which he advances the thesis that love consists in the creation of what he calls a "shared self."[4] "[L]ove involves an actual fusion of selves, a kind of mutual indispensability rather than mere mutual attractiveness and enjoyment." The kind of love he has in mind is romantic love. Other forms of love he largely ignores, even apparently regretting that they are referred to by the same word.[5] Troubled by the idea of the merging of selves, Irving Singer has written: "My difficulty with the concept of merging has resulted from my inability to interpret it in any literal sense . . . . Lovers, however intimate, are separate individuals." Yet literal merging is exactly what Solomon says occurs: "we can and do literally 'merge ourselves' in love, for this, and nothing else, is what love is." "It is the task of this book to make . . . new sense out of 'love' through a literal rather than metaphoric sense of the 'fusion' of two souls."[6]

Solomon's usual formulation is that love simply is shared identity or selfhood: "Love is shared identity." On other occasions, he says (more appropriately) that it is the desire for or the attempt to achieve shared identity: "Love . . . is the attempt to find another person who will give us a sense of our 'true' selves and make us feel complete, once and for all." To confuse matters further, there are places where, noting that we also have a tendency to preserve our own autonomy, he characterizes love in a third, more complicated way: "Love is the dialectical tension between individual independence and autonomy on the one hand and the ideal of shared identity on the other."[7] Since Solomon clearly allows for the possibility of unrequited love, it is best to follow the second formulation and identify love with the desire for or urge to create a shared identity, and view the first and third formulations as descriptions of the love relationship.[8]

What is meant by "shared identity" or "shared selfhood"? In Solomon's view, the self is not fixed and well defined but fluid and continually in process. Rather than a metaphysical substance, the self is a social construct that arises from our interactions with others. In love we redefine or reconstitute our very identity together with another person, becoming a couple or, in Solomon's language, a "shared self."

No doubt Solomon is right that the self in the social-psychological sense is not a fixed entity and is shaped through social interactions. How our parents, siblings, other relatives, friends, and teachers respond to us, how they treat us, what they say about us, all have much to do not only with how we think and feel about ourselves but with who we in fact become. Solomon sometimes acknowledges that the self is constructed through these more formative loves of childhood, but more often he seems to assume that it is romantic love that shapes the self. For example, in a passage where the subject is clearly romantic love, he asserts: "love essentially provides our most basic sense of self-identity." Later he adds: "It is ourselves we choose in choosing our intimacies." "The creation of the self is, more than anything else, the establishing of a variety of roles, romantic *roles* in particular, in which the self is defined primarily in terms of one sensuous, intimate relationship."[9]

It is true that, when we fall in love, we acquire through our beloved a new sense of ourselves. We find new roles to play, new feelings to explore, new strengths and vulnerabilities. Falling in love can be a rebirth experience, in which a new self is seemingly called into being.

Literary evidence for this can be found in the famous balcony scene from Shakespeare's *Romeo and Juliet*:

> Juliet: ... Romeo, doff thy name,
>   And for thy name, which is no part of thee,
>   Take all myself.
> Romeo: I take thee at thy word.
>   Call me but Love, and I'll be new baptiz'd,
>   Henceforth I never will be Romeo.[10]

But do we always undergo such a rebirth experience when we enter a new romantic relationship? Even if we do, has a new self literally come into being? The tradition whereby the woman abandons her family name and assumes her husband's when she marries may suggest that this is so for women, but one wonders how many women (or men) feel that marriage has provided them a new self. Is not the change in identity brought on by romantic love sometimes rather slight? And when this is so, would it not be odd to describe the process as a literal creation of a new self?

Certainly there is a connection between romantic love and personal identity, but what does Solomon mean when he says that lovers share, or seek to share, a self? I find a new self in a manner of speaking, or at least a new way of looking at myself, when I fall in love, but surely my beloved and I do not literally share the same self? To be more precise, as I enter a new romantic relationship, I gain a (somewhat) new image of myself and my partner does the same, but neither my self nor my image of myself is identical with her self or self-image. We speak of "our union," of "becoming one," but all of this is metaphor. We are never literally one, at least on the empirical psychological plane. Even in pathological cases where ego boundaries become hopelessly confused, lovers still know that they are distinct individuals.

As we have seen, however, Solomon does not always identify love—more accurately, the romantic love relationship—with the creation of a shared self. Sometimes he even says that shared identity is an impossibility:

> Shared selfhood is the goal of love, the aim of its every word, caress and gesture, but it is a partial, ultimately impossible goal that must always coexist with the reality of two very different people, each with their own histories and backgrounds, their own battles in life, their own personalities.[11]

Even when denying the possibility of full union, however, Solomon insists that lovers want to fuse. This lends his vision of love a tragic cast, as if it were a kind of Sartrian hopeless project in which lovers pursue what can never be.

Do lovers really yearn for a literal fusion of selves? Psychiatrist Ethel Spector Person insists to the contrary that a love relationship is always with an other.[12] If there were no other (as would be the case with literal fusion) there would be, she tells us, no relationship. Solomon allows that love has otherness as its precondition. "[T]he independent individual is the presupposition of love." He immediately adds, "and this independence is just what love wants to overcome and deny." The passage continues:

> Making love is a desperate and temporarily successful attempt to be one, but we are painfully aware, even in our most satisfied moments, that there is still an abyss between us. And so we always want more, love being not satisfaction but desperation, for the true end of our desire is never satisfied.[13]

There are compelling reasons for doubting that sexual lovers wish to overcome their separateness. Much of the charm of lovemaking resides in the fact that the lovers are not literally one. I caress my beloved, giving her pleasure, and she caresses me. If she were not other, my caress of her would be a self-caress, which is something quite different. I experience her caress as a gift only because it does not come from me and is not controlled by me. It is given to me by another. Sexual lovers like romantic lovers in general, seek to preserve difference and otherness even in union. Where there is no other, not only is there no relationship (as Person urges), there is no union, only a single solitary self.[14] I value my beloved's otherness, the ways in which her body is different from mine. I surrender to her and to the pleasure she gives me, yielding to her as other, not as an extension of myself. Far from wanting to literally merge, I cherish how she is both different and separate from me. A large part of the joy of romantic and marital relationships is being able to watch close up how another, always somewhat mysterious being, thinks, feels, and lives.

There can be no doubt that personal identity is altered by love, but Solomon both exaggerates and misconstrues how this alteration takes place. Lovers often speak of "we"—"we think," "we feel," "we did"—indicating that they view themselves as, in some sense, joined. At the same time, however (as Solomon often observes), lovers realize that they are still two reasonably distinct individuals. The I-self is not replaced by the we-self as Solomon's language sometimes suggests. Rather, a new shared identity is established alongside, within, or surrounding an earlier, more individual, or more family-of-origin-based, identity.[15] In fact, part of the social and psychological function of romantic love in modern Western culture is to help young people extricate themselves from the families in which they grew up through an intense identification with someone outside the family. In this way, falling in love actually contributes to the formation of a more independent sense of personal identity. Seen in this light, every human being participates in several different identities. Solomon writes:

> The contemporary self . . . is notoriously *underdetermined*, in the sense that who we are is always an open question. In a single day we may play a multiplicity of roles, each with its own self—parent, child, teacher, student, friend, nemesis, intruder or center of attention. Within this confusion and occasional conflict of roles we try to pick out our "true" selves, give priority to some over others, denying some ("I wasn't myself last night") entirely. But there is rarely a "right" choice in such matters; there is no "true" self that dominates all others and, even if one self, one set of roles were to dominate, that identity is still always a choice, always an option.

There is much truth in this description but one cannot help wondering, Who is playing these various roles? Who is doing the choosing, if there is no self underlying the multiplicity of role-selves? Solomon's answer is, No one. "Every self is composed of *roles*, not as a front or facade, but as its very essence. . . . [T]he truth is that the self is . . . the wearing of masks—[there is] nothing behind them."[16]

Fellow philosophers will sympathize with Solomon's reluctance to posit the existence of some mysterious, unknowable transcendental ego as the owner of our thoughts and perceptions, but Solomon's solution, though less metaphysical, is no less mysterious. Besides, are we not, all of us selves, aware of choosing and playing roles? If so, once again we must ask, Who does the choosing and the playing? Another role? Some particular "package" of roles? If the latter, what gives this package its coherence? What differentiates package me from package you? Solomon observes that the roles lovers play are often clichés.[17] True, but then what differentiates one self in love from another, if not that they are played by different individuals, different agents, different selves? Are we to believe that the only thing that distinguishes us from one another is that each of us belongs to some unique constellation of roles?

More troubling, if "self" simply means "role," where is the originality of Solomon's thesis that love reconstitutes the self? Becoming a new self would then mean only playing new roles. That we acquire new roles when we enter a new love relationship is hardly a novel idea, let alone a new theory of love. Even if the self is simply a collection of roles, the problem remains that we do not play the same role as our lover plays, as a literal shared-self theory would seem to require.

Maybe Solomon does not mean, as his language leads us to expect, that lovers share or seek to share the very same self. Some passages suggest a quite different, less radical, interpretation: "there is nothing mysterious about shared selfhood, self-identity conceived through identification with another person, or group, or institution. Being on a team with 'team spirit,' for example, is a sharing of one's self, at least for a few hours, perhaps for the season."[18] Here it seems that shared selfhood or identity, Solomon's defining characteristic of romantic love, is only a matter of identifying with or sharing one's self. If so, we may wonder once more what is new in Solomon's theory. Few will be surprised by the idea that romantic lovers identify with or share themselves with one another. I am not the first to be confused by Solomon's view of a literal fusion of selves. Singer has written, "I find this analysis unacceptable because it seems to confuse the sharing of self with an actual merging, which is what Solomon means by 'shared identity.'"[19] The frustration in trying to understand Solomon's identity theory of love is that, as he sometimes formulates it, it seems fantastically extreme, whereas on other formulations it appears little more than a commonplace.

There is a legitimate sense in which lovers share an identity, a way in which they constitute a "we." Through identification, through the sharing of selves, and through the private performance of romantic roles—all of which Solomon elucidates brilliantly—lovers participate in an identity to which outsiders have only limited access. Robert Bly offers a poignant description of such an identity in his poem, "A Third Body":

> A man and a woman sit near each other, and they do not long
> at this moment to be older, or younger, nor born
> in any other nation, or time, or place.
> They are content to be where they are, talking or not-talking.
> Their breaths together feed someone whom we do not know.

The man sees the way his fingers move;
he sees her hands close around a book she hands to him.
They obey a third body that they share in common.
They have made a promise to love that body.
Age may come, parting may come, death will come.
A man and a woman sit near each other;
as they breathe they feed someone we do not know,
someone we know of, whom we have never seen.[20]

As important as this we-identity is, I remain uncomfortable with Solomon's description of it as a literal shared self. His formulation is troubling because selves are also, in a very legitimate sense, individual and reasonably distinct. In this familiar sense of "self" no two people are ever literally one. Notwithstanding his sometimes unfortunate choice of words, Solomon often acknowledges this impossibility but then, as we have seen, claims that lovers wish to be one. To the contrary, I propose that the "we" lovers seek (and find) is one that embraces separation and individuality within it; and when they say otherwise, they are speaking metaphorically—or possibly metaphysically.

If a literal union of selves on the psychological plane is not the goal of union-love, then what is? This is the question that will occupy us throughout the rest of this chapter and the next. It will turn out that there are many answers, many kinds of union that lovers seek, some simple and pedestrian, others elusive and more complex. Let us begin by considering some of the commoner forms of interpersonal union.

COMMON FORMS OF INTERPERSONAL UNION

One of the simplest forms of interpersonal union arises from the sharing of interests, tastes, and values. With such common ground two individuals may feel themselves united in contrast with or in opposition to others who do not share the same tastes, values, or interests. If, while talking to fellow passengers on a cross-country bus trip, for example, I encounter someone who shares my admiration for Shostakovich's string quartets or my aversion to consumerism, we will experience a boundary closing around us excluding others. Such a sharing of interests does not necessarily result in love, not even the love we call friendship. Yet union based on shared interests, tastes, and values is common in love relationships and usually constitutes part of the basis for them. Our more superficial friendships may be based on little else.

If I come to find my fellow traveler's manner of relating to me uncomfortable (excessively remote, say, or too intimate and personal for my liking), a desire for friendship will probably not emerge. I may even break off the conversation despite the interests and tastes we have in common. On the other hand, even if my traveling companion and I differ significantly in our moral and aesthetic values, but I find his way of discussing those disagreements agreeable—if, for example, he listens carefully and respectfully to what I say, responds intelligently, and offers his own opinions in a manner that leaves room for mine—I may end up feeling a greater affinity with him than would be engendered by any commonality of beliefs. Here we move from shared interests and tastes to something deeper. Let us call it compatibility of relationship styles. What I have in mind is the overall character of relating—how one listens and talks, the quality and duration of eye contact, the degree of intimacy, the degree of emotional interaction, or any of a host of other factors to which we respond, even if only subliminally.

Compatibility of relationship styles is not always a matter of similarity; frequently complementary styles work better together. For example, a very talkative individual and a reticent one may find themselves comfortable partners because they can then each do what they do best, or avoid doing what they are reluctant to do. Thus, those who particularly dislike talking about themselves may choose to spend time with individuals who rarely ask and, perhaps, do not care. It is obvious that our choice of companions is not necessarily made with the objective of maximizing intimacy. The opposite may even be the case: I may spend time with people who talk only of facts, precisely because I am uncomfortable with anything else. Yet even in this there is a kind of union. I am united, in a distant but for me familiar and comfortable way, with my fellow fact-lover or feeling-avoider. A boundary is formed keeping us on the inside and others, those who might come too close, on the outside. Here we have what might be termed a nonintimate union.

Another form of union often found in love relationships is that which arises with mutual sexual attraction. Let us return to the fellow travelers with similar moral or artistic sensibilities. Suppose my companion is someone I find sexually attractive. In time, I notice that she is responding to me in a similar way. Now we have something in common that is potentially more powerful than a mutual interest in Shostakovich. Indeed, sexual attractions can be so powerful they cause us to ignore other differences, even when those differences are considerable. Perhaps I never really paid that much attention to

Shostakovich's quartets before but have only convinced myself that I love them because of my alluring companion's contagious enthusiasm.

Sexual attractions, when mutual, are highly effective at breaking down personal boundaries. Even without sexual union itself, individuals who are drawn to one another are united by a shared desire that, again, leaves others on the outside. Their fascination with each other cuts them off from the rest of the world, causing their attention to focus almost exclusively on each other. They are foreground, all else is background. Because of their mutual interest, they are present and engaged to a heightened degree. The intensity of this desire often leads us to seriously misperceive who or what the other person is, projecting onto them qualities they may not possess.

We have already seen one example of union based on complementary differences in our discussion of relationship styles, but the phenomenon merits further examination. Through complementary differences, individuals are united not by what they have in common but by dissimilarities that allow them to fit together—forming, as it were, a greater whole. This kind of union is common in marriages and in romantic relationships but plays a significant role in friendships as well.

Traditional sex roles seem to have been designed to force men and women together artificially, as if there were not already enough in the way of differences, attraction, and commonality to do so. Men who could not cook, iron their pants, or sew a button on a shirt were ready-made for women who were not able to drive a car, balance a checkbook, or replace a fuse. Potentially more troubling than unions based on deficiencies in skills, however, are those based on deficiencies in emotional development, such as that between an individual incapable of care-giving and tenderness and another capable of little else. In the parlance of the day, we call these "codependent relationships," relationships in which both partners are in some sense diminished by the way they need one another. Not all attractions based upon complementary differences are debilitating, however. A shy and inward-looking individual might be attracted to a more extroverted one, or an energetic and gregarious person who has a tendency to get out of control may be drawn to a more rational but moderately boring mate who provides stability for the more excitable partner. These kinds of complementary differences often work very well in love relationships.

We have noticed how care-love and union-love can conflict, but when caring is mutual, and particularly when there is a commitment to mutual caring, a strong bond comes into being that unites the individuals. They do not become completely fused, however, for mutual caring presupposes distance even while it fosters union. This mutual commitment to care is one of the forces that holds families and friendships together. In marrying, husband and wife make such a commitment to each other and then, if the marriage is fruitful, to their children, who in turn may end up caring for their parents in old age. Often familial unions based on reciprocal caring—and other factors as well—endure and deepen over time despite profound differences in values, tastes, and beliefs.

Two closely related factors leading to union between people are compassion and fellow-feeling. "Compassion" refers to fellow-feeling based on suffering or sorrow, while the latter expression has a wider range of meaning, including sharing in another's joy or triumph. Earlier we noted how Nel Noddings distinguishes between "compassion" and "empathy" on the grounds that the latter involves asking ourselves how we *would* feel if we were in another's shoes; it is, she says, essentially a mental act. Through compassion, however, we engage emotionally, actually feeling how the other feels. Similarly, in feeling-with others' joy, we join with them in a real, if temporary, union. An important feature of compassion and fellow-feeling is that they do not depend on any established personal relationship, nor do they necessarily lead to any. One may feel compassion almost instantly with someone one does not know and will never meet, as when a news story on the radio suddenly moves us to tears. When this occurs a genuine experience of union breaks through our emotional boundaries. This can happen almost any time and with almost anyone or anything—complete strangers, characters in a novel or play, people we normally dislike, or other species of animals.

Not all of the forms of interpersonal union discussed thus far necessarily constitute union-love, although they all may exist within union-love relationships and contribute to their formation. Nor is the above list anywhere near exhaustive. These are merely some of the ways in which people may experience union. Let us now consider two kinds of union that have much to do with love.

ROMANTIC LOVE AND THE COUPLE

Romantic love is prototypically union-love: when we fall in love, we desire to be one with our beloved and are invested in preserving and protecting that union once it is established. We have seen how Robert Solomon accounts for this form of union with his theory of shared identity. Psychiatrist Ethel Spector Person's understanding of romantic union is quite different. Many psychologists and psychiatrists have judged romantic love to be suspect, on the grounds that it weakens or even dissolves the ego boundaries that are essential to sound mental health. Person agrees that romantic relationships alter our ego boundaries but in ways that are not inherently pathological or regressive. She characterizes this alteration as an expansion or transcendence, not a collapse or dissolution. In romantic union the difference between self and other is not obliterated:

> One may seek merger, but one seeks it with an Other. If one were successful in achieving complete and total merger (what we would then call fusion), there would be no Other. The concrete fulfillment of fantasies of merger carries with it the threat of the symbolic annihilation of the self *and* of the Other. Love, by its nature committed to the preservation of the beloved as well as the self, cannot press through to its goal.

Expressed in the language of the present study, healthy romantic love is facilitated by a generous admixture of care-love and appreciation-love, both of which are highly respectful of otherness.

In Person's judgement, the union established through romantic love is only partial, and is also temporary:

> [E]xperiences of merger must be fleeting. While the impulse to self-surrender—as part of the impulse to merge—must be regarded as an essential component of passionate love, it can only be realized for brief moments. In such epiphanies the lovers experience their separate selves as mingled, enriched without compromise of the essential autonomy and integrity of either. The transcending of ego boundaries enlarges and enhances the self rather than obliterates it. Paradoxically, then, intermittent self-surrender can be a form of self-assertion, a kind of giving of oneself that is the ultimate expression of one's will as a free agent. Rather than being demeaning, self-surrender is experienced as an empowering act. This may be because the lover is surrendering more to the power of love than to the power of the Other.[21]

There are several ideas worth examining here. For Person, healthy passionate love involves a surrender of the self, a surrender that is simultaneously an expansion and a transcendence. Rather than being diminished by this process, the self enlarges to embrace the other. It does not collapse in weakness, but surrenders voluntarily, more with than to the other. In healthy romantic surrender, then, I neither submit to nor attempt to appropriate my beloved. I do not become a part of her, nor she of me. We expand and join, intermingling, giving ourselves over to the power of love that envelopes us.

Surrender, thus construed, is more an expression of strength than of weakness and is to be distinguished from submission. Only when the self is strong and reasonably whole does one have the courage to surrender. Submission, on the other hand, is devious: "It has a covert agenda, to manipulate the Other in order to maintain the self."[22] We could say then that submission is more a survival strategy, employed under difficult circumstances, than a voluntary letting go in love and trust. Because of a real or imagined inequality of power, one partner submits in order to preserve the self or meet its needs for security or protection. Such submission, Person implies, is more an expression of fear than love. Realist that she is, however, Person admits that surrender and submission may be mixed in the same relationship. It is easy to see how one might slip from one into the other. An individual might surrender, for example, only to find that his or her partner has not. Realizing this, and in the effort to win the other's surrender, the lover might attempt to manipulate the beloved through submission—"if I abandon myself utterly, you will have to love me."

Person also addresses the intriguing question of gender differences in surrender. Her view (with which I concur) is that surrender is essential to healthy romantic relationships—equally so for both sexes. Yet men and women differ in how they are apt to fall short of this ideal.

> There may well be a gender difference in the common neurotic distortions of the capacity for surrender: men are often inhibited in that capacity, women only too proficient at it. As a consequence, men may be relatively inhibited in their ability to fall in love (particularly during their competitive, striving years), whereas women may too readily resort to surrender as the primary mode of establishing their identities. However, the male propensity to hold back from surrender is as much a liability as is the female propensity to rush into it. Many men appear so constricted by the need to assert the self at any cost (as a corroboration of their masculine gender identity) that they miss out on the transformative potential of passionate love. On the other hand, by taking men as devotional objects, an act which requires a corresponding devaluation of self, women may focus so exclusively on the transformational aspects of love that the very core of the self is put at risk.[23]

It follows that, in healthy romantic relationships, surrender must be reciprocal and approximately equal. When it is lopsided, one party surrendering significantly more than the other, dominance and submission is the likely result.

We have seen that what Person characterizes as the union of romantic love is, by nature, fleeting. Lovers do not spend their entire lives ecstatically joined; there is a quality or degree of merger experienced by them that is intermittent and could not possibly be sustained for years on end. Person seems to miss, however, what Solomon understood: that there is also a kind of union found in ongoing romantic relationships (and even in love relationships we might be reluctant to characterize as romantic, such as friendly, companionate marriages) that often does persist throughout their entire history. There is a sense in which lovers participate in a shared identity. Because this kind of union is not intermittent, it is probably more important to the lovers' ongoing identity as a couple than the passionate but temporary union that was Person's focus.

Identity, as Solomon argued, has to do with where boundaries are drawn. Much as a boundary separates me from you, so for the couple there is a boundary between us and them. Since individuals have no fixed, permanent boundaries, they have no single identity. I have an identity as a separate individual that in some measure excludes you and everybody else, but if you and I are in love (or even if we are committed partners but not passionately in love), we also have a dyadic identity as a couple. I am who I am partly by virtue of my participation in this dyad. It does not seem helpful to say, with Solomon, that we share a self—I am not literally you—but we do participate in a common identity insofar as we both belong to the same dyad. My individual identity and the identity I share with you as my partner may not always fit together harmoniously, and I may have to set aside some of my personal pursuits for the betterment of our union, but individual and couple identity can also support and reinforce each other. Because I am your partner I may feel more alive and "connected" as a part of your world and family, or simply more secure and valued.

My identities do not stop here. I also have an identity as a male, as an American, as middle-aged, as a professor of philosophy, each with its own distinctive boundaries. As a philosophy professor, I am united with other philosophers by shared interests and a common language, which in turn separate us from nonphilosophers. The point is that we all have a multiplicity of identities, ways in which we create boundaries, joining with and separating ourselves from others. Given that this is so, let us now consider what marks off the identity of a couple in a successful, ongoing love relationship such as a marriage. The term "marriage" is used here not in its legal or ecclesiastical senses but in a social-psychological sense. Our goal is to see which characteristics or qualities serve to make two individuals a couple. It matters not whether the relationship is heterosexual, homosexual, or for that matter nonsexual. Although our focus will be on dyadic relationships, it may be that similar identity structures could exist involving three or more participants.

These kinds of unions may begin in a variety of ways: with intense sexual attraction, the recognition of common interests, a sudden feeling of having been "made for each other," a positive response to each other's personalities or character, or through an arranged marriage for that matter. Regardless of how the unions start or how fast they develop, common features emerge insofar as they are healthy, working partnerships. Thus we will not be concerned with what holds people together who despise each other or who stay together for reasons of financial necessity or purely formal obligation.

Many of the forms of union discussed above are apt to be present (mutual sexual attraction, shared interests, complementary differences, and so on), but what is it that makes two people a couple? Alan Soble—in consideration of a different but related question, that of love's alleged exclusivity—discusses briefly something he calls "joint interests." He has in mind not the shared interests and tastes considered above, but the joining of interests of two or more people, such that each assumes the other's interests as if they were his or her own. Soble quotes J. F. M. Hunter: "When we profess love, we can be expected to give ungrudgingly, and to treat the loved one's interests as if they were our own. . . . [Love involves] the wish to unite one's interests with those of another person."[24] Although this is a familiar feature of love relationships, it is not peculiar to the kind of relationships we are analyzing. Robert Nozick has written:

> The general phenomenon of love encompasses romantic love, the love of parent for a child, love of one's country, and more. What is common to all love is this: Your own well-being is tied up with that of someone (or something) you love. . . . When something bad happens to one you love . . . something bad also happens to you. . . . If the loved one is hurt or disgraced, you are hurt; if something wonderful happens to her, you feel better off.[25]

What Nozick is describing is very close to the union based on fellow-feeling, analyzed above, with the additional provision that the fellow-feeling be mutual. Nozick uses the concept "love" more narrowly than I do. In the passages deleted from the above quotation, he distinguishes love from friendship on the grounds that, when something bad happens to your friend, you feel bad for your friend, whereas when something bad happens to one you love you feel bad yourself. His point is not that love and friendship are mutually exclusive, simply that we do not necessarily love friends; love involves a stronger identification. Nozick's generic notion of "love," therefore, seems to correspond, roughly, to my "union-love." Both care-love and appreciation-love, at least in their less personal forms, would evidently fall outside the domain of Nozickian love.

Nozick proceeds to analyze what accounts for the specific kind of union we are investigating. He calls the love that makes for such union "romantic love." This concept, too, he employs quite differently than I. Following his usage, the love experienced by couples in successful long-term relationships is romantic love, whether or not the individuals entertain for one another those more passionate feelings we generally denominate "romantic." It would seem that, for Nozick, even the love that exists in traditional arranged marriages would qualify; whereas, in my usage, romantic love is that most strongly associated with courtship in modern Western culture, but which often ceases or exists only intermittently within marriage itself. Despite this difference in usage, however, we are both attempting to account for the same phenomenon: the union of a couple in a successful long-term love relationship. Nozick characterizes romantic love very much in the same fashion as Robert Solomon, except that his position is more carefully and consistently articulated. For Nozick, romantic love is not the attainment of union but the desire to create union with a particular person. It is the desire to create what he calls a "we" or a "we identity." He never speaks of a "shared self." Also, Nozick makes it clear that this we identity does not supplant each person's individual identity: "The individual self can be related to the *we* it identifies with in two different ways. It can see the *we* as a very important aspect of itself, or it can see itself as part of the *we*, as contained within it."[26]

What are the characteristics of this *we*? First, Nozick tells us, it shares with other forms of love relationships the property Soble referred to as "joint interests." "Your own well-being is tied up with that of someone you love romantically." Second, decision making becomes joint: "Each transfers some previous rights to make certain decisions unilaterally into a joint pool; somehow, decisions will be made together about how to be together." Third, returning to the theme that each partner acquires a new identity through love, he offers the reason: "To love someone might be, in part, to devote alertness to their well-being and to your connection with them." So lovers will be hypervigilant regarding matters that pertain both to each other's well-being and to the well-being of their relationship. Finally, Nozick adds to this list of features that there may also be "a certain kind of division of labor."[27] He has in mind not arrangements such as "I'll cook if you'll wash the dishes," but how a woman might, for example, cut out of the newspaper an article that she knows is of interest to her partner.

This list of characteristics, especially the third, taken together is similar to the understanding of the unity of the couple I had arrived at before encountering Nozick's analysis, although I described it somewhat differently. Union in healthy marriages and similar committed relationships has principally to do with how and to what degree each partner values the other and their ongoing relationship. It is a matter of priorities in interpersonal concern and focus. Indeed, with the possible and perhaps temporary exception of their own children, partners in this kind of love relationship have agreed at least tacitly to place each other first. Each is, in the other's life, the most important other person—although possibly not the most important objective or value, for either or both parties might be more devoted to God, the Communist party, or IBM than to each other.

This is intended as a normative criterion, not a necessary condition of union in committed relationships, which after all may be held together by a variety of factors: habit, fear of change, financial advantage, the influence of religious or moral rules, and so on. But when healthy love keeps a couple together, it is, I believe, this ordering of priorities that is largely responsible for the couple's sense of oneness. Conversely, when it is absent, couple identity is either weakened or distorted. We can imagine, for example, a man saying to his wife, who he believes values her best friend more than him: "You're not married to me; you're married to her." A tactless remark, perhaps, but he has a point. A couple's union is threatened by a greater (even by an equal) attachment outside the family. We are understandably protective of our committed union-love relationships. They are not just now; they involve a shared past and intentions regarding a shared future. So if my partner develops an intense interest in someone else I may well wonder just where I stand, what her priorities are, how secure our future together is. Insofar as my identity is tied to hers, this too is threatened; and for those lacking a strong individual identity alongside or within their we identity, individual identity will be profoundly threatened.

It is often said that, in love, we place the other's interest ahead of our own or make it equal to our own. Neither of these would seem to be essential to healthy, committed union-love relationships. How could such things be measured, any way! It is also sometimes said that, in love, each regards the other as indispensable to his or her own happiness. Certainly, lovers often feel this way, but there is an air of desperation about indispensability that is actually threatening to the quality of love, and to the relationship itself. Insofar as I regard you as being essential to my happiness, I am bound to you by fear, the fear that I might lose you and thus be deprived of my happiness. Although the terror of separation certainly can keep two people together, it does so in ways that almost certainly will be detrimental to the care and appreciation dimensions of love. If I feel that I cannot live without you, insofar as I value my own life, I must hang on to you at all costs. Any need for distance on your part will be followed by panic or rage on mine as I struggle to hold onto what I see as necessary for my own well-being. In response to my clinging, you might well feel an even greater need for distance.

This matter of priorities in interpersonal concern and focus becomes more complicated, and may have to be altered somewhat, as children enter the picture. Parents commonly give more time and attention to a child than to one another, but the love given their child need not be viewed as competing with the parents' love for each other in the way that a comparable attachment to someone outside the family almost certainly would.[28] It is after all their son or daughter, not some external priority. Moreover, the child can be viewed as the product and symbol of the parents' love for one another, or even as an extension of their joint identity. The question of who is loved more need not arise at all.

The child-parent relationship is different in kind from the relationship between the parents. The parents' relationship, ideally, is one of full mutuality, each giving and receiving in roughly equal measure and each responding to the other's needs as an adult. This a child cannot do. When a child is asked to meet the adult relationship needs of a parent (a condition psychologists call emotional or psychological incest), the child has been co-opted to play an unnatural role in the parent's life, from which the child may have difficultly extricating himself or herself. The analogy with incest is appropriate because a child is scarcely better equipped to meet a parent's needs for adult love than to meet a parent's sexual needs. So if a father conveys to his daughter how disappointed he is in his marriage, the empathic child may feel she has to step in and fill the gap, attempting to meet his needs for love and companionship. This, in the very least, is an unfair burden on the child and may lead her to prematurely abandon her own girlhood in the effort to become an emotional partner to her father.

Ideally, parents love their children without being dependent upon the children's reciprocation, allowing them to give and withhold their own love in accordance with their needs and levels of maturity. To the degree that a parent becomes dependent on a child's love, it is the parent's welfare rather than the child's that governs the relationship. This is, of course, the ideal. Few parents are so mature, self-contained, or happy in their marriage that they never use their children in these ways. Finally, in the modern Western family, husband and wife have typically made a commitment to remain together until death, whereas children will normally leave their parents, often to form a stronger union-love relationship with someone outside the family.

Union's Hidden Nature

❖ The classic expression of union-love in Western philosophical literature is the speech attributed to Aristophanes in Plato's *Symposium*. In accordance with his poetic gift, Aristophanes expounds on the nature of love by mythmaking. He begins with an account of the origins of our own nature, thereby suggesting the astonishingly modern, almost scientific, thesis that love is essentially human, and human nature essentially erotic. We were originally, he tells us, twice our present size, the size, in fact, of two human beings fused together, belly to belly. These extraordinary "sphere-shaped original beings,"[1] had four arms, four legs, two sets of genitals (of the same or of different gender making for three sexes in all), and a single large head with two faces, enabling them to see in all directions at once. Fearing their power and self-sufficiency, the gods had them cut down to a more manageable size. The result, after some further surgery, was the two-armed, two-legged half-beings we are today. Zeus next ordered that their heads be turned around, so that they might contemplate their missing parts and be reminded of their insufficiency.

Forlorned, these wounded creatures ran around looking for their other halves. When they found them, they would throw their arms around each other, "longing to grow into one."[2] Alas, they did little else but embrace day and night until the entire race was in danger of dying off. Recognizing this, but not wanting to lose the sacrifices people offered him, Zeus arranged to have their genitals moved from the back to their present position on the front of the body. Now, when lovers embrace, they could attain temporary satisfaction at least and no longer sow their seed on the ground like locusts.

What does this myth tell us about human nature? "Each of us . . . is but the indenture of a man, and he is always looking for his other half." And what is it that we desire from one another?

> [T]he intense yearning which each of them has toward the other does not appear to be the desire of lover's intercourse, but something else which the soul of either evidently desires and cannot tell, and of which she has only a dark and doubtful presentiment. Suppose Hephaestus, with his instruments, to come to the pair who are lying side by side and to say to them, "what do you people want of one another?" they would be unable to explain. And suppose further that when he saw their perplexity he said: "Do you desire to be wholly one; always day and night to be in one another's company? For if this is what you desire, I am ready to melt you into one and let you grow together, so that being two you shall become one, and while you live, live a common life as if you were a single man, and after your death in the world below still be one departed soul instead of two—I ask whether this is what you lovingly desire, and whether you are satisfied to attain this?—there is not a man of them who when he heard the proposal would deny or would not acknowledge that this meeting and melting into one another, this becoming one instead of two, was the very expression of his ancient need. And the reason is that human nature was originally one and we were a whole, and the desire and pursuit of the whole is called love.[3]

So love, then, is "the desire and pursuit of the whole," the desire to "melt . . . into one and . . . grow together, . . . becoming one instead of two." But what does it mean for two to become one? Aristophanes' answer, to "live a common life as if you were a single man, and after your death in the world below still be one departed soul instead of two," brings us back again to Solomon's theory of the shared self. Indeed, Solomon sees his identity theory of love as a reformulation of this pseudo-Aristophanic myth. This time, however, we have not an explicit philosophical theory concerning the literal merging of selves, but a poetic vision, which certainly is metaphor. Could we actually fuse with another and become a single self, I have already suggested, we might end up feeling alone all over again, ready to embark once more on the pursuit of union. The quest for union is a paradox: we desire to merge with another, yet were fusion actually achieved, we would be back were we started—alone and separate.

In apparent denial of this paradox, the paradigmatic lovers of literature often proclaim absolute fusion as their goal. In the famous love duet in act 2 of Wagner's *Tristan and Isolde*, for example, we find the lovers singing about how the little word "and" that joins them also stands between them as a barrier. The scene concludes:

Isolde:	No more Isolde!
Tristan:	No more Tristan!
Both:	No more naming,
	no more parting,
	newborn knowledge,
	newborn ardors,
	ever endless,
	both one mind,
	hotly glowing breast,
	love's supreme delight![4]

This is passion indeed. What these lovers yearn for, as in Aristophanes' myth, is far more than the familiar joining of bodies. In Wagner's radical reworking of Gottfried von Strassburg's thirteenth-century version of the legend, sexual fulfillment seems all but irrelevant. His lovers come to the realization that the union they so ardently seek is not possible as long as they live in a world such as this where existence is inescapably individual. For fusion to be achieved, the entire phenomenal world must be left behind. Theirs is a truly metaphysical passion. As the next scene demonstrates, the lovers are prepared to pay its price—death. Hence the famous Wagnerian *Liebestod*. Nearly forty years earlier, Goethe had written in one of his most passionate love poems:

> I praise what is truly alive,
> what longs to be burned to death.
> . . . .
> And so long as you haven't experienced
> this: to die and so to grow,
> you are only a troubled guest
> on the dark earth.[5]

What are we to make of proclamations such as these? Solomon's theory of a literal merging of selves does not help. Nor do we get much assistance from Denis de Rougemont's suggestion that the ultimate—but hidden—objective of love is death.[6] One may be sympathetic with de Rougemont's misgivings about Tristan and Isolde's passion and agree that there is a deep connection in Western literature (and consciousness) between love and death; but his thesis that an unconscious desire for physical death lies behind passionate love is once again too literal. He is right, however, to this extent: the un-compromising search for union that is characteristic of passionate love does require a kind of death in which purely individual identity must be sacrificed. Here we encounter one of the striking parallels be-tween romantic and spiritual love. Both present us with the paradox of death and rebirth.

In opposition to the literalism of both Solomon and de Rougemont, I suggest that the language of romantic love needs to be read symboli-cally. Like the language of myth, it points to deeper, hidden meanings not necessarily grasped even by lovers themselves, and like all genuine symbolic discourse it admits no definitive interpretation. In what fol-lows we will explore some of the ways in which romantic discourse and romantic union itself can be understood employing well-known psychological and metaphysical theories.

THREE ACCOUNTS OF ROMANTIC UNION

According to psychiatrist Margaret Mahler and her associates, the newborn infant is far from being a psychologically separate individual. Becoming so requires a long and difficult process of separation and in-dividuation. After a brief sleeplike autistic stage lasting about two months the infant enters a phase of "psychological symbiosis" with its mother, in which the boundaries between inside and outside, self and other, are quite vague. Mahler explains: "the infant behaves and func-tions as though he and his mother were an omnipotent system—a dual unity within one common boundary."[7] The state is evidently a pleas-ant one, corresponding to what Freud called the "oceanic feeling." (It is also the condition to which an older child may regress under the ex-treme disturbance known as symbiotic child psychosis.)

Only after the symbiotic phase ends around the sixth month does the separation-individuation process proper begin, a process that will occupy the child for approximately the next three years. During this period, the child gradually learns how it is separate from its mother. Experimenting with its growing sense of separateness, the child de-lights in games like peekaboo or hide and seek. As it begins to crawl and walk, it explores its independence, running off from its mother, challenging her to pursue. In all these games the child is playing with the same fundamental pattern of separation from, and union with, mother. Finally, as the separation and individuation phase comes to an end, with what psychoanalysts call object constancy, the child has internalized a sufficiently stable image of its mother so that it can function with reasonable independence and security, even during her temporary absence.

Mahler recognizes that the separation and individuation phase is open-ended and does not come to any absolute termination. Young adults, leaving home for the first time, are still not fully independent of their parents and may turn to them often for assistance and emotional support. But young women and men are also psychobiologically "programmed" to turn to one another and establish adult sexual and love relationships. These new relationships are in part modeled on and are influenced in various complicated ways by the previous symbiotic bond each of the partners experienced with his or her mother, and, usually to a lesser degree, with the father. Psychoanalyst Martin Bergman writes, "The wish to merge, to be one with the beloved, can be understood as a yearning for the very early symbiotic phase even though this phase was so early that it left no clear-cut memories." He immediately adds the precaution: "It is a longing that can never be entirely satisfied in a state of love."[8] Bergman recognizes, however, that adult love relationships may be helpful in healing wounds left over from the earlier mother-child relationship. The kinds of psychological wounding each of us brings with us into our adult loves profoundly affects not only our behavior as lovers but whom we select as partners.[9]

The games of hide and seek we learned during the individuation and separation phase continue to occupy us, in different configurations, throughout life. Even as adults we may enjoy moments of regression to a quasi-symbiotic form of relationship, but then we pull back inside our more normal adult boundaries. It is significant that adult sexual-romantic play is filled with activities similar to those that occupied us during the symbiotic and separation-individuation phases: kissing, sucking, holding and being held, biting, cuddling, even baby talk. Certainly, part of what makes these so pleasing is the way in which they recapitulate the delicious symbiosis we knew long before. A famous remark of Freud's sums up this psychoanalytic perspective: "the finding of an object [love object] is in fact a refinding of it."[10] All adult love is, at least in part, an unconscious quest to return to the first love relationship.

Adult love games are not necessarily regressive in any pathological sense. If they were they would be more frightening than they normally are. To be able to regress, playfully, one must have a reasonably secure sense of individual identity. If not, the regression involved in romantic surrender would be quite threatening. Impersonal sex or union through appropriation would feel safer. Indeed, many resort to this alternative for precisely this reason.

What is the relevance of this psychoanalytic interpretation of love for our present purposes? Each of us has already experienced a symbiotic union with another human being but have largely forgotten it. Consequently, many of our fantasies and much of our love talk are really about this earlier, forgotten love. When as adults we express the desire to fuse with our beloveds, when we find ourselves saying "I want you to hold me forever" or "I want to melt inside you," we are not describing what we literally want in the present, rather we are expressing our longing for an earlier stage of life when we knew or almost knew the bliss of a perfect union. In this earlier union we felt safe and whole; now we recover those feelings once again, experiencing the union through a direct "bodily reciprocity."[11] Hence the thesis that lovers' discourse constitutes a kind of mythology or nonliteral language, the real meaning of which lies hidden beneath the surface. Psychoanalysis, especially object relations theorists, gives us some clues for interpreting this language.

Erich Fromm offers a different perspective on why and how human beings seek union. Rather than reduce this quest to personal psychological history (the mother-child bond), Fromm accounts for it in terms of a more general, quasi-evolutionary theory:

> What is essential in the existence of man is the fact that he has emerged from the animal kingdom, from instinctive adaptation, that he has transcended nature—although he never leaves it; he is a part of it—and yet once torn away from nature, he cannot return to it; once thrown out of paradise—a state of original oneness with nature—cherubim with flaming swords block his way, if he should try to return.[12]

According to Fromm, we alone among the creatures of the earth are aware of the circumstances in which we live and this awareness separates us from the rest of nature as well as from one another. All creatures come into being, feed off other living beings either directly or indirectly, and die, becoming in the process food for other forms of life. (The "mutual eating society" Alan Watts once called it.)[13] No doubt other animals are more directly engaged than most of us in this life-and-death struggle, but they presumably lack comprehension of the whole picture, and of their own eventual and inevitable end. Human consciousness, while not in the least removing us from the common pattern, places us in the unique and troublesome position of being able to observe the whole tragicomic scene. All of this, Fromm urges, makes our "separate, disunited existence an unbearable prison" and gives rise to anxiety, shame, and guilt. Separateness, in his view, is the source of all anxiety. Man "would become insane could he not liberate himself from this prison and reach out, unite himself in some form or other with men, with the world outside." Here then is the origin of the quest for union: "The deepest need of man . . . is the need to overcome his separateness to leave the prison of his aloneness."[14]

In our ingenuity, Fromm believes, we have devised a variety of ways to cope with the problem of aloneness. We pursue orgiastic states through drugs, alcohol, trance, dance, or sex. Through conformity we attempt to submerge ourselves in groups, seeking to be like everyone else. By means of creative activity we unite ourselves with the materials with which we work. These attempts to overcome our aloneness, however, are not really successful—orgiastic states are temporary, conformity costs us our individuality, productive work gives us union with things but not with other people. Fortunately, there is a solution that does work and this, Fromm tells us, is love: mature love unites us with others in stable bonds without the loss of individual integrity. Not all interpersonal fusion is love, however. A condition resembling love, and sometimes referred to by that name, he calls "symbiotic union." This condition resembles Mahler's mother-child symbiosis and presumably results from some failure to complete the normal separation-individuation process. It can take either a passive or an active form; the passive form he calls submission or masochism and the active form, dominance or sadism:

> The masochistic person escapes from the unbearable feeling of isolation and separateness by making himself part and parcel of another person who directs him, guides him, protects him; who is his life and his oxygen, as it were. . . . The sadistic person wants to escape his aloneness and sense of imprisonment by making another person part of himself. He inflates and enhances himself by incorporating another person, who worships him.[15]

Masochism and sadism are attempts to achieve union but at the price of independence or integrity. The sadistic partner is as dependent as the masochistic one; they need each other. A person who is sadistic in one relationship is likely to be masochistic in another—sadistic at home, for example, and masochistic at work. Mature love, in distinction from its perverse cousins sadism and masochism, is union with integrity. (When speaking of mature love, Fromm uses the word "union" rather than "fusion.") How this union is achieved and what it consists of, Fromm does not say. He seems to regard it as something of a mystery:

> Mature *love is union under the condition of preserving one's integrity*, one's individuality. *Love is an active power in man*; a power which breaks through the walls which separate man from his fellow men, [a power] which unites him with others; love makes him overcome the sense of isolation and separateness, yet it permits him to be himself, to retain his integrity. In love the paradox occurs that two beings become one and yet remain two.[16]

Here we have another explanation of why human beings seek union: it is solace for the human condition of separation and alienation. As in Aristophanes' myth, we are portrayed as having fallen away from some original unity to which we wish to return. What we need to recover is not symbiosis with our personal mothers but oneness with nature itself. The original rupture of our union with nature—our primal wound as it were—is caused by nothing less than human consciousness itself which enables us to imagine the future and anticipate our own death. We observe the world only by standing apart from it, as a separate self or ego. Thus it is precisely the subject/object structure of human consciousness that is at fault—to be conscious of is to be separate from.

If this interpretation of Fromm is correct and subject/object consciousness is the root of our sense of separateness, two questions emerge. (1) Is human love sufficient to heal it? (2) Is it true that human consciousness is inherently in the subject/object mode? It is interesting to note that subatomic physics has had to abandon the ideal of the objective observer and hence, some have argued, subject/object duality itself. Moris Berman goes further in claiming that subject/object consciousness is far from universal. It is, he tells us, a recent Western development preceded everywhere by what he calls "participatory consciousness," in which subject and object are united rather than separated in the act of knowing.[17] If Berman is right about this, perhaps it is the ascendancy of subject/object consciousness in Western society that has led, in part, to our acute sense of alienation and hence to our cultural preoccupation with romantic love since the late Middle Ages.

So far the question as to why human beings seek oneness has been examined from two different—but essentially naturalistic—points of view. Mystically inclined thinkers have accounted for the allure of union quite differently. They agree that love has a hidden objective, but rather than mother or nature it is the divine itself that beckons us in love. What Aldous Huxley called the perennial philosophy "finds in the soul something similar to, or even identical with the divine Reality."[18]

In the West we are most familiar with this point of view in the Platonic and Neoplatonic theory that the soul seeks to return to its place of origin: the Good, the One, or God. According to Plato, even sexual desire has as its ultimate goal not pleasure or the beauty of the beloved's body but the transcendent Idea of the Beautiful, which the soul knew before it became incarnate. Love is a quest for immortality through union with this Idea. In its Augustinian variation, which was almost universally accepted throughout the Christian Middle Ages, the love that God has placed in the human soul draws us ever toward Him in whose image we were created. The Indian metaphysician (the Advaitan Vedantist, at least) sees the Self (Atman) as never having been separate from ultimate reality (Brahman). The goal of mystical love, then, is not to return to the creator but to awaken to the Self's own true nature as Atman-Brahman, the undifferentiated reality that precedes subject/object duality.

The difference between these two mystically influenced philosophies, which may loosely be identified as Western and Indian—is that, in the latter, complete union between the soul and the Absolute is the objective whereas, in the West, mystics are more apt to speak of a communion or marriage in which the individual identities of both parties are preserved. Our present task is not to decide which—if either—of these is correct but, simply, to note that both of them fit within Huxley's definition of the perennial philosophy. Moreover, each proclaims an ideal of union and of union-love, the goal of which is attained only through surrender of the individual self or ego—a surrender characterized everywhere as death. We are back once again to Wagner's *Liebestod* and Goethe's longing to be burned to death. Rather than clinging to its worldly identity, the ego abandons itself in surrender to the divine, much as romantic lovers surrender when they fall in love.

Here we have a metaphysical rather than a psychological interpretation of the urge for union. What is of interest at present, however, is not mystical love itself, but the way in which mystical longings can be concealed within human love, even when we do not recognize the existence of such longings. Perhaps the presence of this transpersonal dimension of love should be suspected whenever our longing for the beloved is unusually intense, or whenever the beloved is so idealized that all manner of perfections are attributed to him or her.

THE THREE THEORIES we have considered, each of which accounts in a different way for the desire for union, are not necessarily mutually exclusive. Martin Buber weaves the first and the third together when he writes:

> The prenatal life of the child is a pure natural association, a flowing to-ward each other, a bodily reciprocity; and the life horizon of the developing being appears uniquely inscribed, and yet also not inscribed, in that of the being that carries it; for the womb in which it dwells is not solely that of the human mother. This association is so cosmic that it seems like the imperfect deciphering of a primeval inscription when we are told in the language of Jewish myth that in his mother's womb man knows the universe and forgets it at birth. . . .
>
> Every developing human child rests, like all developing beings, in the womb of the great mother—the undifferentiated, not yet formed primal world. From this it detaches itself to enter a personal life, and it is only in dark hours when we slip out of this again (as happens even to the healthy, night after night) that we are close to her again. But this detachment is not sudden and catastrophic like that from the bodily mother. The human child is granted some time to exchange the natural association with the world that is slipping away for a spiritual associa-tion—a relationship.[19]

For Buber the natural bodily and psychological reciprocity with the mother rests upon a deeper metaphysical reciprocity with what he refers as "the great mother." The metaphysical account of the quest for union underlies the psychological.

All three of the theories we have investigated see human existence as in some way estranged from its original nature. Aristophanes' myth concurs, as does the biblical story of the Garden in Eden. The belief that we have fallen from some original state of unity would seem to be firmly embedded in human consciousness, regardless of whether any of the three theories we have examined adequately accounts for it. Each also testifies to a deeply felt sense of the incompleteness and insuffi-ciency of ordinary human existence and to a belief that we once knew something better. Each embraces a myth of paradise lost.

Seen in this light the hope and the burden of love are nothing less than paradise regained. Given the weight of this hope and that it is usually unconscious, it is not surprising that love is so often attended with disappointment. Taken together, these theories suggest that through our all too human loves we are attempting to regain our blissful symbiosis with mother, reenter the paradisiacal garden of nature from which we were expelled with the birth of human consciousness, and reunite ourselves with the even more primordial oneness of Being itself. Such, it seems, is the hidden agenda of passionate human love.

Perhaps our three theories have even more in common: each can be read as presupposing an original state without subject/object duality, without the conventional division of reality into self and not-self. The infant, Mahler tells us, does not see itself as separate from its mother, or even from the surrounding environment; Fromm speaks of a oneness with nature preceding the emergence of subject/object consciousness; and mystics proclaim a union in which the division between subject and object does not exist at all. All three theories are predicated on the idea that we have come from and seek to return to, at least proximally, a nondualistic state.

Here, however, we must be careful. Should a unity that precedes the emergence of normal human consciousness (as in the first two theories) be equated with one that comes after? Once the question is raised, the difference is apparent: the first two theories give to love an essentially regressive objective; the third theory describes a union that is transcendent. Ken Wilber calls the confusion of these two views the "pre/trans fallacy." He explains:

> The essence of the pre/trans fallacy is itself fairly simple: since both prerational states and transrational states are, in their own ways, nonrational, they appear similar or even identical to the untutored eye. And once pre and trans are confused, then one of two fallacies occurs:
>
> In the first, all higher and transrational states are *reduced* to lower and prerational states. Genuine mystical or contemplative experiences, for example, are seen as a regression or throwback to infantile states of narcissism, oceanic adualism, indissociation, and even primitive autism. This is, for example, precisely the route taken by Freud in *The Future of an Illusion*.
>
> In these reductionistic accounts, rationality is the great and final omega point of individual and collective development, the high-water mark of all evolution. No deeper or wider or higher context is thought to exist. Thus, life is to be lived either rationally, or neurotically . . . .
>
> On the other hand, if one is sympathetic with higher or mystical states, but one still confuses pre and trans, then one will *evaluate* all

prerational states to some sort of transrational glory (the infantile pri-mary narcissism, for example, is seen as an unconscious slumbering in the *mystico unio*). Jung and his followers, of course, often take this route [as did Buber in the passage quoted above], and are forced to read a deeply transpersonal and spiritual status into states that are merely in-dissociated and undifferentiated and actually lacking any sort of inte-gration at all.

Wilber's position is that "Spirit is indeed nonrational; but it is trans, not pre. It transcends but includes reason; it does not regress and ex-clude it."[20]

Mystical union is not a preconscious state but, many mystics tell us, the attainment of a higher consciousness or of pure consciousness itself. This distinction is often ignored or rejected by scientifically minded Westerners who tend to see in the nondualistic state of con-sciousness described by mystics nothing but unconsciousness. Per-haps it is this attitude that lead de Rougemont to accuse passionate lovers of seeking death, and that lead Freud to see in the oceanic feeling little more than an unconscious desire to return to the womb. To the mystics—the only ones who have actually "been there"—nonobject consciousness is nearly always described as a higher level of consciousness.[21]

It is not appropriate, then, to assimilate the mystical ideal of union to the psychological theories and conclude that it too must be regres-sive. Moreover, if this mystic perspective is taken seriously, even pas-sionate human love may turn out to have a profound, if hidden, mean-ing and may after all be a quest for literal fusion. The fusion is not that of two empirical selves, however; this is but the symbol of another, deeper union.

THE RELATIONSHIP BETWEEN MYSTICAL AND ROMANTIC LOVE

The similarity between mystical and romantic love has often been noted. Mystic and historian of mysticism Evelyn Underhill describes this similarity:

> Attraction, desire, and union as the fulfillment of desire; this is the way Life works, in the highest as in the lowest things. The mystic's outlook, indeed, is the lover's outlook. It has the same element of wildness, the same quality of selfless and quixotic devotion, the same combination of rapture and humility. This parallel is more than a pretty fancy: for mys-

tic and lover, upon different planes, are alike responding to the call of
the Spirit of Life.[22]

Underhill expresses the parallel very well, but her choice of language—"in the highest as in the lowest things"—will not please cham-
pions of ardent human love. A few metaphysically inclined theorists of
love, however, have portrayed the relationship between these two passions less invidiously.

Historically, at least in the Latin West, most Christian thinkers
have seen passionate human love as an impediment to the love of God
and the spiritual life. In keeping with Saint Jerome's dictum that "He
who too ardently loves his own wife is an adulterer,"[23] and with the
Augustinian ideal that God alone should be loved as an end and
everything else only as a means, romantic love came to be viewed as
competing with and detracting from what ought to be the sole object
of devotion. The emergence of courtly love at the end of the eleventh
century may be seen as a rebellion against this exclusion—what psychoanalysts might call a return of the repressed. Here, nearly for the
first time, heterosexual romantic love is extolled as a value in its own
right. By the end of the thirteenth century, in what at least looks like
an attempt to reconcile the secular troubadour ideal of *fin' amors* with
orthodox belief, we find Dante describing his passion for Beatrice as a
vehicle to the love of God—"whoever speaks with her shall speak
with Him." For this reconciliation to be accomplished, however, it was
essential that the love be emptied of all sexual intent, and marriage
with the beloved was never a consideration. Possibly it was even necessary (as Maurice Valency ironically observes) that the lady die before
the lover could realize the transcendental meaning of his adoration.[24]

Other attempts at reconciling romantic and spiritual love have been
made both before and after Dante. Among the most thorough and systematic of them was that undertaken toward the end of the nineteenth
century by the great Russian philosopher, mystic, and poet Vladimir
Solovyov. Solovyov sees love—especially sexual love (his term for romantic love)—as the only power capable of undermining egoism:

> The meaning and worth of love, as a feeling, is that it really forces us,
> with all our being, to acknowledge for *another* the same absolute central
> significance which, because of the power of our egoism, we are con-
> scious of only in our own selves. Love is important not as one of our
> feelings, but as the transfer of all our interest in life from ourselves to
> another, as the shifting of the very center of our personal lives. This is

characteristic of every kind of love, but predominantly of sexual love; it is distinguished from other kinds of love by greater intensity, by a more engrossing character, and by the possibility of more complete overall reciprocity. Only this love can lead to the real and indissoluble union of two lives into one; only of it do the words of Holy Writ say: "They shall be one flesh," i.e., shall become one real being.[25]

This becoming "one real being" Solovyov intends quite literally. He conceives of the Absolute as a living organism, of which we are the members.[26] Our egoism, however, prevents us from realizing this truth and we come to see individual life as self-justifying. Only the powerful experience of falling in love awakens the realization that we are part of a larger whole, which eventually includes the whole universe and even the Absolute itself. "Truth as a living power that takes possession of the internal being of a human and actually rescues him from false self-assertion is termed Love. Love as the actual abrogation of egoism is the real justification and salvation of individuality." Notice that individuality is set in opposition to egoism. The true individual for Solovyov is universal; it is not the separate, empirical ego, but (as in Vedanta) the universal Self or individual that we all ultimately are. Solovyov writes: "The meaning of human love, speaking generally, is *the justification and salvation of individuality through the sacrifice of egoism.*"[27]

Sexual love not only resembles mystical love on a lower level, as in Underhill's thesis, it is both preparatory and participatory. It prepares us for the love of the Absolute by overcoming the ego, while at the same time we participate in the divine through union with the human beloved. Christians have often made extreme claims for love—consider Augustine's summation of Christian morality: "Love and do what you will." But it is extraordinary, and beyond the wildest dreams of Augustine, Aquinas, or Luther that such claims should be made for sexual love. Solovyov does precisely this: "For good reason sexual relations are not merely termed love, but are also generally acknowledged to represent love *par excellence,* being the type and ideal of all other kinds of love." And why is it that sexual love has this unique power?

God *is* all, i.e., he possesses in one absolute act all positive content, the whole fullness of being. A human being (in general and every individual being in particular), being in fact only *this* and not *another,* may *become* all, only by doing away, in his consciousness and life, with that internal boundary which separates him from another. "This" may become the "all" only *together with others;* only together with others can an individual realize his absolute significance—become an inseparable and ir-replaceable part of the universal whole, an independent, living and original organ of the absolute life. The individuality is a certain specific likeness of the unity-of-the-all, a certain specific means of receiving and appropriating to oneself all that is other. Asserting himself apart from all that is other, a human by that very act divests his own real existence of meaning, deprives himself of the true content of life and reduces his individuality to an empty form. In this way egoism is by no means the self-consciousness and self-affirmation of individuality, but on the con-trary its self-negation and destruction.

In Solovyov's view we must join with others in order to join with God; we have no access to the divine as separate egos. Regarding the role of sex in sexual love, Solovyov is not as explicit as we have come to expect of authors a century later, but he does offer the following: "Exclusively spiritual love is quite obviously as much an anomaly as an exclusively physical love. . . . False spirituality is a denial of the flesh; true spirituality is the regeneration of the flesh." The last part of this quotation—that "true spirituality is the regeneration of the flesh"—is perfectly orthodox, but rarely had it been taken to apply to the sexual act itself.[28]

LOVE AS REGRESSION AND LOVE AS TRANSCENDENCE

Perhaps Solovyov exaggerates the role of sexual or romantic love in overcoming egocentricity, much as others exaggerate in the opposite direction in calling it narcissistic or an *égoïsme à deux*. Yet Solovyov performs a great service in pointing out that passionate human love can be a pathway toward, rather than an obstacle to, the spiritual life. In not seeing how romantic love can open us to the divine, we have sometimes mistaken the human beloved for the divine, or at least for something more magnificent than he or she is. This idolatry and the tragic consequences stemming from it have been a major theme in Western literature and life for the last eight centuries, so much so that many of our mental health professionals can find in this passion little more than a disturbing symptom of some underlying disorder.

Scott Peck, whose book *The Road Less Traveled* was on *The New York Times* best-seller list for twelve years, writes of what he calls the myth of romantic love: "As a psychiatrist I weep in my heart almost daily for the ghastly confusion and suffering that this myth fosters. Mil-lions of people waste vast amounts of energy desperately and futilely attempting to make the reality of their lives conform to the unreality of the myth."[29] In a similar vein, the Italian philosopher Francesco Alberoni argues:

> No one can fall in love if he is even partially satisfied with what he has or who he is. The experience of falling in love originates in an extreme depression, an inability to find something that has value in everyday life. The "symptom" of the predisposition to fall in love is not the conscious desire to do so, the intense desire to enrich our lives; it is the profound sense of being worthless and of having nothing that is valuable and the shame of not having it.[30]

Much can be said in support of these authors' points of view. Romantic love often is immature, obsessive, and neurotic. Indeed it is nearly inevitably so for those who are immature, obsessive, or neurotic—and all of us are at least the first for awhile. Moreover, it is doubtful that romantic love alone can free us from these conditions. Doubtless it sometimes does produce the bizarre and excessive behavior that so fascinates our novelists and readers of novels and occupies so much of the time of psychotherapists.

Notwithstanding the truth in these critiques, E. S. Person also has reason on her side when she characterizes romantic love as a transcendent experience. Acknowledging love's destructive possibilities, she argues:

> Nonetheless, romantic love remains one of the most worthwhile and transcendent human experiences, its inherent dilemmas and the fact that it serves as a magnet for psychopathology notwithstanding. Despite the general cautions of traditional wisdom and psychoanalytic theory, I am certain that romantic love is generally more enriching than it is depleting. It is a magnificently human condition, and yet not everyone will experience it. Despite its (usually) transient nature, it offers access to the unconscious, lights up the emotional life, and brings internal change in a way that often far outlives the experience itself. Romantic love is the preserve of hope and imaginative longing; it is one of the passions that moves us, that initiate the great quests and adventures of our lives. Like so many other human gifts, romantic love has the potential for both good and evil, but should not be judged by its corrupted forms or dismissed on account of its transience.[31]

Romantic love is so various and so rich in the possibilities it presents for interpretation that some readers may find truth as well in the vision of it offered by the English novelist and theologian Charles Williams when he proclaims that falling in love is a miracle, a true revelation, in which through God's grace we are allowed to see another human being *sub species aeternitatus*. When we fall in love, Williams believes, we have been granted a momentary participation in God's own vision of the beloved, seeing the adored one as he or she would have been before the Fall. As Williams sees it, falling in love is not projection, overvaluation, delusion, or idealization; it is a divinely assisted act of perception.[32]

What emerges from this discussion of romantic love is that romance is a complex, multi-leveled phenomenon. It is inherently symbolic, at times more and at times less than it seems. Moreover, it can take a variety of forms, and the form it takes—whether regressive and obsessive or transcendent and transforming—is largely a consequence of where the lovers are in their own emotional and spiritual development. According to a widely held psychological theory, a man still fixated in Oedipal love is virtually doomed to fall for someone who psychologically resembles his mother, and then to superimpose the earlier pattern on the new relationship. Because we tend to choose partners on about the same developmental level as ourselves, his partner will probably be acting out complementary problems from her own past. As a result, both will be attempting within their present relationship to resolve childhood difficulties of which they may be quite unconscious. As long as they remain unaware that this is happening, they almost certainly will experience disappointment and misunderstanding. Should they become conscious of the reasons they have selected each other, however, they can actually help one another in this process and may—with time and perhaps a little outside help—go a long way toward healing the wounds stemming from their parental relationships.[33]

According to the prevailing wisdom among many of our mental health professionals once love has been freed from these regressive tendencies, once projections have been recalled and transferences resolved, then "mature" (that is, nonromantic) love is possible. This mature love, we are advised, is realistic: lovers see each other as they really are. Alas, the ideal of mature love they commend turns out to be quite passionless—"stirring-the-oatmeal love," Jungian analyst Robert Johnson calls it. "Romance and friendship," he assures us, "are utterly opposed energies, natural enemies with completely opposing motives." If friendship is to prevail, then, romantic love must go.[34]

There is much to be said for stirring-the-oatmeal love, but the conviction that romance is inherently disturbed and will inevitably end after a few months or years of living together is at best a half truth. We might expect from Jungians such as Johnson a nonreductive approach to romantic love. Instead, they most often view it simply as a consequence of projection—the lover projects his/her anima/animus onto the beloved and falls in love with the projected image, failing to see him or her accurately. No doubt something like this often does happen but the analysis overlooks something crucial: we can project onto another only what is, in some sense, within us. So if a woman projects her animus onto her beloved, she must actually in some sense "possess" that archetype.[35] But if the lover can possess the archetype, why cannot the beloved? And if he does, then her seeing it in him is not necessarily, or not only, projection; it could be perception as well. Similarly, if a lover sees his beloved as the eternal feminine, this could be because in some sense she is. Interpreted in this way, an archetypical account of romantic love does not have to reduce it to an illusion resulting from unconscious projections.[36]

What seems to lie behind reductionist critiques of romantic love such as Peck's, Alberoni's, and Johnson's is the idea that passionate interpersonal love must rest upon a distortion of reality. No human being could be everything the romantic lover supposes. The psychotherapist, therefore, proposes to cure lovers by sobering them up and ridding them of their illusions. As Irving Singer and Robert Solomon have both argued, however, romantic love is not so much delusion as an act of the imagination—or, in the language of the present study, it is a matter of responding to the beloved (partially) as symbol. And symbols, as an older, more metaphysical tradition understood them, do not necessarily point backward; they can point forward and upward as well. Or they may point in both directions at once, as is more often the case. The symbol leads us away from reality only when we fail to see it as symbol—when, for example, we take our enhanced perception of the beloved for objective fact.

As an alternative to the reductive analysis of romantic love, my suggestion is that falling in love is not only a way of working out problems stemming from unresolved parental attachments, healing childhood wounds, or projecting archetypes onto undeserving objects. Even those who have successfully addressed their parental attachments and gone a long way toward healing the wounds of childhood can and do fall in love. The beloved still functions symbolically in these cases, but now the symbol points more to a higher than to a lower developmental level. On this view, enduring interpersonal love does not have to be the lukewarm companionship so often commended by our mental health professionals. Rather, passion, freed up through the resolution of inner conflict and liberated from its backward-looking tasks, is now available for the real work of adult life—moving beyond the ego level of psychospiritual development.[37]

Once again the beloved is symbol—but not mere symbol, not symptom. Genuine symbols, Paul Tillich argues, "participate in the reality of that to which they point."[38] Understood in this light, calling the beloved divine may convey a profound truth. Perhaps something like this was the meaning of Saint Paul's teaching in his letter to the Ephesians (5:25–33) that husband and wife, as members of the body of Christ, become one flesh through marriage.[39] The passage suggests that marital sex can be viewed as a celebration or ritual enactment of the Christian couple's oneness in the body of Christ.[40] If this is what the author of Ephesians intended, he presumably thought it an exclusively Christian mystery; but this seems excessively provincial. I prefer to think there is but one "mystical body," whatever name we might give it, and we are all members of that body regardless of religious party affiliation. This was Solovyov's view, and Buber affirms something similar with his thesis that in every encounter with a Thou one meets the Eternal Thou. To the voice of the Christian and the Jew can be added that of the Sufi, Jelaluddin Rumi, when he proclaims:

> The minute I heard my first love story
> I started looking for you, not knowing
> how blind that was.
>
> Lovers don't finally meet somewhere.
> They're in each other all along.[41]

CHAPTER 5

Love and Value

❖ The claim that the human beloved actually in some sense is divine is bound to strike many readers as fatuous in the extreme, yet in much of Asia the standard form of greeting consists in placing the hands in prayer posture over the heart chakra. This gesture—and its verbal accompaniment in modern India and Nepal, *nomaste*—is understood as an acknowledgment of the divine within the other. Regardless of who the other is empirically, he or she is seen as divine. Thus an idea that seems strange to many of us in the West is integrated into the daily pattern of much of Asian culture. Here, of course, we have moved well beyond the domain of romantic love which was our concern in much of the last chapter.

Belief in the divinity of the person is far from unknown in the West. We have had occasion to note Martin Buber's view that the Eternal Thou is present in every encounter with a Thou. Mother Teresa makes a similar point more dramatically. At a panel discussion at the United Nations several years ago the moderator, Jean Houston, found herself asking, "Mother, how does it happen that you are able to do so much, and why are you in this state of joy?" Houston records the rest of the conversation:

> "My dear," she said, "it is because I am so deeply in love."
> "But Mother, you're a nun!"
> "Precisely," she said. "I am married to Jesus."
> "Yes, I understand, you're married to Jesus. All nuns are."
> "No, you don't understand," she countered. "I really am. I am so in a state of love that I see the face of my Beloved in the face of the dying man in the streets of Calcutta. I see my Beloved in the day-old child

who's left outside our convent, and in the leper whose flesh is decaying; and I can't do enough for my Beloved! That is why I try to do something beautiful for God."[1]

What are we to make of this? An extreme literalist response might be, "The woman is deluded. Jesus has been dead for twenty centuries, so she could not possibly be married to him. Moreover, the leper she finds on the street is not Jesus, but a completely separate person from a different culture and time. If she sees Jesus' face on this individual, she must be hallucinating."

Such a response is almost comically inappropriate. Mother Teresa knew she was not married to Jesus in the ordinary sense: it is a mystical marriage, not a social or legal one. But what is a "mystical marriage"? Is it an illusion? an act of self-deception? a metaphor? And what are we to think of Mother Teresa's claim that she sees the face of her Beloved in everyone she meets? The behavior occasioned by this belief (or experience) is so obviously above the general level of human morality we should hesitate to dismiss it out of hand. Were I to encounter a leper on the street my response would probably be one of revulsion. I might feel compassion as well, but I would want to keep the leper at a distance out of fear that I might be contaminated or harmed, even though I know leprosy is not particularly contagious and is easily cured in the early stages. So should I, with my fear-based, self-protective response, judge my perception of the leper to be more accurate than that of Mother Teresa? Should I say to myself, "I see what the leper really is—an object of disgust or a 'poor bloke'—whereas Mother Teresa is the victim of some delusion"?

To take another approach, could Mother Teresa's way of seeing and loving be explained as projection and then be dismissed as symptomatic of some psychological disorder that you and I, with our more realistic perception of how things are, have managed to escape? But do we, unlike Mother Teresa, see the leper as he really is? What exactly is the leper? or anyone? We frequently laugh at lovers because they fail to see how banal their beloveds really are; we mock them, thinking ourselves superior, or we smile condescendingly at their projections or idealizations. Could it be, however, that the lover sees something we do not?

Not that lovers never suffer from illusions; they certainly do. But why should we believe the disinterested perception of an "objective observer" more accurate than that of the lover? Is the father deluded when he calls his infant "the most beautiful baby in the world"? His judgment, especially if he misconstrues it, treating it, for example, as an objective fact, may lead to folly. He would then expect other fathers to respond to his baby as he does—rather than to their own babies as he does to his. What we need is a better way of understanding lovers' valuations, a way which recognizes that they are not necessarily either objective facts or subjective illusions, or some combination of both. We cannot understand the nature of love until we find a credible alternative to this dichotomy.

LOVE AS APPRAISAL AND BESTOWAL

Irving Singer has given much attention to this problem and proposes an ingenious solution. Love is neither delusional nor is it only a response to objective value. Rather, it involves the interaction of two different kinds of valuation. Singer shares the general view that love has to do with value—that what we love we value—but valuations, he tells us, are of two distinct kinds: appraisal and bestowal.

In appraising an object, we assess its value relative to how it meets preexisting needs or desires. There are, in turn, two kinds of appraisal: objective and individual. Objective appraisal is a matter of estimating value in a way that is "open to public verification."[2] The appraiser of a house, for instance, might determine the square footage of the structure, the construction cost per square foot, the price of comparably sized building lots in the area, and so on, and from these facts determine the market value of the house. Another appraiser would use approximately the same system and come up with a similar result. The house, of course, may be worth either more or less to different potential buyers, depending on how it meets their particular needs. This Singer calls "individual appraisal." The two forms of appraisal are not completely distinct, however, objective appraisal being a function of averages of individual appraisals.

Both objective and individual appraisals are objective in the epistemological sense because they are simply a matter of determining how well prior needs or interests are satisfied. Singer writes: "As estimations of worth, appraisals are in principle no different from what a scientist provides when he makes judgments about matters of fact." The difference between objective and individual appraisal lies not in the epistemological objectivity of the judgment but in the standpoint from which it is made. Individual appraisals are made relative to the interests of the individual who makes them. "Objective appraisals estimate a person's [or any love object's] value in relation to the interests of some prior community."[3]

Singer sees appraisal as a necessary condition of love, but it is not a sufficient condition. It is the second, quite different form of valuation, bestowal, that gives love its distinctive character. Through bestowal a new value, not a function of prior needs, is brought into being.

> I suggest that love creates a new value, one that is not reducible to the individual or objective value that something may also have. This further type of value I call bestowal. Individual and objective value depend upon an object's ability to satisfy prior interests—the needs, the desires, the wants, or whatever it is that motivates us toward one object and not another. Bestowed value is different. It is created by the affirmative relationship *itself*, by the very act of responding favorably, giving an object emotional and pervasive importance regardless of its capacity to satisfy interests. Here it makes no sense to speak of verifiability; and though bestowing may often be injurious, unwise, even immoral, it cannot be erroneous in the way that an appraisal might be. For now it is the valuing alone that *makes* the value.[4]

For Singer, both appraisal and bestowal are necessary conditions of love; neither alone is sufficient. By itself appraised value might produce liking or desiring but not love; a love based on bestowal alone, without prior appraisal, Singer regards as "foreign to human nature." Yet bestowal does not result in the creation of any objective value. When a man says of the woman he loves that she is beautiful, sensational, or perfect, "His superlatives are expressive and metaphoric. Far from being terms of literal praise, they betoken the magnitude of his attachment and say little about the lady's beauty or goodness."[5]

CRITICISMS OF SINGER'S THEORY

Singer's ingenious way of accounting for valuation in love avoids the objective-value/subjective-illusion dichotomy, but his solution presents problems of its own. First, it seems phenomenologically false in that I, at least, do not experience value as emanating from me when I love. That I bestow this special value on my beloved is simply not how it feels. I find the value, it comes to me (or seems to) from the beloved herself. Her cherished qualities and the value I find in them seem to belong to her. Singer writes, "For me the loving stare of one human being visually glued to another signifies an extraordinary bestowal of value, an imaginative (though possibly excessive) response to the presence of another person. The lover's glance illuminates the beloved."[6] This description certainly fits some cases, especially those loves or that stage of love we call infatuation. But is it not also possible that, rather than my stare or glance illuminating the beloved, my receptive eyes and open heart receive *her* illumination? This, at least, is how I experience enamorment. Moreover, if I came to believe that the special value I attribute to my beloved were actually created by my own imagination, I might well have second thoughts about loving her. Almost certainly I would love her less—"she is not as wonderful as I thought; it was only my imagination that made her seem so." Is this not, in fact, what happens when infatuation comes to an end? But does all love involve such an imaginative creation and bestowal of value? To say with Singer that love is "sheer gratuity," or that it is "a creative means of *making* . . . [the beloved] more worthy," diminishes the beloved; for it is necessary to bestow value on her only to the extent that she lacks it.[7]

There are deeper problems with Singer's theory of love than these phenomenological considerations. After all, my way of experiencing love may be peculiar. Perhaps everyone else experiences it just as Singer describes. Even if most were to experience it as I have suggested (with the value seeming to come from the beloved), the reality of the situation might be quite different. It could be that love arises when lovers make the mistake of thinking objective something only created by them in their enthusiasm. To pursue this matter we must examine more carefully Singer's theory of bestowal. The lover, he tells us, employs the creative imagination in much the same manner as an artist:

> [L]ove may be best approached as a subspecies of the imagination. Not only does the lover speak in poetic metaphors, but also he behaves like any artist. Whatever his "realistic" aspirations, no painter can duplicate reality. The scene out there cannot be transferred to a canvas. The painter can only *paint* it: i.e., give it a new importance in human life by presenting his way of seeing it through the medium of his art and the techniques of his individual talent. These determine the values of his painting, not the external landscape that may have originally inspired him. The artist may vary the scene to his heart's content, as El Greco did when he rearranged the buildings of Toledo. What matters is his way of seeing as a function of the imagination, not the disposition in space of stones and mortar. Similarly, a lover sees a woman not as others might, but through the creative agency of bestowing value. He need not change her any more than El Greco changed the real Toledo. But he renews her personality by subsuming it within the imaginative system of

his own positive responses. Through her he expresses the variety of feelings that belong to love. Artists, even the most abstract, do not create out of nothing: they re-create, create anew. So too, the lover re-creates another person. By deploying his imagination in the art of bestowing value, by caring about the independent being of another person, the lover adds a new dimension to the beloved. In relation to him, within his loving attitude, she becomes the object of an affirmative interest, even an aesthetic object. She is, as we say, "*appreciated*"—made more valuable through the special media and techniques in which love consists.[8]

This is a penetrating passage. Singer is right both about the role of imagination in love and in his analogy between the lover and the artist. At the same time, however, his account of artistic imagination seems seriously incomplete. It is not just a "re-creation," renewal, or "rearrangement." The imagination of the artist like that of the lover has also to do with perception, discovery, and with penetration into deeper levels of reality. Placing an image on a canvas, however novel, is not necessarily an act of creative imagination, or at least not a notable one. The crucial aesthetic questions are: What makes the image significant? What makes it work? What gives it artistic merit? Surely not every rearrangement of the buildings of Toledo would have been equally satisfactory. In some sense, El Greco's rearrangement was "right." Moreover, artists' works also may offer insights into other levels of reality. Consider how Cézanne's paintings of Mont Sainte-Victoire reveal something about the underlying structure of the mountain, of mountains in general, even about three-dimensional space or our perception of it.

What I am proposing is that artistic imagination has epistemic significance. The painter does not merely invent; he or she discovers and reveals what is hidden or unnoticed. This is why, or partly why, works of art have value. It is the same with the writer of fiction. We do not commend a novelist for creating an unbelievable character. The character must in some sense be "true" if we are to admire the writer's power of invention. The situation is much the same with the lover who does not so much "add a new dimension to the beloved," "renew her personality," "re-create" her, or see her "through the creative agency of bestowing value" making her "more valuable." The lover sees deeply into who the beloved is, discovering depths and complexities that are missed by mere acquaintanceship. At least, this is how it works when love goes beyond infatuation. Consider the following passage from Annie Dillard's novel, *The Living*:

Clare knew that common wisdom counseled that love was a malady that blinded lovers' eyes like acid. Love's skewed sight made hard features appear harmonious, and sinners appear saints, and cowards appear heroes. Clare was by no means an original thinker, but on this one point he had reached an opposing view, that lovers alone see what is real. The fear and envy and pride that stain souls are phantoms. The lover does not fancy that the beloved possesses imaginary virtues. He knew June was not especially generous, not especially noble in deportment, not especially tolerant, patient, or self-abasing. The lover is simply enabled to see—as if the heavens busted open to admit a charged light—those virtues the beloved does possess in their purest form. June was a marvel, and she smelled good.[9]

Clare understands June's limitations; there is no delusion here. Instead we find a highly individual perception, guided by love, that Clare realizes others will not share. As Dillard views her characters, Clare does not bestow this value on June.

Perhaps it is Singer's naturalistic approach that leads him to see love as the bestowal of value. A naturalist presumably would be reluctant to speak, as have many of the authors whose views we have explored, of levels of reality. From a naturalistic perspective, each person is what he or she is empirically, and nothing more. The one who claims to see more—to find illumination, radiance, the sacred, or "those virtues the beloved does possess in their purest form"—must be creating these qualities or their value.

The approach followed here, however, is not limited to naturalism, but presupposes that there are levels of reality, and these levels are hierarchical or holarchical, some being higher or more encompassing than others. Borrowing the term "holon" (part-whole) from Arthur Koestler, Ken Wilber sees reality as holarchical. Each holon is nested inside the one above it—for example, atomic particles within atoms, atoms within molecules, molecules within compounds, chemical compounds within cells, cells within organs, organs within bodies, bodies within ecosystems, and so on. The relationship between higher and lower levels is not one of dominating but of including and embracing the lower levels. As Wilbur puts it, it is holons all the way up and holons all the way down.[10]

No argument will be offered here to prove that reality is hierarchical except to note that denying it altogether would seem to make the most remarkable lovers of all, individuals such as Mother Teresa, seem rather foolish. Either saints see more deeply into others than the rest of us, or they do not. If they do not, then their claim to find Jesus, the Buddha nature, Lord Krishna, or the Eternal Thou within the individuals they meet, must be judged an error; they claim to see something that simply is not there. Yet, who would deny that the love the saint manifests is, ethically and spiritually, a higher love? The rhetorical questions are unavoidable: Are we to suppose that a higher love rests on an inferior metaphysics, on a less veridical perception of reality? Is the leper on the street of Calcutta only a leper so that anyone who sees him as Jesus or Buddha is either mistaken or is creating something from out of his or her own imagination?

Even without proof that there are higher or deeper levels of reality, I submit that the awesome morality of the saints and the near unanimity of their conviction on this matter give us reason to take their metaphysical claims seriously. Singer writes of the saint's love:

> The saint is a man whose earthly needs and desires are extraordinarily modest; in principle, every human being can satisfy them. That being so, the saint creates a value-system in which all persons fit equally well. This disposition, this freely given response, cannot be elicited from him: it bestows itself and happens to be indiscriminate.[11]

If I may hazard a rejoinder in behalf of saints: their earthly needs are modest because their deepest needs, which are anything but modest, are met in their relationship with the divine. This is what the saints tell us, and their behavior supports what they say. It is not that "every human being can satisfy them." Rather, because their needs are met elsewhere, they are able to relate to others in terms of the others' needs rather than their own. Furthermore, it is not that the saint "creates a value-system in which all persons fit equally well"; the saint discovers an absolute value in each. Finally, rather than labeling this saintly love "indiscriminate," could we not say that the saint discriminates very well indeed? He or she discriminates between the empirical other and the divine presence within that other, seeing both without confusing them. The ordinary lover often confuses these different levels and ends up feeling cheated and disillusioned, whereas saints see both without confusion and remain steadfast in their love.

It may be that Singer's rejection of this metaphysical, levels-of-reality perspective—along with its corollary that deeper levels can somehow be detected through the more mundane ones—makes it difficult for him to appreciate Plato's theory of love as well:

I fail to see how Plato could be talking about the love of persons when he says that the lover sees in the beloved an "image" or "representation" of absolute beauty. Plato uses this idea to argue that all lovers are really in love with the absolute. Might we not also say that the lovers he has in mind are simply incapable of loving another person?[12]

As an alternative to this reading of Plato, I propose that the Platonic theory of love must be understood mystically, even incarnationally. It is not that the human beloved is a means to some transcendent absolute, but rather, each human beloved is an incarnation of that absolute. In Platonic language the beloved not only imitates the Beautiful, he or she participates in it. In loving his beloved for his beauty (read: perfection, divinity, sacredness), the platonic lover loves him for what he is, not as a means to something else. This was certainly Dante's reading of Plato. More recently L. A. Kosman has written, "surely it is such a mystery to which Diotima alludes: the mystery of loving being itself incorporate in the world, of loving in my very beloved himself humanity incarnate."[13]

Far from being "incapable of loving another person," Plato dramatizes for us, in the remarkable final speech of the *Symposium* (215A–222C), just how the Platonic lover does so. He shows us first, by way of contrast, how Alcibiades loves Socrates—rather in the style of Pausanias, seeking sexual pleasure from him together with the ego gratification of seducing such a famous and elusive man—but then goes on to reveal the love Socrates has for his young friend. Socrates wants nothing at all from Alcibiades but tries to tease and nudge him toward a higher perception of the Good. This is the reason for Socrates' ironical, pedagogically motivated flirtation with the proud young man. He loves him in the only manner his theory allows one to love someone lower than oneself on the Platonic scale of values; he loves him benevolently, one might almost say agapistically, attempting to lead him upward toward the Good. This is eros conceived as striving to give birth in beauty (206B) not as desiring to possess it (206A).

It is germane to recall here another episode from Plato's dialogues. In the *Phaedrus* (242B–C), when Socrates reaches the conclusion of his speech on love as a form of madness, he is ready to depart but is stopped by a divine sign informing him he is guilty of blasphemy against Love. He must atone by offering another speech in which the error is corrected. Love is not madness; it is *divine* madness.

For those who find all this talk of mysticism, incarnations, participation, and levels of reality entirely too metaphysical, there is, fortunately, a way in which the general idea behind the preceding discussion can be expressed in language that is quite naturalistic. All that is required for the general theory I have been advocating to make sense is the recognition that we can experience valued universal qualities within particulars. Those who may never have experienced anything they would be comfortable calling "sacred" or "holy" may nonetheless perceive, more fully in one individual than in any other, some quite naturalistically construed universal—humanity, for example. What I have in mind is this: through my relationship with my wife, I experience more completely than in any other way what it means to be human. It may not be that she is objectively more human than others or even that I believe her so. Nor am I bestowing this quality on her, not even, to the best of my knowledge, bestowing its value. Yet through knowing and loving her I receive my deepest awareness of this important universal quality. She allows me to see so much of her: her struggles and hopes, her pride and fears, her heroic courage and childlike insecurities. I know these same qualities exist in others, including myself, but it is through her that I encounter them most completely and forcefully.

In this example, no transcendental reality is presupposed, no levels of reality implied. Nor need it be supposed that I am under any illusion in my assessment of who my wife is. As far as I can see, no bestowal has taken place either. I love my wife (partly) because of qualities she objectively possesses even if no one else sees them as fully, as consistently, or with the same intensity as I do. Why this vision is granted to me may seem mysterious, but perhaps it is only that she lets me see more of her. Then again, maybe my loving allows me to see more deeply, or gives her the safety to be more fully herself. Regardless of the reason, I am grateful for the gift. I suspect that each of us learns most fully what it means to be human from such special cases.

LOVING THE OTHER AS-IS

There are further, perhaps more serious, difficulties with Singer's theory. Remember the passage previously quoted: "Individual and objective value depend upon an object's ability to satisfy prior interests— the needs, the desires, the wants, or whatever it is that motivates us toward one object and not another." Objective appraisals give us the value of an object relative to the interests of some prior community; individual appraisals are a matter of determining how the object will meet the needs of the appraiser. When the love object is a person, objective appraisals are never sufficient. They "are always supplemented by individual appraisals in which we decide what another person is worth in relation to our *own* interests or needs."[14] It follows that any appraisal of a person is solely a matter of determining the value of the person relative to prior needs, and these must include the needs of the one doing the evaluation. Appraisal, then, can never be a matter of assessing the intrinsic worth (real or imagined) of a person or object. Yet Singer is emphatic that in loving persons we value them for their own sake and accept them as they are: "In relation to the lover the beloved has become valuable for her own sake." Or, "Love is indeed an acceptance of another as she is in herself. In that respect it is 'unegoistic.'" More recently Singer has added: "Certainly my concept of bestowal implies an acceptance of the other as-is, as he is in himself, his indefeasible autonomy being and remaining paramount in the loving relationship."[15]

Loved ones, then, are valued as ends, but from whence comes this end value? There can be but one answer: it is bestowed by the lover. To repeat (with emphasis added): "*In relation to the lover* the beloved *has become* valuable for her own sake." Thus I do not love you because you *have* end value to which I respond; rather, you *become* valuable for me through my bestowal. It could be argued that loved ones already in some sense possess the end value others have bestowed upon them (or have bestowed upon themselves), but since bestowal creates no objective value to which another might respond, whatever end value you "have" from yourself or others can play no direct part in my appraisal of you. Finally, remember that for Singer bestowal always follows a prior appraisal, and individual appraisals, which are necessary when the love object is a person, are always in terms of the prior needs of the appraiser.

Putting this all together we get the following:

1. Love requires both appraisal and bestowal.
2. Appraisal must precede bestowal.
3. When the love object is a person, the appraisal must include individual appraisal.
4. Finally, individual appraisal is solely a matter of determining how the one appraised meets the needs or interests of the one doing the appraising: "Our evaluation is an 'individual appraisal' if it is based on the object's utility for ourselves alone, as the ones who make the evaluation."[16]

It follows, rather awkwardly, that no one could ever value another as an end without first determining that the individual is good for the valuer.

There are two questions that must be asked about this way of looking at love. First, is it true that we never bestow value on people we have not already appraised as good for us? Second, is such an analysis adequate for ethical notions of "love"? Singer's theory is most convincing when applied to what I call "personal love." I use this expression not to refer to love between persons, better called "interpersonal love," but to those loves (whether of persons or things) that arise from attraction to, preference for, or attachment to the loved. In those sections of *The Nature of Love* that present the theory of appraisal and bestowal, Singer's discussion centers on objects of personal love. Further, the love object is nearly always a person, and the love itself generally of a romantic or quasi-romantic character.

Clearly Singer does not intend his theory to apply only to personal love, however. The first volume of his work contains an extended discussion of religious love in the Middle Ages and the Reformation. So we are justified in wondering what happens when this theory is applied to a nonpersonal love such as love for one's neighbor. Is it reasonable to suppose that, here too, the lover appraises the loved in terms of his or her own needs? When a Sister of Charity encounters a dying man in the streets of Calcutta, for example, does she first appraise him? Presumably she determines that he is a human being and that he is in need; but these are not appraisals in Singer's technical sense of the term because they have nothing to do with the "object's ability to satisfy prior interests—the needs, the desires, the wants, or whatever it is that motivates us toward one object and not another." How would Singerian appraisals come into play in the sister's love for the man? There is one passage in which Singer applies his theory to such cases:

> On some religious views, which I have discussed under the concept of agape, God loves all creatures regardless of how worthless they may be in an appraisive sense and people acquire a similar capacity when godliness is in them. I myself have never held this belief. I am convinced that wholly nonappraisive love is foreign to human nature. Even saints who sacrifice their lives are motivated by evaluations that account for their behavior and that constitute an appraisive substratum for their ability to love. At the very least, they are appraising those for whom they die as suitable beneficiaries of their self-sacrifice and as more deserving of life than they themselves.[17]

Several things must be noticed about this passage. To begin with, many Christians would agree that "wholly nonappraisive love is foreign to human nature." Nygren, for example, insists that agape is God's love, pure and simple.[1] Second, Singer gets into trouble when he tries to account for what he calls the "appraisive substratum" of the saint's love. The saint, he tells us, appraises the value of the one for whom the sacrifice is made, determining that he or she is a suitable beneficiary. Perhaps. But again this does not qualify as appraisal in Singer's technical sense. He fails to show how the saint makes an appraisal of the loved relative to the saint's own interests.

Finally, Singer tells us that the saint must have appraised the life he or she saves as being more valuable than the saint's own. Here too the appraisal does not accord with Singer's definition of that concept: X's judgment that Y is more valuable than X is not very plausibly a judgment made from the perspective of X's own interests. Moreover, I doubt that the saint would claim that the one saved is more deserving of life. Most probably he or she judges all human life to be equally valuable. Yet, because the saint is the one at hand, the duty of the sacrifice falls to him or her. Surely the saint need make no claim beyond this.

It seems safe to conclude that, regardless whether wholly nonappraisive love is foreign to human nature, it does exist. Saints at least practice it. But how about the rest of us? Do we ever love without first appraising the loved relative to our own needs? Consider the following passage:

> In my description bestowal involves benevolence toward its one or many objects, for value is being created in them, but bestowal equally appears as a means of *enjoying* these objects or some of their attributes. Through bestowal we accept them, not as we accept a trial offer of some household article that arrives in the mail but rather in treating them with respect and in recognizing a dignity in them they have not necessarily earned and that we accord them on our own. Their sheer presence as participants in the universe is highlighted, given special importance. Our bestowal addresses itself to what they are "in themselves," as-is and not in reference to whatever valuational ranking they may also merit from an appraisive point of view.[19]

This seems an accurate description of how we treat those we love. But does it apply only to those we have selected and appraised as *good for us*? Most of what Singer says (with the exception of the loved one being "highlighted" and "given special importance") applies sometimes to our relations with people we have just met and whom we have not yet had the opportunity (or lack the motive) to appraise. On a good day, I suspect, most of us are quite able to treat with benevolence; to accept and respect, to recognize a dignity within people we have not appraised in Singer's sense of the term. To take a commonplace example, suppose a woman you have never seen before comes to your office or place of work and asks something of you. Can you not listen to her attentively, take what she says seriously, treat her with respect, accept her as she is, and then benevolently offer whatever assistance you reasonably can? Surely you would not first have to appraise how she is likely to meet your needs. Indeed, you might treat her as described even if you did not especially like her. Singer is quite right that the person in question has not earned the respect and dignity you show her. So it could be said, as Singer does, that you have bestowed the dignity and given her respect. But then, is this not the bestowal of value without prior appraisal and thus an instance of that "wholly nonappraisive love" that Singer thinks "foreign to human nature"?

A defender of Singer could agree with the description of how we behave in such cases but deny it has anything to do with love, possibly on the grounds that love is inherently preferential. My justification for classifying the behavior in question as "love" is the two criteria employed throughout the present work—ordinary usage and the existence of precedents in the history of love theory—both of which allow that nonpersonal benevolence can be called love. Moreover, it is not certain that Singer believes all love is preferential. That love for persons must be follows from the fact that it presupposes the judgment "good for me." Singer has written: "As bestowal, love accords a person preferential status that is unearned in any appraisive sense." Yet a recent book of Singer's contains a chapter on religious love in which we find the following: "so too can religious love be seen as the imagination reaching beyond the limitations of self, friendship, family, nation, or humankind in a supreme attempt to embrace and accept all reality."[20] It is difficult to see how this reaching out to embrace and accept all reality could be preferential. If nothing is excluded, there is no preference. But then, if preference is not a necessary condition of love, why does bestowal presuppose appraisal?

Having spent so much time with the first question regarding the existence of nonappraisive love, we can dispose more readily of the second: the adequacy of Singer's analysis for ethical notions of "love." Are the requirements of ethical love satisfied by loving only those whom we have previously appraised as good for us? It seems clear that they are not. Ethical love requires, minimally, that we acknowledge the dignity of, or show regard for, the life and welfare of all human beings irrespective of whether they are useful to us. This position is based on the familiar moral principle that each possess, or is granted by us, an intrinsic worth that must be acknowledged. It follows that every individual we meet, not just those we personally love, ought to be treated as an end. Singer agrees that loved ones must be treated as ends, but on his analysis the obligation to do so arises only after end-value has been bestowed upon them. And this, as we have seen, presupposes a prior appraisal of the loved relative to the appraiser's own interests.

There is a great difference between love based on the response to intrinsic value (or what the lover takes to be intrinsically valuable) and love as the bestowal of value. It is far more difficult to found an ethic of love on the latter. A theist might be able to circumvent this difficulty by claiming that God has already bestowed value on all. In this case, everyone we meet could be said to possess this divinely bestowed value prior to any personal appraisal on our part. For a Singerian, however (where bestowal is purely human, and individuals can be loved only after being appraised as valuable relative to the interests of the appraiser), any ethic of love would have to be a highly constricted one. We could have obligations—more accurately, obligations based upon love—only for those who have passed the test of individual appraisal.

A FINAL LOOK AT BESTOWAL

Between the first and third volumes of *The Nature of Love*, Singer notes, there is a slight change in the relative emphasis given to appraisal and bestowal: "my former analysis could be taken as magnifying the role of bestowal to the detriment of appraisal." He elaborates:

> In the first volume of this trilogy, the idea that love is appraisal was shown to be the basis of the great eros tradition in Western philosophy. I criticized several of its proponents—Plato, Aristotle, St. Augustine, Freud, Santayana—for having ignored the element of bestowal, thereby misunderstanding the role of appraisal as well. I continue to think my critique was valid. What I now see more clearly, however, is the degree to which these thinkers were right in their insistence upon appraisal as a crucial ingredient of love.[21]

This judgment is correct in the sense Singer intends: the latter work does show greater appreciation for the role appraisal plays in love.[22] At the same time, however, there is a way in which volume 3 gives even more weight to bestowal. He writes: "all appraisals must ultimately depend on bestowal since they presuppose that human beings give importance to the satisfying of their needs and desires. Without such bestowal nothing could take on value of any sort."[23]

It seems to me that this revision requires a significant change in the structure of love. Instead of appraisal (of the love object), followed by bestowal (on the love object), now we have bestowal (on the lover's needs), then appraisal (of the love object), followed by bestowal (on the love object). Surely, all things considered, it is bestowal that has pride of place in this revised version of Singer's theory. It is now more than ever a bestowal theory. Moreover, this alteration is odd. Evidently, needs (no matter how dire) and their satisfaction possess or create no value in themselves; we must first bestow value upon them. One wonders why Singer thinks this the case. The result is a strangely voluntaristic theory of value. We would expect a naturalist to hold that needs themselves create values for the organisms in which they reside. Cannot all animals be said to value that which they need?

In *The Pursuit of Love*, Singer uses as an example of what he calls "primitive bestowal" the neonate's bestowing value on its mother's breast.[24] He suggests that this may be the first act of love. But what exactly do neonates do when they bestow value? It makes sense to say that neonates value the breast, even perhaps that they love it. But what does it mean for the neonate to bestow value upon the breast? Would it not be more to the point to say that the newborn automatically, instinctively values the satisfaction of its need for nourishment and pleasure, and then comes to value and love the breast through association? What is added by introducing the notion of bestowal in this context? In several places in *The Pursuit of Love*, Singer speaks of love in nonhuman animals; evidently they bestow value as well. But what is an animal doing when it bestows value on the object of its desire? Is the animal doing something in addition to desiring the object? If so, what? One begins to wonder whether the concept of bestowal, with its theological heritage, really has a place in a naturalistic theory of love.

It is not my intention to suggest that what Singer calls "bestowal" can in every instance be reduced to or replaced by appraisal (whether objective, individual, or transpersonal). In the domain of personal love, we often simply do value one object over another without any objective or universalizable reason for doing so. If I love my wife more than my neighbor's wife, I do not have to justify my preference by claiming that she is objectively more deserving. I simply value her more. This is part of what it means to (personally) love her. But does the concept of bestowal capture this important feature of personal love? Whether Singer intends it or not, the concept suggests that a value has been created by the lover and then given to the loved. Singer says that bestowed value exists, and even that it exists in the loved one.[25] But what kind of existence does bestowed value have? Remember, he denies that it has objective existence. Does it then have a subjective existence? What could it possibly mean for bestowed value to exist subjectively in the love object?

If the concept of bestowal is out of place in a naturalistic theory of love, we need an alternative formulation. I suggest that rather than the lover bestowing value on what he loves, it would be more to the point to say, simply, that he *values* it. "John values Tim" is not about Tim's value, created or discovered, objective or subjective. It is about how John feels about Tim—he values him. "John bestows value on Tim," suggests that some value has been created by John and then given to Tim. What are we to make of the view that a new value has been created by John, bestowed upon Tim, and now exists in Tim, but is not objectively present in him? What does all this mean? What does it add to "John values Tim"?

Finally, Singer's view is that bestowal is a necessary condition for love, all love. Although personal, preferential love probably always involves bestowal, or what I prefer to call "valuing," nonpersonal ideals of love such as those found in ethical and religious thought often do not. Such loves are more apt to arise either from experiences of transpersonal value or from some belief that each person possesses inherent worth, and possesses it independently of Singerian appraisals. Moreover, as we shall see shortly, the purer forms of appreciation-love do not fit the Singerian model of love either, for they clearly do not require any Singerian appraisal.

Our investigation of Irving Singer's theory of love began with the observation: "What we need is a better way of understanding lovers' valuations, a way which recognizes they are not necessarily either objective facts or subjective illusions, or some combination of both. We cannot understand the nature of love until we find a credible alternative to this dichotomy." Has Singer provided us with a credible alternative? Despite my criticism of Singer's efforts, he has succeeded, in part, and has added significantly to our understanding of love.

Singer's analysis sheds light on personal love, especially on how we value an individual we love preferentially. When a man says that the woman he loves is magnificent, he is not necessarily deluded nor is he offering an appraisal with which he expects others to concur. To quote Singer once again: "His superlatives are expressive and metaphoric. Far from being terms of literal praise, they betoken the magnitude of his attachment and say little about the lady's beauty or goodness." Not only is Singer insightful in seeing the lover's superlatives as "expressive and metaphoric," but also in seeing the whole process as involving creative imagination akin to the artist's.

However, Singer's answer to the objective-fact/subjective-illusion dichotomy does not go far enough. There are things going on, even in personal love, that the appraisal/bestowal theory does not account for. That we sometimes experience in the loved transpersonal value must also be acknowledged. Even if the objective reality of transpersonal value is doubted, the importance of individuals' experience of such value, and its subsequent impact on love, cannot be denied. To say that love consists simply of appraisals (reducible to community and personal interests) to which purely personal bestowed value has been gratuitously added, is not sufficient. Moreover, if we are to take seriously the analogy between the lover and the artist, let us allow that lovers (like artists) sometimes see (not just create) what the rest of us do not. More serious is the way that Singer's theory fails to account adequately for the nonpersonal love that is central to ethical traditions from Christianity to Confucianism. These ways of loving in no way presuppose an evaluation of the loved "based on the object's utility for ourselves alone." Nor, it seems to me, are they well understood as nonappraisive bestowals.

Appreciation-Love

❖   Appreciation-love is more aesthetic and less active than either care-love or union-love. Here, nothing need be done for, to, or with the loved. The lover simply beholds the love object, appreciating it for what it is. There is no clinging, no meddling, no urge to transform. Appreciation-love might be thought of as the spiritual core of all forms of love, and so I would wish to make in a normative theory of love. Since, however, this is not our present goal it must be admitted there are loves that lack the detached respect for otherness that is characteristic of this love.

In its most elementary form, appreciation-love is simply the delight one takes in the presence of a pleasing object or person—or a quality such as an aroma or a color one especially enjoys. As that wise woman of contemporary American fiction, Shug Avery, remarks: "Listen, God love everything you love—and a mess of stuff you don't. But more than anything else, God love admiration. . . . I think it pisses God off if you walk by the color purple in a field somewhere and don't notice it." Or as Rilke proclaims in an unforgettable opening line of one of his sonnets to Orpheus: "To praise is the whole thing!"[1] When experienced to the full, appreciation-love is at peace with the universe, embracing all without the need to change anything. It comes from that still point at the center which knows but the single word, "Yes!" Hermann Hesse describes this way of loving in one of his essays:

> The eye of desire dirties and distorts. Only when we desire nothing, only when our gaze becomes pure contemplation, does the soul of things (which is beauty) open itself to us. If I inspect a forest with the intention of buying it, renting it, cutting it down, going hunting in it,

or mortgaging it, then I do not see the forest but only its relation to my desires, plans, and concerns to my purse. Then it consists of wood, it is young or old, healthy or diseased. But if I want nothing from it but to gaze, "thoughtlessly," into its green depths, then it becomes a forest, nature, a growing thing, only then is it beautiful.

So it is with people, and with people's faces too. The man whom I look at with dread or hope, with greed, designs, or demands, is not man but a cloudy mirror of my own desire. Whether I am aware of it or not, I regard him in the light of questions that limit and falsify: Is he approachable, or arrogant? Does he respect me? Is he a good prospect for a loan? Does he understand anything about art? . . .

At the moment when desire ceases and contemplation, pure seeing, and self-surrender begin, everything changes. Man ceases to be useful or dangerous, interesting or boring, genial or rude, strong or weak. He becomes nature, he becomes beautiful and remarkable as does everything that is an object of clear contemplation. For indeed contemplation is not scrutiny or criticism, it is nothing but love. It is the highest and most desirable state of our souls: undemanding love.[2]

As a spiritual love, this "contemplation" or "pure seeing" has much in common with neighbor love—it is unconditional, undemanding, and selfless. Neighbor love reflects a more activist ideal, however. As a form of care-love it seeks to help, while this purest form of appreciation-love does little at all save behold. Yet, paradoxically, receiving this love—feeling fully seen, heard, and accepted by one who wants nothing from you—can be more transforming than all the assistance care-love can proffer. It may not be the warmest form of love, nor the most passionate or intimate, but it can be very useful even though it recognizes no notion of utility.

What Hesse describes is only the purest form of appreciation-love, however. Broadly conceived, this love is neither austere nor especially spiritual. There is nothing rare or unusual about it. It need not, like Hesse's undemanding love, be free of desire. The delight one takes in a sunset or the smell of eucalyptus would qualify as appreciation-love, and such experiences normally awaken in us at least the desire to repeat them. Yet this desire has nothing of the grasping about it. Desire may be present in appreciation-love, but it is not its principal feature.

It may be doubted whether we ever experience pure appreciation-love for those we love the most intensely. With them we want union, we engage with care and concern, or we desire reciprocation, hoping they will meet our needs. Nonetheless, we do have appreciation-love for these special individuals. Sometimes we find ourselves standing back, just looking at them, feeling blessed by the mere fact of their existence. In our intense personal attachments, however, appreciation-love is not likely to remain pure for long. After the tranquil moment of appreciation we rush in, seeking to merge or to serve, breaking the detachment of pure contemplation. Still, it is to a considerable degree our appreciation for the beloved that keeps these loves healthy, making it possible to let go, to wait, to allow the beloved simply be who he or she is, honoring the independence the other's soul requires.

One indicator of the presence of this kind of love is the sense of grace that often accompanies it, the feeling that we have been granted a gift, something unexpected and unearned. Suddenly it is just there—the smile of the passing stranger, the sunset, the scent of magnolia blossoms—and we feel, however briefly, the joy of being alive. Nothing has changed, but now life makes sense and we know why we are here—or we simply lose the need to ask.

APPRECIATION-LOVE AND SIMPLE APPRECIATION

Earlier we considered whether care-love differs from the ordinary phenomenon of caring and concluded that, for the most part, it does not. We may now wonder if appreciation-love is the same as simple appreciation; this time the dissimilarity is considerable. As "appreciation-love" will be used here, what is intended is appreciations that are particularly strong, but more especially those in which the object is appreciated as an end-in-itself. Only then are we likely to label appreciation "love." While I may appreciate money, I do not have appreciation-love for it because I do not value it for its own sake. I may appreciate those who are useful to me but not love them, because it is not the individuals themselves that I appreciate, only what they do for me. It is only natural, however, for appreciation of someone's deeds to lead in time to appreciation-love for the one who performs them.

Appreciation-love, like care-love, involves regarding the loved as an end—but in a somewhat different sense. Given that care for another has the other's well-being as its objective, it is a concern that cannot be reduced to the lover's self-interest. It must be other-regarding in the protoethical sense of concern with the loved's well-being. Appreciation-love, on the other hand, does not have anyone's well-being as its objective. The delight I take in a rose is not *for the sake* of the rose. Yet it is *of* the rose. It would be stretching things to say that I am using the rose for my sake, or for the sake of my enjoyment. I am not *using* the rose, I am *enjoying* it; I appreciate it for being what it is.

Consider a slightly different example. Suppose someone were to say "I absolutely love roast beef," and were to demonstrate this by eating it at every opportunity. Here, "love" does not mean "appreciation-love" but is being used as a synonym for "like" or "desire" (or is one of those hyperbolic uses based on analogy with romantic love). Not every attraction to a thing or property of a thing qualifies as appreciation-love. Our appreciation of an object becomes love only when we delight in the object for simply being what it is. Wanting to consume roast beef is rather different.

Returning to the example of appreciating a rose, suppose that in order to appreciate it better I cut it from the bush on which it is growing and take it to my room. Does this cutting of the rose *in order to appreciate it* qualify as love? I think the answer turns on how the rose is being appreciated. If I am appreciating it qua living being, as a part of my reverence for life, it would be more appropriate not to remove the rose from the bush but to contemplate it as it is. If, on the other hand, I appreciate the rose as an aesthetic object, I may be better able to enjoy its form, texture, and fragrance at leisure in my room. In both cases I am appreciating the rose itself, not merely using it as a means to something else. Hence both instances qualify as appreciation-love.

There is a familiar objection to this line of reasoning: the rose, it might be argued, is merely a means to my enjoyment of it. But this way of putting the matter is misleading. It suffers from the same kind of unfortunate subjectivist reduction that leads to the doctrine of psychological hedonism in ethics, and which plagued classical empiricism with doubts concerning the reality of the "external world." My attention is focused on the rose, not on my pleasure. It is true that I cannot appreciate the rose without having an experience of it that I enjoy, but why conclude that the rose is merely a means to this enjoyment? The rose cannot be removed from the circuit by any solipsistic or hedonistic reduction, for it is precisely the rose that is the focus of my contemplation, not me or my enjoyment.

What makes the object of appreciation-love an end-in-itself, then, is not (as with care-love) that its well-being is the objective of the love, but simply the quality of attention given to it. The object is being appreciated for itself, not as a means to something else. Even roast beef might be contemplated for itself by a gourmet, making genuine appreciation-love possible here as well. However, appreciation-love for roast beef would imply that the gourmet enjoys looking at it, smelling it, discussing it with other gourmets, reading or writing about it, much as he enjoys eating it. (Consider how connoisseurs of wine need not actually drink the wines they are savoring.) Ordinary "lovers" of roast beef, however, merely desire it as a means to their own gratification.

This difference between appreciation-love and mere appreciation has significant implications for the theory of love outlined in the present work, for if every instance of appreciation counted as love, appreciation-love would be nothing more than the positive valuation that is a universal feature of love. Appreciation-love would not then be an independent form of love, but a characteristic of love in all its forms. As a matter of linguistic convenience, however, I will sometimes speak of "appreciation," "appreciating," or "the appreciated" and intend by these locutions not mere appreciation but appreciation-love. The context should make clear that these expressions are being used in the more technical sense.

The clearest examples of objects of appreciation-love are those entities with which care or union are impossible or inappropriate, such as ideas, ideals, or abstract qualities. For this reason, much of the following discussion will be concerned with the love of abstract entities, and how this is related to love for persons or things. Unmixed appreciation-love may also be experienced for less abstract objects, especially when they are thought to be beyond the reach of union and care, such as a rainbow or a sunset. With these there is little likelihood that the inclinations associated with our other two loves will arise. Yet such objects are loved; they touch our hearts and thrill us in ways that only the loved can. Appreciation-love objects, then, include not only ideals we admire (truth, beauty, freedom, justice); general qualities or properties of persons (integrity, a sense of humor) or things (cobalt blue); but also persons or things themselves when we value them for simply being who or what they are.

Since our three forms of love differ from one another largely in their objectives (and in the nature of the relationship between the lover and the loved), the objective of appreciation-love is neither caring-for nor union-with. Indeed, such intentions may be inappropriate, impossible, undesirable, or merely irrelevant. Does one, for example, intend the welfare of an ideal such as justice through loving it? In some sense, this might be possible. Lovers of justice would presumably practice it and thereby strengthen its existence in the world, influencing others to love and practice it. Or they might devote themselves to articulating its nature, and thus contribute to others' understanding of it. However, it is not clear that justice itself benefits from such care, nor even that its benefit can be coherently intended. To know whether it could, we would first have to know what kind of "thing" justice is. Fortunately, we do not have to resolve this difficulty in order to understand the nature of appreciation-love. All that is required is the realization that one can love justice appreciatively without believing that doing so could contribute to its welfare. Since this is the case, appreciation-love is logically distinct from care-love.

Does one seek union with justice by loving it? Again, this is a possible way of looking at the matter, depending on how one understands the relationship between persons and ideals. But the point once more is that belief in the possibility of such a union is not necessary to loving justice as an ideal. Some Platonists might hold that loving justice involves fusion with the Idea itself, but one may also love it as an ideal while believing that the merging of persons and ideals makes no sense at all.

Since it is clear that appreciation-love does not have as an objective either the welfare of the loved or union with it, we must ask, what is its objective? The one word answer is "appreciation": the lover appreciates the loved, he or she values or delights in it for what it is. But just as the term "union" turned out to have multiple senses, so does "appreciation." It may consist in aesthetic contemplation, awe, reverence, delight, dedication (as to an ideal), or it may be a simple matter of accepting the loved as is or bestowing one's attention upon it. Thus the term will be used here, in a slightly technical sense, as a stand-in for several different, positive, but relatively nonactive, nonappetitive, and nonappropriative responses to the loved. We can conclude then that there is no single objective and no single relation appropriate to this love, but rather a family of related objectives and responses.

Although appreciation-love cannot be reduced to care-love, the linkage between them is strong. Indeed, it seems probable that if anything one appreciates can be cared for, one will have care-love for it as well. For example, if I have appreciation-love for a child and then learn that the child is seriously ill, I am filled with concern. My impulse is to see what I can do. Even when I am convinced that the object of appreciation-love cannot itself be cared for, as with love of a principle, appreciation may lead to caring for all those beings the principle touches. Thus it may make little sense to have care-love for *ahimsa* (not harming, nonviolation), but my living in accordance with this ideal requires the utmost in caring; I must care for all those things to which the principle applies.

Appreciation-love and union-love are less compatible because the former demands detachment from the loved whereas the objective of the latter is to seek union with the object. It might even be, as Hesse maintained, that the purest form of appreciation-love is free of desire, including the desire for union. Despite the tension between these two ways of loving, however, it is possible and even common to love the same object in both ways. Romantic love is fundamentally union-love but is typically based upon appreciation of some the beloved's qualities and, ideally, of the beloved's very being. So although there is often friction between these two ways of relating to the loved (especially when union-love is possessive in character), we must recognize that there are forms of union that are quite tolerant of otherness, and ways of being united that are not threatened by differences and independence. Lovers united by being first in each other's life or lovers who have made a commitment to care for each other may well succeed in fostering rather than squelching appreciation of each other's individuality. It is the more problematic forms of union such as appropriation, submission, and codependency (see Chapter 8) that work against appreciation by undermining the detachment that is essential to it.

In the West, Plato's is probably the leading historical example of a theory that gives primacy to appreciation-love. Here, the ultimate object of love is the Idea of the Good or Beautiful (the two concepts appear to be used interchangeably in the *Symposium*), which alone is loved as an end. Yet, since Plato also characterizes love as a desire to *possess* the Good/Beautiful, union-love is present as well. His use of the concept "possess" is peculiar, however. On my reading, "possessing the Good" means knowing the Good and then putting this knowledge into practice by performing good deeds and creating good or beautiful things. These beautiful things, because they are images of true Beauty, can be used by others in their own assent to the transcendent Idea. This is possession in an entirely nonacquisitive sense. Regardless, however, Platonic possession is union (the lover and the Good converge, at least in that the lover becomes good), and Plato's, then, is not a pure appreciation-love theory.

When Plato's theory is applied to interpersonal love, one man is said to love another because he perceives beauty/goodness in the other. In Platonic language, the beloved "imitates" or "participates in" the Beautiful. But the real object of love is the Beautiful itself, understood as a transcendent Idea or Form, as "beauty only, absolute, separate, simple, and everlasting, which without diminution and without increase, or any change, is imparted to the ever-growing and perishing beauties of all other things."[3] Persons or things are, therefore, secondary love objects and are loved only because they "imitate" or "participate in" the Beautiful. There has been much criticism of Plato's alleged reduction of the love of persons to the love of qualities.[4] Regardless of where one stands on the matter, the love of qualities figures prominently in philosophical accounts of love because of the role this love plays when it comes to giving reasons for loving.

REASONS FOR LOVING

Appreciation-love in the form of love of ideas, ideals, or abstract qualities often comes into play when we attempt to give reasons for why we love what we do. If I try to explain why I love the music of Haydn, I may refer to the humor found in some of his works, the optimism, the wonderful formal balance.[5] I may explain my love for my best friend by pointing to his integrity, reliability, and sense of adventure. These explanations derive their force from my appreciation-love for the qualities mentioned, at least in some possible combinations and instantiations. (The qualification is necessary because one may admire some qualities only when conjoined with others, or only in certain kinds of persons. Thus, one may not admire restlessness as an abstract quality but admire it in pursuit of an admirable goal such as truth. Or a homophobic man may love physical beauty in women but be uncomfortable or even repelled by the same quality in his own sex.)

There is considerable disagreement among love theorists concerning the importance of the love of qualities within the entire scheme of love. Is the love for something usually or always dependent upon the love for the qualities possessed by that thing? This, it is widely held, was the view taken by Plato. If this interpretation is correct, all love (or all instances of the form of love the Greeks called "eros") is reducible to the appreciation-love of qualities. Whether we are aware of it or not, ultimately, we love only the Beautiful/Good. So if a youth, as yet unschooled in the nature of love, finds himself casting amorous glances at another's body, it is only because the body he sees "participates in" or is an "imitation of" the Idea of the Beautiful that is the true, even if unknown, object of his longing.

As a universal theory of love, this will certainly not do. We love neither our parents nor our children solely because of the personal qualities they embody. Indeed, we sometimes love them despite these qualities. Even less do we love them as mere stepping stones on the way to some transcendent Platonic Form, as Plato is frequently understood to mean. But it would be incorrect to apply Plato's theory of eros to the love between parents and children. This kind of love the Greeks called "*philia.*" Even as a theory of that form of eros we call "romantic love," however, the account is inadequate. I may fall in love with someone because of her beauty and other admirable qualities, but in the long run it is unlikely that attraction to these qualities constitutes the sole basis of my love. Not only is it unlikely, it would be morally troubling as well because, were I to love someone only because of her personal qualities, I would presumably transfer my love to whoever came along possessing those same qualities to an even greater degree. Although this may sometimes happen, human attachments are not usually so fickle. When they are, we begin to wonder about the lover's emotional maturity and moral character.

The issue of commitment comes into play here because, as has been noted, caring for someone gives rise over time to an obligation to continue caring. Yet personal love is never just commitment, it is fundamentally a matter of natural inclination. Still we do make commitments to those we love. As has been noted, should an individual suddenly stop loving someone he or she had loved for a long time, we would feel that something was seriously amiss. Almost certainly we would blame the lover for the failure, unless we could excuse it on the grounds of some temporary emotional disturbance.

At the other extreme, it is sometimes urged that love of persons must have nothing to do with the qualities the persons possess. People must be loved unconditionally, it is said, understanding by this that we love them regardless of their personal qualities. From this perspective, loving an individual because of his or her qualities is taken as evidence of moral failure, or even as evidence for love's absence. This ideal of unconditional love fails, however, as a description of how people usually love, though it may be defensible as an ideal of how one ought to love.

Taking a more analytical look at the question of reducing the love of persons or things to the love of qualities, such a reduction holds only if X's love of Y can be completely reduced to X's loving some set of qualities (say, a, b, and c) and Y's possessing those qualities, or more accurately X's believing Y does. In this case X loves Y, cares for him, appreciates him, wishes to be one with him only because X believes Y possesses a, b, and c. If this reduction holds, it has frequently been argued, X does not really love Y at all; X loves only a, b, and c, which just happen to be instantiated in Y. Or, as some have expressed it, X loves Y only as a means to a, b, and c. The question we must consider is not whether the love of persons and things is *ever* reducible to the love of qualities (whether, for example, an adolescent boy's romantic interest in his favorite movie star might simply be an attraction to certain general qualities he believes the star possesses), but whether it *generally or always* is. Although the answer to the extreme form of the reducibility thesis is fairly obvious, a systematic investigation of just why it fails will reveal much about why we love the persons and things we do. Let us begin by considering whether love for inanimate objects can be reduced to love of qualities, since this would obviously be the easiest position for an advocate of the reductionist thesis to defend.

Before investigating this reductionist thesis, however, a distinction must be made between the qualities or properties of an object and what might be termed its "relational qualities." The latter expression refers to how the object is related to other objects, especially the lover. In speaking of the qualities or properties of an object, then, we will exclude such things as "being the father of" or "being to the right of." These are properties in the technical, logical sense but not in the more ordinary sense of being actual, physical or psychological properties of the thing itself. They are better classified as properties of the relationship between the object and something else. That X is to the right of Y tells us nothing about X's nature (except that it is spatially locatable), only where it stands in relation to Y. X's being the father of Y, although primarily relational, gives us a little more information about X (that it is a male animal), but not much. That X is an attentive father to Y gives us a little more information. Thus the distinction between properties of objects and relational properties is not a clear either/or issue, but is a matter of degree—a relative distinction. As we proceed it will be necessary to keep the distinction between properties of an object and relational properties in mind.

Let us begin with a fairly simple, pedestrian example of love for an inanimate object: suppose my friend John says that he "loves" a particular basketball. John gives as his reasons that it bounces perfectly, it makes the kind of thud he likes to hear when it strikes the floor, and it sticks to his fingers to just the right degree, giving him the grip he desires. If these were the only reasons he loves it, he would "love" any basketball with the same qualities just as well, and his doing so would be reducible to the "love" of those qualities. The ball itself would then be fully replaceable as a "love" object. But suppose instead that John offers the following as his reason for loving the basketball: "This is the ball with which we won the state championship back in 1965 and it's been signed by all the members of the team. For these reasons, I would not part with it for anything." Here John's love of the ball is no longer reducible to love of the ball's qualities.

What has changed is that John now has a unique historical relationship with this particular ball. True, it could have been another ball but it happens to be this one. The historical fact becomes the basis for a sentimental attachment to the individual object. Its having been the ball with which John's team won the big game is not so much a property of the ball—like its bounce, the sound it makes, or its "grip"—but a fact about the John-ball relationship, or (more accurately) about the John-ball-team relationship. Once this is understood, it is apparent that John's love of the ball is no longer reducible to the love of the ball's qualities; nor is the love object replaceable by another possessing the same physical characteristics. Notice also that John's love is now not so much an appreciation-love of the ball's qualities as it is a union-love (leading to care-love), because John's identity with the team and with his own past is symbolized by the ball.

Now we ask why John loves Mary. John met Mary during the season in which they won the big game. Within two years they were married, and they remain so all these years later. He was first attracted to her because of something about her smile and the fact that she did not seem at all frightened by him; she was not intimidated or even overly impressed by his athletic prowess like the other young women he knew. More important, she saw and responded to something deep within him that no one else had noticed—a capacity for tenderness, let's say, of which he himself was only dimly aware. John and Mary quickly fell in love. We will assume for the sake of simplicity that the three qualities just mentioned—the smile, the absence of intimidation, and the perception of a single aspect of his inner emotional nature—were the sole basis of John's love. (This is highly improbable, but the number of qualities changes nothing in the logic of the situation, only its degree of complexity.) So John fell in love with Mary because she possessed three qualities he found attractive. Notice that the second and third qualities, however, are not static universals that just happen to be instantiated in Mary; they are complex but specific phenomena that are already part of the John-Mary relationship, not qualities of Mary but of her manner of interacting with John. This could conceivably be true also of the first quality (her smile), if she has a special smile reserved just for him. Only by an artificial process of abstraction can these qualities be separated from the relationship and be viewed simply as characteristics of Mary.

It might be pointed out that someone else could have possessed the same, or sufficiently similar, relational qualities so that John might have fallen in love with her instead. Indeed, John might have fallen in love with someone possessing quite a different set of relational qualities that he found equally compelling. While both of these are possible, Mary was the one he met and now, after more than thirty years of marriage, he still loves her. Moreover, he now loves her not only because of the many fine qualities she possesses, both old and new, but because they have been together for so long and have become so much a part of one another that he can hardly imagine his life without her. It is not that John cannot imagine any other woman with personal qualities he might find appealing. He may have met such a woman, even entertained the idea of having an affair with her, or actually done so. But with this other woman, the one whose personal qualities he found so charming, there was something missing. What was missing is the shared history of an essentially positive relationship spanning his entire adult life. John could never find this with anyone else for he has shared this history only with Mary.[6]

To the extent that a shared history has been unhappy, individuals may well want to get out of a relationship and start over again with a clean slate, as it were. But when the shared history has been largely good, such as John and Mary's, there is a bond nourished not merely by the present personal qualities of each partner but by years of shared memories and experiences. With no one else could either feel the same sense of continuity. No one else has participated in this history, shared the same joys, sorrows, disappointments, and fulfillments. Factors such as these and not some unique conjunction of abstract human qualities give individuals who have been together for a long time the feeling that their partners are irreplaceable.

Loved ones are not irreplaceable in the sense that we could have loved no other individuals than the ones we have. That a woman has loved her son for decades hardly means that she could not have loved a quite different son (or daughter) who might have been born to her by a different roll of the genetic dice. Her loving him now has more to do with the fact that he is *her* son and that they have been in a mother-son relationship for so many years than with any particular personal qualities the son possesses. Should they be qualities the mother esteems, loving him may be easier. Yet even should the son's most admirable qualities undergo a sudden change, the mother most probably would still love him, even if somewhat differently and with greater difficulty. Indeed, should she discover that owing to some freak error in the hospital records he is not actually her biological son, she would almost certainly—after some serious psychological readjustment—continue loving him much as before. The new revelation does not obliterate the shared history of their mother-son relationship.

It seems doubtful that there is any more robust sense of irreplaceability of love objects than this. A woman may say to her husband after decades of marriage, "You are irreplaceable, I cannot live without you." The fact remains that she might have done just as well, although differently, with someone else. She feels that he is irreplaceable largely because they both are who they now are, partly, because of their life together. The woman who would have been married to another man for the same period of time, in a legitimate sense, is not the same woman. She may even have difficulty conceiving having been married to another because the "she" thereby imagined is not the "she" she now knows. It is here that Robert Solomon's identity theory of love is especially helpful. Notwithstanding Solomon's insight into how love shapes personal identity, however, it must also be admitted that some individuals change very little regardless of whom they share their lives with, and all of us, even if we undergo significant change, are, in a legitimate sense, the same person in two or more successive love relationships. Our different "relational selves," as we might term them, occupy successive segments of the same life history in a way that self and other do not.

What follows from the preceding analysis of the role played by the love of qualities in the love of persons? When fantasy and projection are heavily involved, love for a person may be reducible to love for the general qualities the person possesses or is believed to possess. More normally, however, some of the qualities that draw us toward a particular individual are not so much qualities of the loved as qualities of the relationship between lover and loved, qualities of how they interact with one another. Once the relationship has a history, even a short one, this history becomes a factor in why and how each person loves or does not love the other.

Shared history is not peculiar to romantic and marital love but is a factor in most interpersonal love. Consider, for example, if you would choose to have exactly the parents, siblings, or children that you now have if you were picking a family based solely on personal qualities? How many of your oldest friends are people you would choose to form friendships with were you to meet them for the first time today? Yet consider also what it costs to lose them. It is shared history that binds us together, more than "blood" or any ideal matching of qualities. As we saw with the case of John and his cherished basketball, even the love for things may be influenced by historical and relational factors that cannot be reduced to the love of abstract qualities. We can conclude that the love we have for persons and even things, while often arising from the love of qualities, is only rarely reducible to it. When it is so reducible, the love is of an especially superficial nature that might better be classified as liking, attraction, or infatuation.

With other loves (of family, country, religion, or ethnic group, for example) the love of abstract qualities probably plays little or no role. Because these attachments are largely nonvoluntary, shared history is all or nearly all. We simply happen to belong to this particular family, ethnic group, and so on. Insofar as attraction to qualities enters the picture, it may arise after the loving has begun, more as consequence than cause. For example, an Irishman may come to love the qualities associated with his nationality because he first loved his Irish family.

A LOVE INDIFFERENT TO QUALITIES

There is no doubt that most human love is motivated, partially at least, by attraction to the qualities and relational qualities of the loved. Theologians sometimes call this "natural love." It is human nature, they observe, to be drawn to certain qualities and experiences: to love what gives us pleasure, to love those who love us. But there is another love, they assure us, that is not inherent in our nature but that nonetheless is manifest in the world. In the New Testament this love is called "agape." One of the most influential of modern interpreters of "agape" is the Swedish Lutheran theologian and New Testament scholar Anders Nygren, whose monumental *Agape and Eros* first appeared in Swedish in the 1930s. Nygren's reading of "agape," although extreme and rather polemical, fits our present purposes especially well because he sees agape as unmotivated by attraction to either the loved or its qualities. The traditional Roman Catholic view, as we have seen, is quite different. Agape, or that form of it known as neighbor love, is motivated by the transpersonal qualities of the loved—the image of God that dwells in each of us. Nygren rejects this reading absolutely.

In his view agape is an "unmotivated gift," not a response to any characteristics, personal or transpersonal, of the loved. He views the Catholic understanding of agape as a corruption of the original biblical teaching. Already by the time of Augustine, "agape" had been given a Neoplatonic interpretation, resulting in a blending of "eros" and "agape" that Nygren calls the "*caritas*-synthesis." Nygren's polemical mission is to redeem "agape" from this distortion. "Agape," he insists, refers first to God's love and only derivatively to love for the neighbor. When Christians love their neighbors, it is not with their own love; rather, God's agape flows through the Christian lover employing him or her as a channel of His love.[7]

According to Nygren one of the principle differences between agape and eros is that eros is motivated by the value of the love object whereas agape is "indifferent to value." God does not love us because of our righteousness; he loves the righteous and the sinners alike. Nygren—who never tires of quoting the Gospel passages, "I came not to call the righteous but the sinners" (Mark 2:17) and "He maketh the sun to rise on the evil and the good" (Matthew 5:45)—insists that "God does not love that which is already in itself worthy of love, but on the contrary, that which in itself has no worth acquires worth just by becoming the object of God's love."[8]

It follows that human life taken by itself is devoid of intrinsic value. We are worthless, but God bestows value upon us through the gift of His love. As Nygren puts it: "Agape does not recognize value, but creates it." It is, he says, both "spontaneous and 'unmotivated.'"[9] In the same way, we extend love to our neighbor not because of the neighbor's worth but because of his or her need. Loving the sinner, thus, is more Christian than loving the saint.

Neera Kapur Badhwar has offered an interesting criticism of Nygrenian love: "the denial that the worth or lovability of the individual has anything to do with the love, is precisely the denial that the individual is loved for 'himself.'"[10] Badhwar's purpose is to show that agape cannot be the foundation of friendship love. In this she is certainly right. As love of all, agape is without preference, and for that reason, not personal, whereas friendship is necessarily both preferential and personal. However, I do not agree with Badhwar that agape is the "denial that the individual is loved for 'himself.'" Seeing why this objection is not convincing will reveal one of the strengths of neighbor love.

All agapists would agree that neighbor love is not a response to the loved's personal qualities. If it were, it would be both conditional and preferential. Yet, even if it is not motivated by these qualities, the lover must see them and take them into account. Because the agapist lover strives to meet the needs of the loved, he or she must endeavor to see the loved clearly. If the one in need is starving, this is a simple matter, but under other circumstances knowing what is needed requires considerable subtlety in determining not only the loved's objective situation but who, precisely, he or she is. The love itself is not conditioned by these factors, but the lover's decision regarding what actions are required is. The proper conclusion, then, is that agape loves the individual *for* who he or she is, but not *because* of who he or she is.

This is precisely the strength of a spiritual love such as agape. Not being conditioned by the individual qualities of the loved, it does not alter with them. Agape can see the loved so clearly precisely because it is not distracted by either attraction or aversion. (The same can be said of the purer forms of appreciation-love.) If I love you because of your kindness and then you do something cruel, my love is called into question. I may feel cheated or deceived—"I thought you were kind, but now I see that you are not." If, on the other hand, I love you agapistically, I see and respect your kindness but am not attached to it. If you suddenly act cruelly, I have no urge to withdraw my love. I simply watch and say to myself, "Yes, sometimes he can be cruel as well as kind. How like a human being. How like myself."

Agape is very different from those loves that are based on the attraction to personal qualities, as are friendship (Badhwar's concern) and romantic love. These loves are certainly not unconditional in the strong sense; nor, as Badhwar argues, can agape be their foundation. But is there any inherent incompatibility between unconditional and personal love? As Nygren understands agape, the two loves do conflict—personal love arises in response to the loved's personal or relational qualities whereas Nygrenian love is indifferent to those same qualities; personal love is preferential whereas Nygrenian love is not.

However if we think of unconditional love in its less radical sense (more like the "modified unconditionality" discussed in Chapter 2), the incompatibility vanishes. A woman may fall in love because her beloved possesses attractive personal qualities, but then she may commit herself to accepting her beloved as he is, so that even if he changes significantly she will continue to love him. I am not sure that such loves are ever indefeasible but there is no denying that they sometimes are very strong and withstand substantial changes in the personal qualities of the loved.

This kind of unconditionality is frequently present in or awakened by strong personal loves. How else are we able to account for the fact that the love of ordinary people may persist through profound alterations in the loved, such as those that accompany prolonged physical or mental illness. Such constancy is especially evident within families. Parents may continue to love a child even after he or she has been in a comatose condition for years, or, for that matter, after their child has blown up an airliner full of innocent people. Personal love's qualified unconditionality is not inherently moral.

As another example of the kind of modified unconditionality we find in personal love, consider the case of a man whose wife is terminally ill. The love he demonstrates in caring for her is certainly not purely conditional. Nor, however, is it absolutely without conditions. It is conditioned by the fact that she is his wife and has been for decades. Presumably, he first began to love her because of personal and relational qualities, which also were conditions. But now, a lifetime later and in the final stages of her last illness, many of these qualities are no longer in evidence and, presumably, never will be again. If so, his present love cannot be motivated by these qualities but doubtless is motivated by his memory of them and the memory of their life together—as well as by the gratitude he feels for all she has given him. What is more, he is aware that, if roles were reversed and it was he who was dying, she would love and care for him. In this example, we have a love that is intensely personal yet apparently not motivated by the active presence of personal qualities of the loved or even by the expectation of their return. Relational qualities involving shared history, however, remain profoundly operative. Such a love is not as unconditional as Nygren's agape, but it is unconditional in the less extreme sense of not being much influenced by the present qualities of the beloved.

This kind of unconditional love does not occur only in those special relationships where the love was originally based on attraction to personal qualities. We may experience it for parents, children, and siblings, none of whom were chosen by us because we admired their personal qualities (although personal qualities may have come to influence how we love them). Even more interesting is the way in which we sometimes experience this modified form of unconditional love for someone with whom we have no personal relationship at all. Think of an occasion when you are feeling good about yourself, and about life in general, and a man who is a complete stranger does something toward you that you dislike. This time, however, rather than reacting defensively as you might on other occasions, you just watch what he does without being personally affected. Perhaps you even feel compassion toward the man who treats you rudely or wishes you harm, wondering why he acts as he does, wondering what he might have suffered that could have lead him to act in this way. Here we have an example of a compassionate love and acceptance that seems to operate independently of attraction to personal qualities.

The above is an instance not only of a spiritual form of care-love but of a fairly pure form of appreciation-love. The one offended is not attracted to the personal qualities of the stranger but sees and accepts them without condemnation. Appreciation-love, it will be recalled, may simply be nonjudgmental acceptance. In the example, the stranger's personal characteristics are not appreciated, but very likely some transpersonal or quasi-transpersonal quality such as his humanity is. From such examples it is apparent that we can have respect, even reverence, for a person when none of the individual's personal qualities attract us to him.

People who work in the "helping professions" are able to maintain such an attitude of loving detachment much of the time. They interact with client, patient, or student—understanding, helping, making the welfare of the other their priority. A psychotherapist's patient may strike out in anger, but, realizing that it is transference anger and part of the patient's recovery, far from being offended, the therapist is supportive, even thrilled. Not that such work is selfless: therapists get paid for their efforts and presumably derive self-satisfaction from it as well. No doubt they like some clients better than others, perhaps offering more of themselves because of these preferences. But they are able, more often than not, to focus disinterestedly on the client's well-being for the duration of each session. There may also be moments when the therapist's own ego almost ceases to exist as he or she focuses on the client's needs. On such occasions, the therapist becomes all attention and compassion; technique and professionalism are all but irrelevant. It is as if the therapist has become a channel for a power to heal and understand that she never knew she possessed—and perhaps does not possess. Here we have a love very close to Nygren's agape.

So is there a love independent of the love of qualities? The answer remains inconclusive, but we may be sure that there are loves that operate with a reasonable degree of independence from the attraction to personal or relational qualities. Still, whether there exists a love as completely free of attraction and the love of qualities as Nygren demands may be doubted. None of the cases just discussed unequivocally qualifies. Perhaps (as was suggested in our earlier discussion of unconditional love), it is best to think of completely unconditional love as a limiting case that human love approaches but never quite reaches.

Before leaving this discussion of unconditional love, however, there is a serious theoretical problem with Nygren's notion of agape that must be noted. If agape has *nothing* whatever to do with the qualities of the loved, then why is it extended solely to human beings? Badhwar formulates the objection this way: "But this radical interpretation of agape renders it mysterious [as to] why agape is selectively *directed* at human beings, given that it is not *motivated* by them."[11] It seems that there may, after all, be a quality that conditions even Nygren's agape—the universal quality of being human. This is not a personal quality in the usual sense of that which differentiates one person from another, but a universal quality that distinguishes persons from non-persons. Although Nygren insists repeatedly that agape is unconditional and theocentric, he fails to notice that it is in a crucial sense both conditional and anthropocentric. Nygren's God loves human beings preferentially.

Love's Unity and Universality

❖ Are "care-love," "union-love," and "appreciation-love" logically independent concepts, such that none can be reduced to or derived from either or both of the others? What is the potential for cooperation and for conflict between the three ways of loving? Is the notion of "love" we have been investigating a universal concept or merely an English word? Should the English language be faulted, as it sometimes has been, for employing the word "love" as broadly as it does? Does the human capacity for loving have a biological basis such that love, something as we know it, is likely to exist in all societies? Finally does analysis of the word/concept "love" fully reveal the nature of love itself? These are the questions to be pondered in the present chapter.

THE INDEPENDENCE OF THE THREE LOVES

Our three forms of loves and the concepts referring to them are interrelated in complex ways. They arguably overlap conceptually, presupposing and/or implying one another, but they also may be psychologically or causally linked such that the presence of one kind of love causes or makes probable the presence of another. Moreover, there are occasions in which conflicts arise between these ways of loving, placing them in opposition to each other. Expressed more technically, between these three concepts or between the phenomena they denote we find putative logical entailments (for example, caring for X logically presupposes appreciation-love for it or for its qualities); causal connections linking one form of love to another (for example, appreciating X causes one to care for X, if X is the kind of thing whose benefit can be intended); and conflicts or contradictions (for example, achieving union with X undermines the distance necessary to caring for X as an end). Let us begin the investigation of how care-love, union-love, and appreciation-love are inter-related by demonstrating that the three concepts are logically independent.

That the three senses of "love" are logically independent is a matter of considerable theoretical importance, for, if any one of our three senses of "love" were derivable from the others, there would not be three distinct senses of "love" at all but merely two (or one), to which the other belongs (or the others belong) as a subcase. It is not necessary to demonstrate complete logical independence—that no kind of caring, for example, presupposes appreciation. It is only the absence of complete logical dependence that must be established, such that none of the three loves is fully derivable from either or both of the others. There are obviously three possibilities to consider: (1) that care-love is reducible to appreciation-love and union-love; (2) that appreciation-love is reducible to care-love and union-love; or (3) that union-love is reducible to care-love and appreciation-love. The other cases (that one form of love may be reduced to only one of the others) need not be separately established, since, if A is not reducible to B and C, clearly it is not reducible to either B or C alone.

To start with the irreducibility of care-love: it is easy to show that the conjunction of appreciation-love and union-love does not necessitate caring. A Platonist might have appreciation-love for the Good, for example, and seek union or fuller participation with it while not intending the Good's benefit on the grounds that nothing can benefit it—the Good being already perfect. Were we to allow irrationally intended benefit, however, this argument could conceivably collapse. To conclusively demonstrate logical independence, then, what is needed is a form of care-love that is actually incompatible with union and appreciation. Such an example exists in Nygren's construal of agape. As we have seen, a Nygrenian love for the neighbor has nothing to do with appreciation of the neighbor or the neighbor's qualities. Nor can the desire for union have a place in it, for in Nygren's reading it is eros that aims at union, and the misguided *caritas*-synthesis that sought to incorporate this objective into Christian love. Although agape does seek the well-being of the loved it does so not in response to any quality of the loved, but solely in obedience to God's command. Likewise, if union has a place in a Nygrenian interpretation of neighbor love, it makes its appearance later, as a result not as a cause or precondition of loving. Moreover, Nygren's

God does not care for us because of appreciation of us or desire for union with us but in response to our need and in accord with His own nature as overflowing Agape.

Since the actual existence of Nygrenian love may be doubted, it might be that all actual caring arises in consequence of either appreciation or the impulse for union, causally linking it to its sister loves. Even if this is true, however, we have what is necessary to refute the reductionist thesis—the concept of a form of caring that is logically independent of union-love and appreciation-love, a concept moreover that is not hypothetical, but one of considerable historical importance.

As for the irreducibility of appreciation-love, although caring for something and seeking union with it might imply that the lover also appreciates the loved, appreciation-love is not reducible to the other two loves because it may sometimes exist without them. That appreciation-love can exist without its sister loves is evident from Hermann Hesse's notion of undemanding love examined in Chapter 6. The passage quoted earlier began: "The eye of desire dirties and distorts. Only when we desire nothing, only when our gaze becomes pure contemplation, does the soul of things (which is beauty) open itself to us."[1] With an appreciation-love so pure, desire for union, even the desire for the loved's well-being, would seem to be precluded. If so, at least one form of appreciation-love stands in complete independence of care-love and union-love. As with Nygrenian agape, the actual existence of such an unmixed appreciation-love may be doubted, but once again the concept exists.

It might be thought that appreciating something and caring for it would entail union-love for it as well. After all, care-love seems to presuppose the union of identification; and if merely having a positive attitude toward union is sufficient for union-love, it is difficult to imagine that one would not have such an attitude toward identification with an object appreciated as an end. This is true, but union-love is not reducible to the other two loves. The problem this time is not that it goes beyond them—existing, sometimes, independently. Rather, union-love falls short of caring and appreciation in that the desire for union can undermine the distance and regard for the loved as an end that is required by the latter loves. Distorted forms of union-love may conflict sharply with both care and appreciation. Thus while appreciation-love and care-love will often give rise to a form of union-love (the positive attitude toward identification already present in caring), other forms of union-love clash with caring and appreciation because of the greater detachment these require.

CONFLICTS BETWEEN THE THREE LOVES

The above demonstration of the logical independence of care-love, union-love, and appreciation-love shows as well how intimately related the three loves are, and how numerous and various the linkages between them. More intriguing than these linkages, however, is the matter of conflicts that sometimes arise between the three loves. These conflicts are not logical contradictions between the concepts themselves, since it is evident that the three loves often blend together in perfect harmony, but conflicts between the phenomena themselves. (There may, however, be conflicts between the concepts or descriptions of *specific forms* of the three loves—between the description of pure forms of appreciation-love, for example, and descriptions of possessive or appropriative union-love.) Since there are only three possible dyadic combinations of our three loves—union-love and care-love, union-love and appreciation-love, care-love and appreciation-love—there are three possibilities for conflict we must consider. The two combinations involving union-love clearly have the most obvious potential in this regard, but since these have been mentioned before, a brief reminder will do.

Care-love and union-love conflict with one another when the urge for union erodes the detachment that is indispensable for caring. Care-love, it will be recalled, requires treating the loved as an end, whereas union-love does not. When we over-identify with someone we love, we may lose the ability to conceive of his or her well-being as different from our own—fusion leads to confusion. The conflict is not between care-love and union-love per se, but between caring and a somewhat distorted form of union-love. Such distortions are far from uncommon in union-love relationships, however. To offer just one example: a mother who became pregnant in her teens may convey to her daughter an excessive fear of sex, reading her own past into her daughter's present. The daughter may, in fact, be quite capable of regulating her own sex life, but the over-identified mother cannot see this. Since identification is inherent in union-love, however, conflict can exist even when the union-love is quite healthy, it being no easy matter to distinguish one's own interest from that of a loved one with whom we identify.

Union-love and appreciation-love bump up against each other in similar ways. When the union is too close, or of the kind that diminishes otherness, appreciation suffers. As with care-love, appreciation-love presupposes detachment and valuing the loved as an end. When union is achieved through appropriation of the beloved, or when lover and loved become enmeshed, genuine appreciation-love becomes difficult or impossible. Such lovers might appreciate the beloved narcissistically—as an extension or reflection of themselves—but this sort of appreciation does not qualify as appreciation-love because the loved is not appreciated as an end.

The possibility for conflict between care-love and appreciation-love is less evident, and its existence more problematic. Appreciation is most apt to enhance caring because an appreciated love object will appear more deserving of care. However, strong appreciation of an individual could also give rise to jealousy or envy, thereby diminishing the urge to care, or even undermining it altogether. Seeing how good-looking or brilliant you are might lead me to wish you ill rather than well.

It could be argued that it would not be appropriate to call this kind of appreciation "love." For appreciation to rise to the level of love, not only must it be particularly strong but the object must be appreciated as an end. Thus, if I envy a man because of his brilliance, I am not so much appreciating his intelligence as an end as I am reacting to the shadow his intelligence casts on mine. What is going on here, the counter-argument continues, is the lover's failure to have genuine appreciation-love for the other's intelligence—and perhaps for his own as well. If the lover truly appreciated both, he would have less need to make invidious comparisons. This is an interesting rejoinder, making moral as well as logic sense, but it is not entirely convincing, resting as it does on a somewhat normative interpretation of "appreciation-love." No doubt there is an ideal of appreciation that precludes envy or jealousy, but are there not also less noble appreciations that would qualify as love? Consider, for example, the appreciation Antonio Salieri (as fictionalized by Pushkin, Rimsky-Korsakof, and more recently Peter Shaffer in his film *Amadeus*) has for Mozart's genius—and his subsequent poisoning of him. Could we not say that Salieri kills Mozart partly because he loves his music so much?

One might attempt to save care-love and appreciation-love from conflict by pointing out that they have different objects. Salieri's appreciation-love is not for Mozart (it might be urged) but for his music, whereas his hatred is for Mozart the man. But this different-objects argument may not work either. Mozart's musical genius is, after all, a part of Mozart the man, not something completely separate. Still (the objector may persist), they are not the same objects—loving one of a person's qualities is different from loving the person.

There is a stronger argument for the conflict between care-love and appreciation-love, however, that completely circumvents the different-objects objection. We can imagine a character similar to the fictionalized Salieri burning Mozart's compositions after he kills him. Here the music itself is the object not only of an intense appreciation but also of a violent hatred. He loves Mozart's music, even loves it as an end, but his humiliation and hatred override his appreciation-love of Mozart's compositions. This argument, it seems, has no ready answer. Apparently even these two forms of love can conflict, at least through the medium of envy.

There are other possibilities for tension between care-love and appreciation-love. Appreciation could mitigate against caring if, say, a man's appreciation for a woman were so exalted that he could not conceive of anything he might do to show his care—"she is too perfect, too devoid of needs." The objection might be made that, even in this case, care-love may be present in the form of the disposition to care; it is simply that the lover cannot find an occasion for exercising it. While this is true, over time even the lover's disposition might cease, precisely because of the absence of such opportunities. Almost certainly he would come to care less. In this case, an extreme and perhaps idolatrous appreciation has led to at least the diminution of caring.

There is one more way in which caring might impinge upon appreciation-love. Just as care-love can promote union-love by drawing us closer to the one we care for, so caring often contributes to a deeper appreciation-love. But the reverse can also happen; as we care for some people we might discover things about them that we do not appreciate at all. We might end by appreciating them less or not at all. Imagine, for example, an idealistic young man who chooses nursing as a career because he cares deeply about human suffering, but then after years of working in his chosen field he comes to appreciate people (or sick people) less and less. All his labor on their behalf has somehow damaged his ability to value them as ends in themselves. Is not this what happens sometimes when people in the helping professions "burn out"?

English Word or Universal Concept?

In our analysis of "love" no account has been taken thus far of the distinction sometimes made between words and concepts. Words belong to specific languages whereas concepts, it is alleged, are common to different languages. "Love," "*liebe*," "*amour*" are three different words, but, some would say, they represent the same concept. Given this distinction, it seems appropriate to ask whether the thesis that "love" has three fundamental senses is a claim made about just the English word or about some more universal concept potentially present in all languages. If the preceding analysis concerns simply the English word, it has less philosophical significance than otherwise, for it would then provide us with insights only into a particular linguistic culture.

There is considerable disagreement within philosophy regarding the status and even the existence of concepts. Rather than argue that there is a universal concept of "love" (a dubious thesis that would generate needless controversy), let us be content with the claim that the three kinds of phenomena denoted by the English word "love" are universal, or nearly so, even if they are shaped by and valued differently in the cultures in which they exist, and even if they are not always referred to by a single word. The question we must ask, then, is whether there are human societies in which the three phenomena here identified as love—caring for as an end, seeking or valuing union with, and appreciating for its own sake—are unknown. To ask the question this way is to know the answer: these phenomena would have to exist and would have to be linked together roughly as has been described if a society is to be recognized as human (and also, I believe, if it is to endure for a reasonable length of time).

The argument has been made already with respect to care-love. It was said in Chapter 2 that caring is fundamental to the human way of being-in-the-world. An analogous argument can be made with regard to appreciation-love, and for a similar reason. One can scarcely conceive of human beings who appreciate nothing as ends—who take no delight in one another or in the things, events, and qualities they encounter or in the ideals they proclaim. Such a state of affairs, should it exist in any single individual, would be grounds for classifying the person as abnormal in the extreme. That it be the general condition of a culture would require nothing less than rethinking what it means to be human.

Union-love is similarly ubiquitous. Life devoid of identification with others, with no positive experiences of intimacy and (more to the point) with no desire to establish or preserve any of the forms of union investigated above, would scarcely be recognizable as human. Human beings need to belong, to feel connected, to experience themselves as parts of larger wholes such as families, clans, tribes, geographical or geological regions, or natural ecosystems. To constrict the ways of meeting these needs is to diminish human life; to eliminate them altogether would render it unrecognizable. I submit then that our three ways of loving are as universal as any of the other widely regarded universals of human culture such as the family, technology, economic structure, myth, or religion, and are as well, no doubt, among the dispositions that have evolved for its survival.

Given the importance of these phenomena in human life, it is reasonable to assume, further, that some way of referring to them must exist within all natural languages. It is likely, therefore, that a book such as the present one could be translated into other languages, even if it proved necessary to use different words for the phenomena here called "love," and even if some of the particular ways of loving we have considered might seem foreign to people from other cultures. There can be no doubt that the ways in which people love are profoundly influenced by culture and history. Yet the human capacity to love is informed by biology as well, and by those features of the human condition that are universal—the tendency to live in groups in which cooperation plays an essential role; the need to reproduce and, more importantly, the necessity of raising children to the age at which they too can reproduce; and the need to transmit to the young the values, traditions, and skills essential to both physical and cultural survival. It is safe to conclude, then, that most (though perhaps not all) of what we call "love" would be familiar to human beings wherever and whenever they have lived.

Romantic love is probably the most variable of the human ways of loving. There can be no doubt that modern Western societies have cultivated it, refined it, and made of it both an art and an obsession in ways that would seem peculiar to many other cultures. Until recently, on the few occasions when anthropologists addressed the question of romantic love, they tended to judge it a peculiarity of the modern West. In 1992, however, William R. Janowiak and Edward F. Fisher (defining "romantic-love" as "any intense attraction that involves the idealization of the other, within an erotic context, with the expectation of enduring for some time into the future"), discovered evidence for its existence within 146 of the 166 cultures for which ethnographic data existed. More recently, Jankowiak has discovered evidence for existence of romantic love in two of the cultures that were previously classified as inconclusive.[2]

Evidence is also accumulating regarding a genetic basis for romantic love. That this form of attachment has evolutionary origins and functions have been claimed by many, but perhaps most carefully and cogently by the English anthropologist Sydney Mellen.[3] He calls the phenomenon simply "love between men and women" rather than "romantic love," but it is apparent that what he has in mind is the long-term emotional bonding or attachment that occurs between sexual partners. The argument, briefly put, is that species survival required not merely that hominid females have offspring and care for them but that their sexual partners bond emotionally with both them and their progeny. Obviously, the young who receive this additional protection would have a greater chance of passing on their genes. In this way, a biologically based tendency to pair bond must have been established early in hominid evolution. Recently, this biological perspective on romantic love has received significant support from research into the biochemistry of romantic (as well as other forms of) love.[4] The researchers report that when we fall in love, chemicals are released in the brain producing pleasurable and potentially addictive sensations. Hence, the well-known euphoria of love has an organic basis.

As early as 1959 sociologist William J. Goode had ingeniously reached the conclusion that romantic love must be "a universal psychological potential." He defines "romantic love" as "a strong emotional attachment, a cathexis, between adolescents or adults of opposite sexes, with at least the components of sex desire and tenderness."[5] Agreeing with the general view that romance is only rarely the basis of marriage, Goode called attention to what others had overlooked: that in societies where marriage is not based on personal choice and attraction, social structures or practices exist that serve to discourage either the formation of romantic attachments or marriage based upon them. Goode's point is that there would be no need to devise controls to prevent romantic marriage unless such an eventuality were likely. In the earliest periods of human evolution, then, it is probable that pair bonding was determined by the personal preferences of those directly involved. However, once social stratification, lineage patterns, totemic relationships, and the transmission of property become social values, marriage based on the choice of the parties themselves would have become socially disruptive.

Putting all this together, the once widely held view that romantic love is the invention of the poets of the late Middle Ages, and exists nowhere outside of Western civilization, has to be rejected. Even this most variable of human loves is more widespread than once thought. In light of the evidence, the only way to make the case that romantic love is a Western invention would be linguistically, that is, by defining the concept not in terms of its most generic features but in some culturally specific fashion—linking it, for example, to Troubadour conceits or to some ideology of the Romantics. The more culturally specific one makes the concept, the less widespread the phenomenon.

IT HAS OFTEN BEEN SUGGESTED that it is a deficiency of the English language that a single word is used to cover the diversity of feelings, attitudes, dispositions, and responses that are embraced by our word "love." I do not share this view and hope that the preceding pages will have shed some light on the parallels and interconnections between romantic love, parent-child love, mystical love, and the ideal of neighbor love, mystically construed. Although these loves are certainly not the same, neither are they altogether different. Following the Augustinian tradition, Mother Teresa conceives of neighbor love as the mystical love for Christ in the neighbor which she expresses, in turn, through the metaphor of romantic love and marriage. This is not sloppy thinking on her part, but shows a deep grasp of the interrelationships between apparently divergent ways of loving. In the present study we have explored as well the parallels and interconnections between marital love, unconditional spiritual love, friendship, the love of beauty, and the regard sometimes shown to strangers. Notwithstanding all these resemblances, however, it is not necessary to employ a single word so broadly; and the use of separate words would help us avoid some of the confusions that arise so readily in the English-speaking world. Yet the clarity gained would come at a price, the price of obscuring connections between phenomena that actually are related.

Finally, amidst all this discussion of words and concepts we must not lose sight of the fact that love itself is neither. Even if the preceding analysis (or any analysis) of the meanings of "love" is convincing, the realities to which it points are not thereby fully disclosed. Concepts and words are at best mere tools of discernment, which distort even as they reveal. At worst, they are idols masking what they purport to represent.

> Between the idea
> And the reality . . .
> Between the concept
> And the creation
> Falls the Shadow . . . .[6]

Concepts point to what lies beyond this shadow, but they do not take us there.

The Dark Side of Love

❖ To investigate love as a natural phenomenon rather than as a normative ideal is to acknowledge that love itself does not have to be good. Indeed, love is subject to a variety of distortions. Any analysis of distorted forms of love will obviously be normative. In my attempt to identify love's dark side, the norms used are my own, or sometimes those of the authors whose ideas I borrow. Others would no doubt draw lines between healthy and distorted love in different places and in accordance with different norms. Had the analysis of "love" pursued in this work been a normative one, these distortions of love would be ruled out by definition. Yet we know that what at least passes for love can frequently be harmful to those who undergo and receive it. As much as we extol love, there is no escaping the fact that great evils are sometimes committed in its name. Lovers are frequently more cruel to one another than they would ever be to strangers; and families often conceal within their interiors horrors justified in the name of love. Moreover, what evils have not been committed for love of country, race, religion, party, or principle!

In contemplating the darker dimensions of our subject, we must remember that love is sometimes passionate, and where there is passion there is intensity, extremity, and unpredictability. In addition, love speaks to our deepest and often least conscious needs. In some of its many forms love marks off a danger zone of life, a place where pain and cruelty, as well as joy and generosity, reside. Moreover, we may seriously misconstrue not merely the nature of love but also its attendant obligations, thinking that it demands perfect loyalty, obedience, or the need to ignore every conflicting obligation or value, as though any deed performed in its name were sanctified.

Jill Tweedie in her disquieting book, *In the Name of Love*, tells the story of Teresa Stangl who faithfully stood by her husband, Fritz, for thirty-five years through all the vicissitudes of his life and career. Sounds familiar, even commendable, but theirs is a love story with a hideous twist: her husband's work involved supervising the extermination of nine hundred thousand people at Nazi death camps in Poland. A devout Catholic, Frau Stangl was upset when her husband became a Nazi and, again, when he left the church. Both these events put a strain on their marriage, but Teresa was a dutiful wife. In time, she learned what was taking place in the camps where her husband worked. When she found out, she was horrified and sobbed uncontrollably for hours, withdrawing from him, unable to bear his touch. He explained that he was only in charge of construction work; he was in fact the Commandant. Years later she explained: "He just kept stroking me softly and trying to calm me. Even so, it was several days before I . . . let him again."[1] Once more she managed to accommodate her life and values to the man she loved. In 1971 an interviewer asked her:

> Would you tell me what you think would have happened if at any time you had faced your husband with an absolute choice; if you had said to him: "Here it is; I know it's terribly dangerous, but either you get out of this terrible thing, or else the children and I will leave you." If you had confronted him with these alternatives, which do you think he would have chosen?

Frau Stangl took more than an hour to answer the question. She lay on her bed and cried, but when she composed herself she said:

> I have thought very hard. I know what you want to know. I know what I am doing when I answer your question. I am answering it because I think I owe it to you, to others, to myself; I believe that if I had ever confronted Paul [her pet name for Stangl] with the alternatives: Treblinka or me; he would—yes, he would, in the final analysis, have chosen me.

Tweedie comments:

> Though she loved her husband deeply—*because* she loved her husband deeply—she did nothing. No one had ever suggested to her that love has some morality, that to be "in love" did not excuse horror outside the cozy family circle, that responsibility to the outer world must intrude. Blinkered, devoted, worried but faithful, whenever she had the opportunity she

received her man into her bed, fresh from the naked shit-stained Jews, clutching their babies, whipped into the chambers. And in so doing, she lived out to the extreme the article of our faith: love conquers all.[2]

This belief, that love conquers all, may be an article of faith for many; but it takes only a little reflection to recognize that if any claim for its truth can be made it applies only to the most spiritual and selfless forms of love, not the kind of love that dominates the hearts and minds of worldly lovers. The kind of love Teresa Stangl had for her husband, rooted in fear of separation and loss, conquers little, unless it be the integrity of the lover herself.

In this particular example of love's perversity, more to the point than the "love conquers all" ideal that Tweedie identifies as the source of the problem is the belief that love requires of us, or of women, complete loyalty—where loyalty is understood as supporting the one we love in all he does. Such unflinching "loyalty" may, of course, be the height of disloyalty, as when we stand by and say nothing, not wanting to rock the boat, while the one we love indulges in what is lowest in his or her nature. As Germaine Greer once remarked of a far milder form of this kind of disloyalty: "Every time a woman makes herself laugh at her husband's often-told jokes she betrays him."[3] If we cannot count on the one we love most to tell us when we are being self-destructive, or merely acting like an ass, who can we count on? And what use is love? It becomes, then, little more than a means of fostering a false self-image that keeps us locked in illusion and denial. Love in some of its forms is only too good at fostering illusions—and whenever it does it becomes, to that degree, a distortion of what love can and should be.

Frau Stangl's story illustrates how we can be disloyal to ourselves in love. We somehow get it into our heads that a love relationship must be preserved at all costs but then, gradually, both partners abandon more and more of their essential selves (or perhaps only one of them does the abandoning) to make the relationship "work." In her desire to be loyal to her husband, Frau Stangl sacrificed not only her personal interests but her very humanity. Once this is sacrificed, all possibility of healthy love is gone.

C. S. Lewis has observed that love has a way of making an absolute of itself or of its object. St. John's formula "God is love," Lewis tells us, had long been balanced in his mind against the remark of Denis de Rougemont, that "love ceases to be a demon only when he ceases to be a god," or (stated without the negatives) love "begins to be demon the moment it begins to be a god." Lewis explains:

Every human love, at its height, has a tendency to claim for itself a divine authority. Its voice tends to sound as if it were the will of God Himself. It tells us not to count the cost, it demands of us a total commitment, it attempts to over-ride all other claims and insinuates that any action which is sincerely done "for love's sake" is thereby lawful and even meritorious. . . .

Now it must be noticed that the natural loves make this blasphemous claim not when they are in their worst, but when they are in their best, natural condition; when they are what our grandfathers called "pure" or "noble." This is especially obvious in the erotic sphere. A faithful and genuinely self-sacrificing passion will speak to us with what seems the voice of God. Merely animal or frivolous lust will not.[4]

Love, in Lewis's view, is more dangerous than lust. His point is that it has a way of taking upon itself a claim of absolute authority: "God is love" is replaced by "love is God." He continues: "Our loves do not make their claim to divinity until the claim becomes plausible. It does not become plausible until there is in them a real resemblance to God, to Love Himself. Let us here make no mistake."[5]

Lewis distinguishes between "Need-love" and "Gift-love"—between a love that is based in the needs of the lover, and the attempt to meet those needs, and a love that, as Saint Paul declares, "gives itself away":

Our Gift-loves are really God-like; and among our Gift-loves those are most God-like which are most boundless and unwearied in giving. All the things the poets say about them are true. Their joy, their energy, their patience, their readiness to forgive, their desire for the good of the beloved—all this is a real and all but adorable image of the Divine life. In its presence we are right to thank God "who has given such power to men." We may say, quite truly and in an intelligible sense, that those who love greatly are "near" to God. But of course it is "nearness by likeness." It will not of itself produce "nearness of approach." The likeness has been given us. It has no necessary connection with that slow and painful approach which must be our own (though by no means our unaided) task. Meanwhile, however, the likeness is a splendor. That is why we may mistake Like for Same. We may give our human loves the unconditional allegiance which we owe only to God. Then they become gods: then they become demons. Then they will destroy us, and also destroy themselves. For natural loves that are allowed to become gods do not remain loves. They are still called so, but can become in fact complicated forms of hatred.[6]

There is much to consider in these interesting passages. Contrary to what Lewis claims, not "every human love" has the potential to proclaim itself divine. There are loves that are intrinsically cool, detached, and balanced; they make no absolute claim upon us. It is passionate love that has this difficult nature whether it be romantic love; love for country, party, and principle; love between parent and child; or, indeed, love for God or for what one takes to be God. There is a paradox in these loves, they stem from our deepest needs yet they tend at the same time toward self-sacrifice. A man may want to possess his beloved, believing she will make him whole and happy, and be willing to throw away all he holds dear to win her. His love is at once both selfish and self-sacrificial, or so it seems.

The self-sacrifice of passionate love is frequently a sham, however, and its resemblance to divine love less than Lewis claims. When we make sacrifices for what we love passionately we often, perhaps always, want something back. This becomes evident when our sacrifices are followed by bitterness or resentment. We give and give, maybe unaware of our own expectations of return, but then when our expectations are not met we become furious. Heloise, one of the most sacrificial of passionate lovers, abandons all in obedience to Abelard. She even gives him up and enters a convent, though she has no vocation, binding herself to God before he does, solely in obedience to his will. Years later, when communication between them is restored, her letters are filled not only with proclamations of love but also with resentment. She writes:

> At your bidding I assumed a new habit, and a new heart to match, as a way of showing you that you were undisputed master of my heart as well as of my body. Never, as God is my witness, did I seek anything from you but yourself: it was you alone I loved, not your possessions. I had no thought for the circumstances of married life, or for the smallest dower, or for my own enjoyment, or for my personal wishes. It was your wishes, as you well know, that I was concerned to satisfy. The term 'wife' may seem at once holier and more substantial, but another was always dearer to my heart, that of your mistress, or even—allow me to say it—of your concubine, your whore. It seemed to me that the humbler I made myself in your eyes, *the more I should be entitled to your love*, and the less I should impede your glorious destiny.[7]

Were self-sacrifice and aspiration ever more intertwined? Seen in the light of modern psychology and feminism there is much here that is disturbing. Of special interest are the words: "the more I should be entitled to your love." Her sacrifice, it seems, had a hook on it; she wanted to earn Abelard's love. Believing she could do so by abandoning herself utterly, she subordinated every need, ambition, and desire of her own to the service of what she calls his "glorious destiny." Such surrender may be meritorious in the love of God; it is misplaced and dangerous in human relationships. Predictably, when her sacrifice failed to win its desired effect her love turned to bitterness, or at least became tainted by it. Those with less spiritual strength than the remarkable Heloise may well be left with nothing but resentment.

There is a truly self-sacrificial form of love that is in no way perverse, but it endures only with difficulty in our need-based personal relationships. The purer forms of altruistic love probably require regular spiritual practice if they are to be sustained over time without resentment. They require a genuine subordination of the ego to something higher. In our more personal loves, there is always, I suspect, something we want back—and it is dangerous when we forget it. For these reasons, it seems to me, Lewis exaggerates the resemblance between divine love and its human counterpart. The element of self-sacrifice in personal love is sometimes little more than a concealed manipulation. We submit, subordinate, or sacrifice ourselves to another, with the unexpressed and possibly unconscious goal of winning something in return even if it is only the other's gratitude. This does not mean the lover's sacrifice is only a strategy to gain something—the lover usually also wishes the good of the beloved—but in these human loves it is doubtful that the lover ever lets go of all expectation of return.

To achieve a truly sacrificial love, one must practice what *The Bhagavad-Gita* calls "relinquishment" *(tyaga)*, the ability to act while "relinquishing all fruit of action."[8] Krishna counsels Arjuna to take his stand in the world, to have goals and objectives, and to act in such a way as to bring them about, yet not to be attached to things working out as he desires, for we can never fully control the consequences of our actions. In the more pedestrian spirituality of modern twelve-step programs, this is called "turning it over" or "letting go." What is required is that we accept what we cannot change; surrender the need to control what, in fact, we cannot control; and have faith that our destiny is in the hands of a higher power.

Lewis is quite right when he says that we must not allow our human loves to become absolute. "Then they become gods: then they become demons. Then they will destroy us, and also destroy themselves."[9] But there is a problem with absolute claims even when motivated by love for the Absolute itself. How do we know when they are directed to the true Absolute? How can we be certain what the Absolute wants us to do? Many Jews believe it is the will of God that Jerusalem belong to Israel, while many Palestinians think God wills that Jerusalem belong to them. It is difficult to see how both could be right; although both, to be sure, might be wrong. Those who speak for religion often direct us to love God and do His bidding, but history shows that horrendous things are often done by those who believe they are following this path.

Toward a Typology of Love's Distortions

What follows is not an attempt to provide an exhaustive analysis of pathological love, a task best left to psychologists and psychiatrists. Thus, rather than considering psycho-pathologies one by one and then describing the distorted forms of love associated with each, we will simply consider how care-love, union-love, and appreciation-love are each subject to specific perversions or distortions. The emphasis will be on the darker aspects of loving itself, not on all of the distortions that can creep into love relationships, as, for example, pathologies in how we receive love.

Distortions in Care-Love

A common distorted form of care-love might be labeled "care-taking" or "inappropriate care-taking." The qualifier "inappropriate" is important because there are times such as periods of physical illness or emotional depression when even normal adults cannot adequately take care of themselves. On these occasions caring-for may actually require care-taking. Under normal conditions care-taking is apt to be inappropriate, however, and may even be harmful to the cared-for. If my friend lacks confidence in his ability to manage his own finances, for example, I might further erode his confidence by "helping" him in a way that implies he lacks the capacity to do it for himself. Here I am encouraging his feeling of inadequacy rather than assisting him to become more self-reliant and competent.

Admittedly, the line between appropriate and inappropriate care-taking is not always easy to discern and disagreement about particular cases is to be expected. The general principle is clear enough, however, and turns on the question of whether the care-taking fulfills the objective of caring—the well-being of the loved. Even when it does not, the care-taker may care but his or her motive might be impure.

Sometimes we wish to make ourselves indispensable to the ones we care for. As Germaine Greer puts it: "As soon as we find ourselves working at being indispensable, rigging up a pattern of vulnerability in our loved ones, we ought to know that our love has taken the socially sanctioned form of egotism."[10]

In more extreme cases, one may use care-taking as a way to humiliate the cared-for by demonstrating how incompetent or needy he or she is, or by displaying one's own superiority. Believing that it is better to give than to receive, I may see to it that I do most of the giving in order to take or hold the moral high ground. Every act of giving then might be used as further proof of my superiority. In cases such as these, care-taking may actually be a subtle form of abuse.

A second distortion of care-love involves presuming to know what another person needs and then imposing it on him or her. Let us call this phenomenon "paternalistic" or "invasive caring." An especially egregious example would be the manner in which Medieval Christians came to construe the commandment to love their neighbors—as an injunction to convert them and ultimately as a justification for the Crusades. It was reasoned that since loving one's neighbor meant meeting his or her needs, and since the needs of the soul take precedence over those of the body, then, given that the principal need of the soul is salvation, which is only possible through Christ, converting one's neighbor was precisely what loving him required. (It was, as well, an all but sure path to one's own salvation.) If any neighbor happened to object, force could be used to compel him, for whatever harm might befall the neighbor's body would be offset by the potential good promised his soul, temporal survival being nothing compared to eternal salvation. In this way, the noble ideal of neighbor love was subverted from the simple acts of healing found in the Gospels into violence against the neighbors of Christendom.

Another possible distortion of care-love, "abstract caring" we will call it, might be thought not so much a distortion of caring as a failure to get there. Yet, if distortions of love can be matters of deficiency as well as excess, this counts as well. Abstract caring involves caring about someone or something only as an abstract intention while failing to recognize the concreteness of genuine care. I may profess myself a humanist, write treatises on the subject, protest loudly against the inhumanity of others, for example, but then proceed to treat my wife, children, and/or colleagues abominably. Many self-proclaimed humanists have at least been charged with this moral failure as has, for example, Jean-Jacques Rousseau who wrote the great eighteenth-century treatise on the education of children but forced his mistress, and later, wife, to send their own children to an orphanage soon after they were born. Nel Noddings intends her "feminine" ethic of caring (see Chapter 2) as a corrective to this distortion or failure.

Distortions in Union-Love

The dark side of union-love also takes a variety of forms, three of which have to do with the failure to preserve appropriate boundaries between the lover and the loved. The first has been alluded to often throughout the current work and might be called "union through dominance," "possession," or "appropriation." Here the lover attempts to merge with the beloved by appropriating or taking possession of him or her. A man might, for example, fail to see or value how his wife is separate and different from himself. It is only his life and needs that matter. Perhaps he fears her autonomy—if she becomes too independent, she might leave him. If so, he is actually dependent on her dependency and must do everything possible to perpetuate it. Another possibility is that the lover might unconsciously or just secretly feel inferior and attempt to dominate his beloved as a strategy for repressing or concealing his own sense of inadequacy. Whatever the exact circumstances, he violates her separateness in the effort to make her an appendage of himself. This is the distortion of love that Fromm labels "sadism" or "dominance," and that E. S. Person also calls "dominance." (Person, it may be recalled, believes it more typically male than female.)

People with narcissistic personality disorders are especially prone to this distortion. Clinical psychologist James F. Masterson describes the condition: "The narcissist defines love as the ability of someone else to admire and adore him, and to provide perfect mirroring." The mirroring Masterson has in mind is not of the real self but of the narcissistically inflated self. The narcissist sees intimate unions as just another way to gratify narcissistic needs and cannot see the other as a separate, autonomous being:

> The narcissist is unable to relate to other people except in terms of his own inflated self-image and his unrealistic projections of himself onto others. Every relationship involving a narcissistic personality requires adulation and perfect responsiveness from the partner or an idealization of the partner so that the narcissist can bask in the other's glow. Whenever these requirements are frustrated, or appear to be lacking from the

narcissist's point of view, he resorts to rage which is always externalized and projected onto the other.

The next step is to devalue the partner since she is not living up to the narcissist's wishes. The narcissist's overblown sense of entitlement makes it almost impossible for him to see what he is doing in these situations since he cannot imagine that his own projections onto the partner are causing him such severe dissatisfaction in the relationship.[11]

A particular disturbing form of union through domination is the attempt to forcefully appropriate another's body. Probably most people are convinced that rape could never have anything to do with love, no matter how perverse. Rape, as it is generally understood today, is an act of violence intended to harm and humiliate the victim. Although this is true, it must be remembered that the desire to hurt and humiliate is hardly foreign to love relationships. Indeed, such urges frequently accompany disappointments in love and perceived slights or rejection. Granting this, the objection may still be made that it is not the love element in a relationship that gives rise to rape; no one could ever rape *because* of love. To suggest they could, the objection continues, is another instance of overgeneralization (a misuse of "love" discussed in Chapter 1), a matter of attributing to love everything that transpires between lovers.

In countering this objection, I propose we consider Soames Forsyte's rape of his wife in John Galsworthy's novel *The Forsyte Saga*. Soames, a Victorian man of property, marries a beautiful and intelligent woman, Irene, whom he pursued relentlessly before she consented to marry him. She did so only after he promised to let her go should she ever request it. There can be no doubt that Soames has a powerful appreciation-love of many of Irene's qualities, especially her beauty; and she remains the passion of his life, even years later when he has married another, more tractable woman. Yet Soames fails to appreciate Irene for herself, not just for her remarkable beauty.

After their marriage Irene finds she cannot love her husband. She withdraws both sexually and emotionally, finally falling in love with an architect named Bosinney. When this happens Irene reminds Soames of his promise to let her go, but he denies having made it. Convinced he is the victim of a grave injustice and that his wife is ungrateful, in a desperate moment of passion (whether of love, hatred, lust, jealousy, proprietariness, or some combination of all of these), he takes her by force.

Soames's rape of his wife is anything but a loving act in any normative understanding of the concept; it has nothing to do with care or appreciation for her as a person, but it has very much to do with his appreciation of some of her qualities, and (our present concern) with his understanding of union. Soames thinks of his lovely wife as his property, and as he likes to reminds her, she had nothing when they met. In his view, no woman has the right to withhold herself from her husband, especially when she has been provided for as well as Irene has. To do so is in violation of the marital contract, and contracts (unlike love) Soames understands. In his way of thinking, he merely takes back what is rightfully his. Soames sees his rape of Irene as "the first step towards reconciliation." As Soames's cousin George wryly remarks: "Soames had exercised his rights over an estranged and unwilling wife in the greatest—the supreme act of property."[12]

The problem resides in Soames's understanding of love and marriage, both of which he views in a highly proprietary fashion. To be sure, his action is one of violence and hostility—he wishes to punish and humiliate both Irene and her lover—but he is also obsessed with her and is unable to tolerate that he cannot own and display her as he does his fine collection of paintings. Indeed, Soames is greatly drawn to beauty and loves Irene very much as he loves his paintings. Both are forms of property attesting to his own worth and accomplishment.

Incest, and perhaps occasionally other instances of sexual abuse of children, may also be the expression of a distorted love. It will no doubt be protested that a parent's sexual abuse of a child should never be called love. That it violates any defensible normative notion of love cannot be denied. Yet a father, say, who sexually violates his daughter *may* at the same time love her, and further, he may violate her *because* he loves her, because he loves her perversely. He loves her, and shows his love, in a way that would be appropriate were it directed toward a consenting adult—his wife, say—yet is hideously inappropriate when directed toward his child. It is this analogy with normal love that makes it tempting to classify some incestuous love (yes, we do use the expression) as "love."

Both incest and rape certainly involve a failure in caring, but since they are not the result of any intention to care they should not be classified as distortions of care-love. They may, however (and this is the point of the preceding analysis), be the result of a misguided quest for union. Soames seeks a union with Irene similar to the union he has with the paintings he loves—he wishes to own her and show her off. The incestuous father seeks a union that perversely resembles the union sought by normal sexual lovers. (Incest and rape might also involve distorted appreciation-love, in that select qualities of the victims are appreciated, but the victim as someone who is an end both in and for herself is not. The perversion lies in the fact that the perpetrator fails to appreciate the victim appropriately.)

The complementary distortion to possession or dominance Eric Fromm calls "masochism" or "submission." The latter, less psychoanalytic name will be used here. E. S. Person maintains that this distortion of love is more typically female than male. The one who submits fails to value her own individuality sufficiently or lacks the power (whether for cultural, financial, or personal psychological reasons) to hold her own in a love relationship. She gives way, submitting to her lover, subordinating her interests to his in order to preserve their union, to avoid abandonment or abuse, or simply to escape from the burden of self-responsibility. This distortion we have already considered in Jill Tweedie's account of Teresa Stangl and her husband and in the story of Heloise and Abelard. Recall, however, Person's insights that submission may also be a covert way of manipulating the one to whom one submits, and how submission differs from the normal requirement of passionate love, surrender, which is both intermittent and more with than to one's partner. Submissive love is, of course, quite normal in children and in mentally incompetent adults. Indeed, part of what makes union through submission a distortion of love is its resemblance to the child's manner of loving. When adults love childishly, something is amiss.

The term "codependency" can be used to refer to both these distortions of union-love, because dominant and submissive people are codependent with one another. "Codependence," however, also refers to a more general condition in which neither partner dominates yet both are confused regarding what belongs to whom—neither feels alright without the other or each gets caught up in the other's problems, attempting to resolve them as if they were their own. When she is angry, he feels it must be his fault. When he fails in a task having nothing to do with her, she tries to fix it. Or when one feels confused, depressed, or angry, the other joins in, sharing the partner's emotional state.

The kind of sharing of another's emotional state involved in codependency differs from healthy compassion or fellow feeling. Through these we feel our way into another's situation, knowing clearly that it is not our own. We do not get stuck there, but are simultaneously intimate and separate, present and detached. The codependent individual, on the other hand, identifies so entirely with the other's condition that he or she is of little help. As a result both end up in the same place. If I am depressed, for example, the last thing I need is for my friend to become depressed too. I need my friend to feel my depression with me, but not to get caught in it. If the depression is severe then he will be concerned, even upset or frightened; but we are both in trouble if he enters my depression too deeply.

It must be admitted that it is difficult to discern just when a relationship becomes codependent. This is because there is no consensus regarding what degree or quality of separation between individuals is normal. Nor should we expect any such agreement. Is it the goal of life that each person attain maximal autonomy? Or should we seek wholeness through relationship, through union with a complementary other or with a larger social unit such as a family? What are the normal boundaries between lovers, between parents and children? Are human beings metaphysical or psychological monads, or is our condition one of mutual interdependence? Is responsibility purely individual, or can it be collective as well? On questions such as these, both individuals and cultures will always differ. Nonetheless, whatever standard is adopted as normal, it is possible to conceive of it not being kept. When this is the case, codependency exists relative to that particular norm. I submit, therefore, that the concept is coherent even if there will never be universal agreement regarding particular cases.

Extreme instances of codependency are not likely to be controversial, however. Consider the archetypical case of the alcoholic husband and his codependent, "enabling" wife, who takes upon herself the responsibility not only for stopping his drinking but for concealing it from friends, relatives, and work associates. Typically, she feels or half-feels that he drinks because she is doing something wrong; at least she thinks she ought to be able to fix the problem. If she complains enough, or hides his bottle, or makes other changes in how she behaves, maybe he will stop and everything will be fine. Actually, however, she may be as much an "addict" as he, addicted not to alcohol but to him and the role she plays in his life. Quite possibly, she grew up in a family where she had to enable one or both of her parents. She may even have unconsciously chosen a partner with whom she can continue her accustomed role. Given her psychological history, this is what it means to love; she needs to take care of someone who mismanages his life.

The first lesson taught by Alanon, an affiliated organization of Alcoholics Anonymous devoted to the recovery of partners (relatives or friends) of alcoholics, is that the partner did not cause the alcoholic to drink and cannot make him or her stop. The focus of Alanon is to break the pattern of codependency in the partners by encouraging them to concentrate on their own lives and to let the alcoholics live theirs. The point is not that partners (relatives or friends) should be indifferent to the alcoholics' condition but to encourage them to focus on what they can control (how they live their own lives) rather than on what they cannot (the alcoholics' drinking). According to Alanon, alcoholics are more likely to address their problems if the partner breaks his or her pattern of codependency with them. Without the partner's enabling, the consequences of the alcoholic's actions will be more apparent both to the alcoholic and to others. It is emphasized, however, that the partner's motivation should not be the alcoholic's recovery. If it is, the partner is continuing the same codependent pattern of manipulation. Rather, the motivation should be recovery from their own codependency with the alcoholic partner.

Codependency does not arise only with the abuse of alcohol or other substances. Lovers may be addicted to one another or to their relationship, neither one able to make a move without the other. Linked together like psychological Siamese twins, each overreacts to events in the other's life. Separation makes them anxious, each feeling lost without the other. And this anxiety they call "love". Were they to encounter anxiety-free love, they would probably not recognize it. Such lovers have great difficulty in knowing what they want or need, and difficulty expressing it even when they do. In codependent relationships, the boundaries separating one person from another are unclear. The fusion they experience is a confusion, a tangled mess, more than an intimacy between two people who accept and appreciate each other as individuals.

Another interesting case of what might be classified as distorted union-love is provided by those "fated unions" that seem beyond the personal control of the partners. A well-known fictional example is Catherine Earnshaw's passion for Heathcliff in Emily Brontë's *Wuthering Heights*. Catherine does not so much desire to be one with Heathcliff, she simply is, without regard for whether her being so is a blessing or a curse. Theirs is one of those fated *grandes passions* which we find so fascinating. The medieval tale of Tristan and Isolde is another. Here the external, fated character of the passion is symbolized by the love philter:

> Now when the maid and the man, Isolde and Tristan, had drunk the drought, in an instant that arch-disturber of tranquillity was there, Love, waylayer of all hearts, and she had stolen in! Before they were aware of it she had planted her victorious standard in their two hearts and bowed them beneath her yoke. They who were two and divided

now became one and united. No longer were they at variance: Isolde's hatred was gone. Love, the reconciler, had purged their hearts of enmity, and so joined them in affection that each was to the other as limpid as a mirror. They shared a single heart. Her anguish was his pain: his pain her anguish. The two were one both in joy and in sorrow.[13]

Judged from their literary prototypes, these fated unions tend to end tragically. It is as if some supernatural or demonic agency held the lovers together so that nothing can separate them—not time, not physical distance, not even death.

Since, as I have argued, the union of union-love must be sought or desired by the lovers, or at least be viewed in a positive light, the condition described here may be thought not to count as union-love at all. It should be remembered, however, that all distortions of love are borderline cases. Even if Catherine and Heathcliff or Tristan and Isolde do not will or desire union in the manner usual to lovers, it may be said that something within or beyond them does. Perhaps it is this abnormality of the "willing," the way in which it is a given, a fact beyond the lovers' control, that makes for the distortion.

I am not certain that fated unions always qualify as dark love but they are certainly extreme cases. When they are destructive either to the lovers themselves or to those around them, as their literary prototypes suggest, it is tempting to count them among love's distortions. Moreover, fated love resembles the distortion of submission, except that here neither partner is dominant. The lovers have submitted to a force that transcends them, and this force seems to be tinged with the demonic in the way the lovers sacrifice to it all other obligations and concerns. They have made, as C. S. Lewis might say, a God of love, or of one particular love—their fated and often fatal passion for one another.

Note also how the normal process of valuation is distorted in this love. It does not seem that Catherine greatly admires Heathcliff. She does not find him especially good or even handsome. The evaluations, normal to personal love, seem all but irrelevant here. It is as if, regardless of value or worth, the lovers simply are one.

Fated unions are not peculiar to sexual or romantic love relationships. In *I Know This Much Is True*, novelist Wally Lamb explores just such a fated union between identical twin brothers.[14] Born only six minutes apart, in opposite halves of the twentieth century, the brothers, almost from the beginning, differ considerably. Dominick, tougher and more worldly, is better equipped for contending with their stepfather, Ray, who is prone to violence. The weight of Ray's abuse thus falls on the weaker brother, Thomas, who by his twentieth year has become schizophrenic. Loving his brother deeply and feeling responsible for him (a role assigned him by their shamed, emotionally scarred mother), and at the same time terrified that his brother's fate awaits him too, Dominick feels trapped in their shared identity. This is not a union Dominick has sought, not even one he welcomes; it just is.

As the novel opens, Thomas has just cut off his own hand in a courageous but pointless act of protest against the Gulf War with which he has become obsessed. The burden of deciding whether the hand is to be reattached, which Thomas vigorously opposes, falls to Dominick. The plot is complex, but after losing his mother to cancer, his job as a high school history teacher, and a wife he truly loves—and after piecing together their family history with the help of some remarkable psychotherapy and a bizarre memoir left by a maternal grandfather he never knew—Dominick is eventually able to reconcile himself to who he is, in all its strange but very human complexity. This is accomplished, however, only after Thomas's tragic death by suicide. In this remarkable piece of contemporary fiction we find a penetrating analysis of the balancing of shared and individual identities, so important to healthy love.

All the distortions of union-love considered so far have involved union between individuals, but other varieties of union—with country, race, ethnic group, or religion—are arguably even more subject to disturbance. These will be referred to under the heading "overidentification with a group." Here, an individual is so tied to a collective identity that it becomes impossible to see clearly either the group itself or what lies beyond. The zealot, for example, loves his particular sect or nation with such fervor that he is blind to its defects, which he then projects onto outsiders (or some specific group of them).

This form of union-love is the social counterpart of interpersonal submission. Much as the submissive lover yields to the beloved, so the lover we are now considering submits to a larger social entity. In many cultures or subcultures, such submission is admired and may even be deemed essential to group survival. Indeed, this form of union-love is so common that it is difficult to recognize it as a disturbance, except at a distance. Further complicating matters is the likelihood that the disposition to love the group to which we belong with an intense preference is almost certainly rooted in biologically based survival mechanisms dating not merely from our tribal but from our primate and mammalian ancestry.

Considering how natural this love is, then, serious doubts arise concerning its classification as "distorted." When practiced in moderation, doubtless it is not a distorted love, but given the realities of the contemporary world it must be admitted that the tribal morality to which this kind of union-love is linked has become largely dysfunctional. Extreme manifestations of overidentification with a group, therefore, necessitate classifying this love as at least potentially perverse. Moreover, this disturbance of love disrupts not just personal relations but those between nations, classes, races, religions, and cultures.

Consideration of this distorted form of love enables us to see in bold relief the great difference between love as a biologically based impulse and love as an ethical and spiritual ideal. Our capacities and dispositions to love have profoundly different sources, which push or pull us in opposing directions. As tribal animals we seek to protect our own, which leads only too readily to fear and hatred of outsiders. Yet our ethical and religious precepts demand universal regard, equality, or even sometimes that we love our enemies. Part of the difficulty of understanding the nature of love is that the concept embraces both of these ways of loving. Each, moreover, seems essential to our lives. Could a society survive following only the dictates of universal love with parents raising children guided solely by this principle, showing them no preference, just disinterested benevolence? On the other hand, if we embrace only the more attached and grounded forms of love, we are likely to find ourselves in perpetual conflict with our neighbors and will never be able to address successfully the problems that confront us as citizens of one world.

Western culture teaches us that we are animals with a long evolutionary history—a "glorious accident" and repositories of "selfish genes"—but also that we are children of a loving God in whose image we have been created. Whether we consciously embrace either of these ideologies or not, our culture and language have been shaped by them, and so too our conceptions of love. Hence we think of love simultaneously as an instinct to protect our own and as a moral imperative to be concerned with the well-being of all.

As if this were not daunting enough, we are now being asked to extend our love even further to include other life forms. From this perspective, even our identification with our own species appears suspect. Valuing humans over the rest of our extended family, we have been exploiting and exterminating other species for our own short-term advantage. Although it may seem strange to say so, we seem to be well on the way to viewing our preferential love for fellow humans as an instance of the distortion of love we have been investigating. For it must be admitted that this love involves the same process of identification with, and overvaluation of, a particular group and the same inability to identify with what lies outside this group. Following this line of reasoning to its ultimate conclusion, even Western humanism and Judeo-Christian neighbor love may have to be classified as distorted loves—both undervalue nonhuman life.

Distortions in Appreciation-Love

There are two closely related distortions of appreciation-love. The first involves loving the qualities of a person (or, more controversially, of other love objects) rather than the individual himself or herself. This we will call "objectification." The second we will term "excessive idealization" or "overvaluation." These two distortions frequently occur together, but they can be distinguished at least in that the former applies only to persons and animals (and possibly other natural entities), whereas the latter can apply as well to abstractions such as principles.

Although interpersonal appreciation-love, in general, is not reducible to the love of the individual's abstract qualities, such reductions sometimes occur, especially in that form of love (or approximation to it) we call infatuation. An example given earlier involved an adolescent's love of his favorite movie star. The boy has no personal acquaintance with the star but is profoundly attracted to her outstanding qualities. In this case, the young man is probably more in love with his own idea than with the woman herself. He loves her because of a few fairly obvious personal traits—such as her beauty, sex appeal, and talent—perhaps enhanced by his own fertile imagination. This same imagination may even supply relational qualities concerning his fantasy relationship with the star—a kind of fictional shared history.

Given that the lover, in this example, is still a boy, we certainly would not want to label his love "perverse." However, if fifteen years later, he knew no other kind of love, we would be less reluctant to do so. It is a distorted love, we might say, because he has not learned to love a real person. Instead he loves only images, ideas, or abstract personal qualities. We encountered just such a love, already, in our discussion of Soames Forsyte's love for his wife, Irene. Now we can see more clearly how Soames's love exemplifies not only distorted union-love but objectification as well. Soames loves Irene as he loves his collection of fine paintings—for her beauty, not for herself.

It could be argued that objectification should not count as

appreciation-love at all because this love must regard its object as an end and Soames's loving his wife's beauty rather than her self does not meet this condition. This argument has merit but, given that Irene's beauty does belong to her and is not something wholly apart, I prefer to classify it as "appreciation-love," but of a distorted form. We are, at least in part, the qualities we possess.

Objectification is not peculiar to romantic love. Recall the example of a father who loves his daughter as if she were a pretty-little-girl-thing when she is in fact both much more and much less than this. The father has objectified and fictionalized his daughter and, thus, loves the object of his own fancy. When the girl acts contrary to the father's idea of her, he may not be able to love her at all (or perhaps he will simply not "see" her at such times). This is a distortion of love because the father does not appreciate his daughter as she is; he does not love her in her full human complexity. What is more, the child is placed in a very awkward position: she has either to conceal her real self in the effort to be what her father wants or to risk not being loved by him at all. Perhaps she will do both, alternating back and forth, unsure of just what or who she is. Such confused identity can be difficult to correct in later life.

To speak of loving the person, not just some abstract qualities he or she embodies, does not presuppose that there exists some self or person independently of personal qualities. Whether there is such a self is a metaphysical question which may be impossible to answer. Nonetheless, we can distinguish between a person possessing a multitude of (not always consistent) qualities and some very limited (either whitewashed or demonized) subset of them. Nor does the distinction between persons and some small set of their qualities imply the existence of a real empirical self that can be correctly identified with a single, but large and relatively static, set of qualities. Who we are changes over time and at least *appears* differently from different vantage points. The point is simply that we are complex creatures, and a healthy appreciation-love of any one of us is quite different from admiring a few attractive qualities. Although the generic concept of love does not presuppose knowledge of its object, healthy interpersonal love does. Loves falling short of this ideal, then, may reasonably be classified as distorted. Other things being equal, the more simplified the lover's perception of the loved, the more the character of the love is called into question.

As we have seen, loving someone solely because of his or her personal (as distinct from relational) qualities is actually quite rare.

Nonetheless, loving an individual because of a few of his or her personal qualities, while barely glimpsing the more complex person to whom they belong, is very common. This description might even fit the majority of cases of interpersonal love. Hence the familiar pronouncement, "love is blind." Perhaps seeing others in their fullness and appreciating them for being who they are is an ideal we can only approach. If so, it may once again seem odd to classify appreciation based on objectification as a distortion of love. My response to this challenge parallels the response given with regard to overidentification with a group, except that the latter has a positive side (group solidarity in the presence of a real enemy) which objectification of an individual apparently lacks—unless it be that objectification makes emotional attachment to less objectively lovable individuals easier. In any case, my view is that the objectification of a person (whether resulting in love or hatred) is a spiritual/epistemological shortcoming with little redeeming value. To be sure, however, this disturbance does admit of degrees, and only fairly extreme cases are apt to call attention to themselves as distortions.

It would be odd to speak of objectification of wholly inanimate things, which after all are objects. Nonetheless, something analogous occurs when natural entities are seen in an overly reductive manner. The rise of science in the seventeenth century, while freeing us from many crippling superstitions, resulted in just such a reduction of the natural world (which contemporary physics has significantly corrected). The distorted perception and valuation involved here is, of course, the negative kind associated with hatred or indifference, not the positive variety that is apt to accompany love. It is also possible, however, to "objectify" nature in a positive way by sentimentalizing it—seeing it as a benevolent, all-embracing mother, for example, or as a force that is creative and nurturing but never destructive. Certainly neither of these ways of representing nature (the negative or the positive) is what the ecological consciousness of the new millennium requires.

This sentimentalized perception of nature serves to illustrate the other distortion of appreciation-love we will examine, sometimes termed "idolatry" or "idealization." The first label is too strong for the milder cases and perhaps unduly theological, while the latter is too weak for the most extreme instances. So let us call it instead "excessive idealization" or, more simply, "overvaluation." It consists in an exaggerated positive valuation of a love object, resulting in an appreciation that is inappropriately doting, devoted, submissive, obedient, rigid, or unrealistic. Here we have a distortion reminiscent of C. S.

Lewis's notion of making a god of love, except that Lewis's emphasis was on the deification of love itself rather than of the loved. Both are possible. Objectification may also be present whenever we idealize excessively, but the terms "idealization" and "overvaluation" have a wider application because they can be applied to nonnatural objects such as ideals and principles. Also objectification may involve negative valuations (resulting in hatred) as well as positive ones, whereas "idealization" and "overvaluation" imply positive valuation.

In many of the less spiritual forms of love, excessive idealization is common, perhaps more the rule than the exception. As with over-identification with a group, it probably plays a role in all fanaticism and zealotry. These two distortions of love not only tend to occur together, they reinforce and provide justification for one another. Because a highly patriotic man idealizes his country, he overidentifies with his compatriots and views their traditional enemies as evil—they are zealots, we are nationalists; they are aggressors, we are merely defending our own.

Excessive idealization may be even more common in the love of principles or causes than in the love of people. One reason this distortion appeals to us is that it enables us to simplify our moral universe. If I can find the one true cause or faith, my life will make sense; I will know what to do and will be relieved of the burden of having to make many complicated decisions. If I could, for example, effectively reduce morality to a single black-and-white issue, say, the killing or not killing of fetuses, I could be assured of being a good person and would know how to assess the morality of others. Moreover, I could do so without having to address the more daunting issues of poverty, homelessness, world hunger, economic justice, overpopulation, or environmental degradation, and without having to significantly change the way I live—it being not terribly taxing as a rule to avoid killing fetuses. On the other hand, if I start taking economic justice or the environment seriously, not only will I face issues of enormous complexity but I may feel called upon to restructure my personal life. As the world gets more complex, the temptation increases to simplify through this kind of idealizing and absolutizing. Perhaps this is one reason for the recent rise in religious fundamentalism throughout the world.

Once again, there is a problem in determining just when this distortion occurs, when a love object is inappropriately or excessively idealized. There exist no unequivocally correct appraisals of love objects to which we can compare the more subjective ones made through love. Moreover, as we have seen, personal love does involve valuing an object preferentially and therefore, presumably, beyond its strictly objective deserts. Even though it is impossible to create an objective test of overvaluation, its more extreme instances are usually apparent, at least to third parties. Given the enormity of the dangers involved, it is important to devise ways of understanding and avoiding these overvaluations. I would like to propose three such ways.

First, we must recognize the relativity of all valuations and of all principles, at least as we are able to grasp and formulate them. There is limitation, fallibility, and the potentiality for error in every judgment we make and in any principle we hold. Even granted the existence of a genuine Spiritual Absolute, its nature transcends finite understanding so that any formulation of it, any concept or image we might use to express it, is but a partial truth. As a result, any particular formulation, any school of thought, say, or any specific conception of the Absolute, is in some measure an idol. Lao Tzu may be the earliest teacher of this principle—"The Tao that can be told is not the eternal Tao; the name that can be named is not the eternal name."[15]

It might be helpful to think of excessive idealization as arising from a kind of metaphysical error, the error of confusing the individual value of an object with its transindividual or transpersonal ground. Expressed in Platonic language, this would involve mistaking the beauty of the human beloved or of any finite object for the Beautiful itself. For Plato, the Beautiful is in some sense *in* the beloved, but also transcends and thus must not be confused with the beloved. The Beautiful is a transcendent reality in which the loved one only participates.

Alternatively, one might think of overvaluation, when applied to persons, as the result of objectification. While interpersonal love in an ideal, normative sense must be directed toward the person, hatred is typically (arguable, always) directed toward an objectification of the person. Using Buber's language, we could say that love, paradigmatically, involves an encounter of an I with a Thou whereas hatred is an encounter with an It. What happens in the distortion of love we are now investigating is that the loved becomes a kind of glorified *It*. Rather than seeing the loved in his or her fullness, an imaginative construct is laid over him or her, becoming the true love object. Although this kind of idealized objectification is common—and is sometimes even identified as the very essence of love—it is actually a distortion of love. For if I must idealize you in order to love you, either you are not lovable as you are or I lack the capacity to love you for yourself. Recipients of such love are apt to conclude that they must pretend to be other than they are. This is why so many women object to men's tendency to idealize them: life on a pedestal is both precarious and incomplete.

A second precaution for avoiding the dangers of overvaluation is closely related to the first but is simpler and more practical in nature. It consists in the recognition that the things we love do not have to be perfect; the ordinary is quite lovable and may even be especially lovable. My loving you deeply does not require believing that you are perfect, or even that you are more intelligent than you are. This principle has the additional advantage of helping us to recognize that we too are lovable as we are.

Apropos of the dilemma of reconciling the ideal and the actual in love, Robert Creeley offers the following poetic reflection:

> I know two women
>   and the one
> is tangible substance,
>   flesh and bone.
>
> The other in my mind
>   occurs.
> She keeps her strict
>   proportion there.
>
> But how should I
>   propose to live
> with two such creatures
>   in my bed—
>
> or how shall he
>   who has a wife
> yield two to one
>   and watch the other die.[16]

Only when we let go of the ideal does the actual become possible. But notice the phrase "yield two to one"; evidently the ideal does not die altogether but somehow lives on within the actual. I have no idea how to prove or account for it, but my own experience accords with what Creeley suggests. Here we have one of those mysteries of love not readily explained by rational analysis. It can, however, be experienced, as I suspect many readers know.

The principle that the ordinary is quite lovable does not only apply to the love of persons. Loving one's country or religion does not require being blind to its faults or even thinking it better than other countries or religions. I may love my religion because it is mine, because it is a part of me and has provided me much solace. If these are the reasons for my love, it will be entirely credible to me that others' religions provide the same for them.

My third proposal for dealing with excessive idealization concerns the vague and uncritical use of ideals to justify our actions. When formulated at a sufficiently high level of abstraction, ideals may seem to be unmixed goods. We sometimes suppose that anything done in their behalf must be warranted. In fact our ideals are often little more than slogans, buzzwords, or rationalizations that act as covers for less noble motives. One may be prepared to fight (read: kill and die) in order to defend God, motherland, party, democracy, freedom, honor, the people, and so on, without being able to explain just what these ideals mean or how they apply to the present situation. One country may intervene in the affairs of another on the grounds of defending "democracy," when it is really only the economic freedom and privilege of a particular group that is being protected, not democracy in its fuller sense. My proposal, then, is simply that we formulate our ideals as fully and explicitly as we can, weigh them against other competing ideals, and give careful attention to how they are or are not at stake in each situation. In this way we might see how the concept "democracy," for example, is being used in reference to a single economic freedom (say, the right of large landowners or transnational corporations to accumulate wealth), while the equal or even more compelling economic freedom of the poor to own land or make a living wage—together with other democratic ideals such as free speech, freedom of assembly, or freedom of the press—are being curtailed.

IS DARK LOVE REALLY LOVE?

It might seriously be questioned whether the distorted ways of loving just examined are love in any legitimate sense at all. Perhaps they would be better classified as separate phenomena having nothing to do with love, or as instances of the deceptive use of "love" (see Chapter 1), ways of concealing the true nature of our motives or actions under the banner of love? Were the path chosen in this work a normative analysis of "love," I would have wished to build into its meaning a number of criteria that would exclude all of these distortions, factors such as making care-love and appreciation-love (both of which require regarding the loved as an end) necessary conditions of love; the provision that the well-being of the cared-for actually be served, not merely intended; and a requirement that persons not be objectified nor principles excessively idealized. Yet since this analysis has followed the descriptive rather than the normative path, and since there is no disputing that "love" is often used to refer to phenomena that fall far short of this or any other ideal, perhaps all of the phenomena discussed here qualify as belonging to our subject. Such would seem to be the consequence of a nonnormative analysis of love.

Some of the disadvantages of the normative approach were noted in Chapter 1, but there are two positive advantages to the nonnormative approach I would also like to point out. First, it may help us see how normal and perverse forms of love are related. To label as "love" only healthy love and to classify the distorted loves described above under some different category would make it more difficult to grasp how unhealthy loves grow into mature ones or, conversely, how wholesome loves become distorted. Following this separate labels approach, healthy and perverse loves might appear to be unrelated phenomena. Second, just as there are moral dangers in idealizing what or whom we love, so, as we have seen, are there dangers in idealizing love itself. A normative analysis may lead us to do just this, blinding us to the dangers inherent in loving and convincing us that anything desired or done in its name must be good.

In the final analysis, however, there is no objectively right answer to the question of whether the distortions considered above are really love. How one answers this question turns largely on whether one chooses to use "love" as a normative or as a descriptive concept. Both choices are legitimate and can be justified by linguistic precedence. Each choice has its consequences. It matters less which path one adopts than that one is conscious of the difference and clear about the choice.

Ideals of Spiritual Love

❖   As each of the three loves has its darker side so are there spiritual
ideals of love corresponding to care-love, union-love, and
appreciation-love. I will not undertake to explore these three ideals at
length, but simply describe them briefly and show how they too fit into
the typology developed in this book. Should it be that there are no
ideals of spiritual love besides these three or some combination of
them, the legitimacy and appropriateness of the typology developed
over the preceding chapters will receive added support.

The spiritual ideal of care-love has been extensively discussed
above in its Judeo-Christian formulation as love for one's neighbor.
Although this love has been construed in a great variety of ways, the
general idea is of an ethic of concern for the welfare of all human beings, without regard to such variables as race, geography, intelligence,
age, gender, nationality, or even moral deserts. It is an ideal of a universal, unconditional, other-regarding, non-preferential care-love.

Somewhat different formulations of universal care-love can be
found in other traditions. These contrast with the Judeo-Christian
ideal either in the scope of the love or in its precise character. For example, the Buddhist notion of *"metta"* (most often translated as "loving kindness") includes within its range not merely all humans but all
sentient beings. Buddhists give less emphasis than Christians to the
self-sacrificial character of universal love, since they reject the notion
of metaphysically separate selves in favor of the interdependence of all
beings. As a result, the gap between self and other is less extreme for
Buddhists. According to Buddhaghosa, the practice of *metta* should begin with loving kindness toward one's own self. Specifically, Buddhaghosa recommends that the novice begin with the practice of re-

peating to himself: "May I be happy and free from suffering" or "May I keep myself free from enmity, affliction and anxiety and live happily."[1]

In classical Chinese philosophy we find an ideal of universal love (*ai*) in the Mohist tradition. (The founder of the school, Mo Tzu, lived in the fifth century B.C.E.) This ideal of universal love has been characterized as an "unemotional will to benefit people and dislike harming them." Confucianism, the dominant philosophical school of China, however, has long rejected the ideal of a strictly universal love in favor of a "graded" love, which diminishes in intensity as it moves outward from the family to the wider community and beyond. Regardless whether *ai* is seen as universal and non-preferential or as graded, its objective remains the same—the good of the love object. It is, therefore, a form of care-love. *Ai* also contains within it a significant element of union-love, however. "This concept of love in the classical Chinese tradition . . . conveys a sense of appropriation. *Ai* is to take someone into one's sphere of concern, and in so doing, make him an integral aspect of one's own person." Confucianists, like Buddhists, have a more communal, less individualist vision of the human condition than we have in the West.[2]

The spiritual ideal based on union-love sees the goal of the highest love as realizing our oneness with God, the Absolute, other beings, or with Being itself. Mystics do not always portray themselves as lovers but it is certainly not uncommon for them to do so, especially in the West. Regardless, union is what they seek and (if we take their word for it) what they find. Hindu mystics speak less of attaining union than of realizing the union that already is, since non-separation from the divine is our natural condition. It is interesting that the same question arises regarding the nature of mystical union as arose in our examination of romantic union: Is the resulting oneness a complete fusion of lover and beloved, or something less? Western mystics most often speak of retaining a portion of their individual self-identity while experiencing "communion" or "marriage" with the divine. Indian mystics, on the other hand, are more apt to describe a fuller union with reality as a whole, often seen as undifferentiated cosmic consciousness. There are, however, numerous exceptions to these general tendencies, both in the West and the East.

The objective of this union-love-based ideal is more metaphysical than ethical, though an ethic of universal caring is often derived from it; for if I am one with all beings, must I not be as concerned for their good as for my own? For the mystic, self-interest and other-interest tend to converge. But the emphasis of this love ideal is more on union itself than on any ethical consequences that flow from it.

Finally, an appreciation-love based ideal was discussed in our examination of Hermann Hesse's notion of "pure contemplation" or "undemanding love." This is a quieter, less active, more detached love, content to contemplate its object, appreciating it for what it is without any other agenda. Perhaps Zen Buddhists, with their celebration of the ordinary tasks and events of daily life, have given us the fullest expression of this ideal, but it can be found in all traditions.

These ideals of spiritual love imply three fairly distinct conceptions of the spiritual life that might be characterized as the ethical, the mystical or unitive, and the contemplative. The first espouses an activist ideal such as that seen in the work of Mother Teresa. The second is more ontological and emphasizes the experience or realization of oneness between the lover and (usually) some metaphysical absolute. The third envisions a spiritual life of detachment in which the seeker aspires to nothing more than the blissful acceptance of reality as it is.

CARE, UNION, AND APPRECIATION: BACK TOGETHER

In the present study I have endeavored to make clear the distinctions between care-love, union-love, and appreciation-love and to demonstrate that none of the three is fully reducible to the others. It has certainly not been my intention, however, to drive a wedge between these ways of loving or to favor them in their purest states. Indeed, it is not certain whether any of the three ever exists in complete isolation. Even a casual look at the subject makes apparent just how intertwined these three dimensions of love usually are. Consider romantic love, for example. Here, lovers appreciate their beloveds and the qualities they possess, seek union with them, and care for their well-being. All three loves are usually conspicuously present and operate more often than not in harmony with one another. Were any of them completely absent, the result would be at least anomalous.

The three ways of loving are also frequently found together in spiritual ideals of love. We have seen how Augustine constructed an ideal of care-love for the neighbor within the framework of a Neoplatonic appreciation-love for God. Mystically inclined Christians join these with union-love for God or Christ, weaving together caring, appreciating, and union in the same concept. We will now look at how Buddhist love theory effects a synthesis of all three ideas.

Love is generally approached in Buddhist philosophy and practice in connection with the four *Brahmaviharas* (literally, "heavenly abodes"): metta ("love," "loving kindness," or "friendliness"), karuna ("compassion"), mudita ("sympathetic joy"), and upekkha ("equanimity" or "even-mindedness"). These Brahmaviharas are sometimes referred to as the four "immeasurable minds" or "sublime attitudes." They constitute a common theme in Buddhist discourses concerning meditation and practice and are considered essential to the moral life and to salvation. As in the Gospel of Luke (10:25–26), when a lawyer asks what he must do to inherit eternal life and Jesus answers with the love commandments, so too the Buddha, when asked by a Brahman what he could do to dwell with Brahma forever, responds: "you must practice the Brahmaviharas—love, compassion, joy and equanimity."[3]

The first of the four, metta, is fairly general in meaning. It is a disinterested, benevolent wish for the happiness of all beings. Through it we develop a friendly or loving attitude toward others and also toward ourselves. The second, karuna, is more specific. It concerns how one responds to the suffering of others and is expressed by the wish that all beings be free of suffering. Karuna is nearly always translated as "compassion," but the contemporary Vietnamese Zen Buddhist monk, teacher, and scholar Thich Nhat Hanh warns against the suggestion implicit in the English word—that we must suffer with the loved. "[W]e do not need to suffer to remove suffering from another person."[4] The third Brahmavihara, mudita, resembles compassion in that it concerns our response to another's condition, but it is the other's happiness and good fortune, rather than suffering, that occasions it. It is a sharing in another's joy. Sympathetic joy is a more difficult attainment than compassion since it requires mastery of our tendencies to compare ourselves with, judge, and envy others. While practice of the Brahmaviharas begins with loving kindness, it reaches perfection only with the fourth, upekkha, which provides the detachment required by Buddhist spirituality. In the words of the American Buddhist teacher Sharon Salzberg: "Equanimity is a spacious stillness of the mind, a radiant calm that allows us to be present fully with all the different changing experiences that constitute our world and our lives."[5]

The four sublime attitudes can be analyzed and meditated upon individually, but they are very much of a piece. So much so that Nhat Hanh refers to them collectively as "true love": "Love, compassion, joy, and equanimity are the very nature of an enlightened person. They are the four aspects of true love within ourselves and within everyone and everything."[6] This composite ideal weaves together all three of the ideals of spiritual love described in the present work. We will refer to it as "Metta" (with an uppercase "M")—not metta as distinct from *karuna, mudita,* and *upekkha*—a loving kindness that embraces compassion, sympathetic joy, and equanimity. Although Nhat Hanh is the only Buddhist writer I know of who uses "love" as a name for this wider ideal, there is general understanding in the tradition that the conscientious practice of *metta* alone will lead to the other *Brahmaviharas.*

This wider notion of "Metta" invites comparison with Christian "agape." Its metaphysical grounding, however, is quite different. Whereas agape is considered a supernatural love, something not quite of this world, Metta has its roots in the very condition of the world, in what Buddhists call *paticca-samuppada* or "interdependent arising." Some Buddhists might be reluctant to call this grounding metaphysical, especially followers of the Theravadan tradition where much of this teaching on love originated, because Theravadans frequently repudiate metaphysics altogether. As the word "metaphysics" is used here, however, all that is meant is "underlying vision of reality," regardless of whether this reality be thought of as ultimate. Such a vision of reality Buddhism certainly has, even if it is construed as entirely empirical (as many maintain) and even if it is "empty" (as others would have it) in the sense of being a construct imposed by the knower.

Central to Buddhist philosophy, then, is the view that all beings are interdependent; they arise together and cannot exist in isolation. Hence the Buddhist doctrine of no-self *(anatta)*, the view that there is no separate, enduring, substantial self. To underscore this notion of interdependence, Nhat Hanh has coined the word "interbeing" (as a replacement for "being"). According to one reading of "interdependent arising," there is no ontological first cause, no immutable substance, nothing whatsoever outside the system of interdependent interbeings.

The broad notion of "Metta," Nhat Hanh's "true love," brings together in a single concept all three of the ideals of spiritual love we are investigating. Given the Buddhist principle of interdepent arising, it could be said that union (in one sense of this ambiguous concept) is the underlying reality of the world, and that true love is but the affirmation of this union. What one loves is never fully other, but something already interdependent with oneself. In this vein, Salzberg proclaims: "The legacy of separateness impoverishes the spirit":

> When we learn to move beyond mistaken concepts and see clearly, we
> no longer solidify reality. We see waves coming and going, arising and

passing. We see that life, composed of this mind and body, is in a state of continual, constant transformation and flux. . . . Without the rigidity of concepts, the world becomes transparent and illuminated, as though lit from within. With this understanding, the interconnectedness of all that lives becomes very clear. We see that nothing is stagnant and nothing is fully separate, that who we are, what we are, is intimately woven into the nature of life itself. Out of this sense of connection, love and compassion arise.[7]

The same vision of interdependence and union can be found in a poem written by Nhat Hanh while working to assist the boat people of the South China Sea in 1978. The poem concludes:

> I am a mayfly metamorphosing
> on the surface of the river.
> And I am the bird
> That swoops down to swallow the mayfly.
>
> I am a frog swimming happily
> in the clear water of a pond.
> And I am the grass-snake
> that silently feeds itself on the frog.
>
> I am the child in Uganda, all skin and bones,
> My legs as thin as bamboo sticks.
> And I am the arms merchant,
> selling deadly weapons to Uganda.
>
> I am the twelve-year-old girl,
> refugee on a small boat,
> who throws herself into the ocean
> after being raped by a sea pirate.
> And I am the pirate.
> My heart not yet capable
> of seeing and loving.
>
> I am a member of the politburo,
> with plenty of power in my hands.
> And I am the man who has to pay
> his "debt of blood" to my people
> dying slowly in a forced-labor camp.

My joy is like Spring, so warm
it makes flowers bloom all over the Earth.
My pain is like a river of tears
so vast it fills the four oceans.

Please call me by my true names,
so I can hear all my cries and laughter at once,
so I can see that my joy and pain are one.

Please call me by my true names,
so I can wake up
and the door of my heart
could be left open,
the door of compassion.[8]

Compassion and love not only presuppose the union of identification, they foster and heighten the experience of it—our identity with those who suffer, those who are joyous, and those who give rise to suffering and joy. This is union-love, not in the most familiar sense of yearning for merger with a separate other but in the less dramatic, and profounder, sense of embracing the oneness of interdependence that is our mutual condition.

The care-love element in "Metta" is apparent from the objective of loving kindness—the happiness of all beings. In Buddhist monastic training, novices spend long hours meditating on the *Brahmaviharas*. Such spiritual work is understood to have beneficial consequences in itself, but the ultimate goal of *metta* practice, as it is called, is *practice* in the sense of action. Although Metta may not be as interventionist an ideal as agape, it is very much concerned with what we do and how we do it. In the context of teaching his disciples how to avoid anger, the Buddha tells the following story:

> On a remote country road, there is a traveler [a man "whose actions, words, and thoughts are all unwholesome"] who falls deathly ill. There is no nearby village, and he is utterly alone, with no one to look after him. There is no hope he will survive. But suddenly, another traveler passes by. He see the desperate man lying alongside the road, and he stops, his heart filled with compassion. He helps the man up and supports him, step by step, until they reach the next village. Then the traveler finds a doctor and stays with the man for three or four weeks until the illness is cured. The traveler rejoices in the man's recovery. [Com-

menting on his own story, the Buddha adds:] When we encounter someone whose actions, speech, and thoughts are all disagreeable, we can be certain that person is filled with suffering. If we don't love him, if we don't help him, who will? If love is in our heart, we will be able to accept those whose actions, speech, and thoughts are all disagreeable.[9]

While the resemblance of this tale to Jesus' parable of the good Samaritan (Luke 10:32–36) is striking, the emphasis upon what the lover feels—compassion for the injured man, rejoicing in his recovery, sympathy because he is disagreeable—is more pronounced in the Buddhist story. The Buddhist good Samaritan does not only pity and assist the stranger, he feels his way deeply into the disagreeable man's world, loving and accepting him just as he is.

Like Jesus, the Buddha exemplified the love he preached. Moreover, the tradition maintains, he came to live among us for our benefit. The Theravadan philosopher and contemporary of Augustine, Buddhaghosa, offers as explanation:

> He came to be for the benefit, welfare, and happiness not only of gods and humans but also for the remaining beings, such as snakes, wellwinged birds, and so forth. . . . Therefore, it should be understood that he arose for the sake of the happiness, welfare, and profit of these [other beings] as well.[10]

The words "he came" and "he arose" are almost shockingly familiar to those acquainted with Christian teaching, yet how different the sentiments regarding the breadth of scope of the love.

As evident as the union-love and care-love dimensions of Metta are, it is the appreciation-love component that gives Metta its distinctive flavor. The predominance of appreciation-love is apparent not so much in the loving-kindness aspect of this love but in the elements of sympathetic joy and equanimity. Whereas Platonic love (another appreciation-love ideal) presupposes a judgment on the part of the lover (that the loved is deserving), *mudita* requires letting go of judgment: "it slices through our predilection to force the world to accord with our views." The tendency "to feel goodwill only towards those we like" must be overcome, requiring that we give up our habit of comparing ourselves to others and competing with them, replacing these tendencies with what Buddhists term the "sharing of merit": "May the merit of this action be shared by all beings everywhere, so that they may come to the end of suffering."[11]

I can vividly recall the moment in my own life when I realized there was an alternative to envying the accomplishments of others. Rather than feeling resentful because I was not a great philosopher, musician, or poet, I suddenly saw I could rejoice in the fact that I lived in a world where such creative geniuses existed and that I had been granted the gift of enjoying their creations. With a single shift in perspective I found I was able to convert much of the envy and self-rejection I had known into gratitude. However imperfectly I have retained this insight, it represented a momentary victory of *mudita*. Salzberg offers this account of a similar transformation: "The gladness which is the essence of sympathetic joy uproots envy and avarice as the mind fills with the qualities of delight and appreciation for others and the wish for them to be happy." *Mudita*, she assures us, conquers boredom as well, because "it gives us so many reasons to feel happy and connected. Boredom is based on a sense of separateness and a turning away that we feel when we experience certain degrees of aversion." The Buddhist alternative to boredom is to reconnect "to the little things."[12] What Salzberg is pointing us toward in her description of *mudita* is a Buddhist perspective on appreciation-love: "If we simply feel the miracle of being present, a kind of appreciation grows along with a kind of joy. Attending to the small things in front of us becomes a way of self-renewal and self-refreshment." Sam Keen expresses the same insight somewhat differently: "We come to love not by finding a perfect person but by learning to see an imperfect person perfectly."[13]

While *metta* sets us on the path of acquiring the sublime attitudes, *upekkha* is the culmination. Characterizing it as even-minded but not unemotional, Harvey Aronson writes: "Equanimity can be understood to be the peaceful but temporary complement to the first three more concerned dispositions." Salzberg adds:

> The practice of equanimity is learning deeply what it means to let go.
> The four boundless states that we call the brahma-viharas or divine abodes culminate with equanimity. In Pali . . . upekkha . . . means "balance," and its characteristic is to arrest the mind before it falls into extremes. Equanimity is a spacious stillness of the mind, a radiant calm that allows us to be present fully with all the different changing experiences that constitute our world and our lives.

If *upekkha* qualifies as a high form of appreciation-love, much like Hesse's "undemanding love," Nhat Hanh shows us how it is union-love as well:

Upeksha [the Sanskrit equivalent of *"upekkha"*] has the mark called *samatajnana*, "the wisdom of equality," the ability to see everyone as equal, not discriminating between ourselves and others. In a conflict, even though we are deeply concerned, we remain impartial, able to love and to understand both sides. We shed all discrimination and prejudice, and remove all boundaries between ourselves and others. As long as we see ourselves as the one who loves and the other as the one who is loved, as long as we value ourselves more than others or see ourselves as different from others, we do not have true equanimity. We have to put ourselves "into the other person's skin" and become one with him if we want to understand and truly love him. When that happens, there is no "self" and no "other."[14]

This passage is not easy to understand; spiritual teachings can be opaque to those who have not engaged deeply in the practices that engender them. Particularly puzzling is the idea of removing "all boundaries between ourselves and others." Like Irving Singer, I find it difficult to believe this happens. Perhaps Nhat Hanh is engaging in hyperbole when he denies any distinction between self and other, or maybe what he says is true on one level of discourse while, from another, boundaries remain. If so, he has not given us the whole story. The following passage from the twentieth-century Japanese philosopher Kitaro Nishida may shed some light on Nhat Hanh's meaning:

When we are absorbed in something the self loves . . . we are almost totally unconscious. We forget the self, and at this point an incomprehensible power beyond the self functions alone in all of its majesty; there is neither subject nor object, but only the true union of subject and object. Moreover, at this time knowledge in itself is love and love in itself is knowledge.[15]

It is not the oneness of absolute identity that Nishida has in mind but the self-forgetfulness of someone fully absorbed in what he or she is doing. Self-identity is not thereby annihilated so much as it is set aside for the period of engrossment. It seems to me the Buddhist should not say (as does the Advaitan Vedantist) that there are no boundaries at all (on the grounds that all division, all particularity, is illusion and only Atman/Brahman is Real), but rather that individual beings are not independently separate existences. Interdependent beings are not, after all, identical beings.

Nhat Hanh's remarks about union are fascinating in another way, also, for he envisions a union-love with full detachment. This Buddhist conception of union is not a yearning for some perhaps unattainable future state, but the unqualified acceptance of the reality already at hand. Here we find not a trace of the tension that so often exists between appreciation-love and union-love. Indeed, the Buddhist perspective seems to be that this kind of union and this kind of appreciation are indistinguishable from one another.

Nhat Hanh's comments on equality are also significant, especially in light of an experience related by Salzberg. When she was studying *metta* in Burma, her teacher, U Pandita, presented her with the following problem: "Suppose," he asked, "you were walking in the forest with your benefactor, your friend, your neutral person, and your enemy. Bandits come up and demand that you choose one person in your group to be sacrificed. Which one would you choose to die?" Salzberg looked deep into her heart and had to admit that she could not choose. Her teacher then pressed her: shouldn't she choose her enemy; shouldn't she choose herself? He seemed to be pushing especially hard for the second answer, so tempting to those from a culture in which Christianity is the dominant religion. But finally she said, simply: "I can't see any difference between myself and any of the others." He nodded in response and she left his room.[16]

In this Buddhist theory, we find a wonderful coalescence of the three elements of love that has been our subject. In our more personal loves such as romance, friendship, and marriage, all three factors are usually present as well, though not with such perfect harmony, leaving room for the disruptive forces of possessiveness, jealousy, resentment, envy. Yet even in these more personal relationships, when we truly appreciate the one we love, all three loves may work together nearly as harmoniously. After much talk about a nonnormative approach to "love," we end with a norm—it is the detachment inherent in the higher forms of appreciation-love that serves most to keep our loves healthy and vital.

Notes

1. An earlier version of this chapter was published under the title "The Meaning of 'Love'," in *Philosophy and Theology* 2.5 (May 1988): disk supplement 1.

2. All these sentences employ "love" as a verb but there are also noun uses, and to these can be added the adverbial and adjectival uses "lovingly," "loving," and "lovable." In this discussion all of the latter will be treated as if they were derivable from the verb usage.

3. "In love" is sometimes used in these cases as well, presumably because of the passionate nature of the attachment.

4. In the psychological literature on love this similarity between romantic love and addiction is well known. See, for example, Stanton Peele's *Love and Addiction* (New York: Signet Books, 1975).

5. I am indebted to James Munz for suggesting this simple and convenient locution.

6. See Irving Singer, *Plato to Luther*, vol. 1 of *The Nature of Love*, 2nd edition (Chicago: University of Chicago Press, 1984), pp. 3–22, and elsewhere throughout his many books on love.

7. 1 John 3:18–19. All references to the Bible are to *The New English Bible* (Oxford: Oxford University Press, 1961).

8. 1 Corinthians 13:3, italics added.

9. Quoted in Gene Outka's *Agape: An Ethical Analysis* (New Haven: Yale University Press, 1972), p. 126 n. 7. Author's italics.

10. Immanuel Kant, *The Doctrine of Virtue*, pt. 2 of *The Metaphysics of Morals*, trans. Mary J. Gregor (New York: Harper Torchbooks, 1964), p. 62 [400] (author's italics).

11. Immanuel Kant, *Foundations of the Metaphysics of Morals*, trans. Lewis White Beck (New York: Library of Liberal Arts, 1959), pp. 15–16 [399] (italics added).

12. Kant, *Doctrine of Virtue*, pp. 62–63 [401–2] (author's italics).

13. Immanuel Kant, *Critique of Practical Reason*, trans. Lewis White Beck (New York: Library of Liberal Arts, 1956), p. 85 [83].

14. Saint Thomas Aquinas, *Summa Theologica*, pt. 1, Q. 20 art. 1, in *Basic Writings of Saint Thomas Aquinas*, vol. 1, ed. Anton C. Pegis (New York: Random House, 1945), p. 216.

15. It is possible that some forms of union-love (such as the distorted forms discussed in Chapter 8) might be increased rather than diminished by fear of the loved.

16. It might be argued that love and hatred do not really have the same object, on the grounds that interpersonal love must always be of the person, while hatred has as its object some objectified idea of the person. This is an interesting argument, but it presupposes a normative notion of "love," specifically, that love can never be directed toward an objectified construction of its object. (A discussion of the difference between normative and descriptive approaches to analyzing "love" follows.)

17. This distinction was suggested to me by James Munz.

18. Martin Buber, *Between Man and Man*, trans. Ronald Gregor Smith (Boston: Beacon Press, 1955), p. 203.

19. See, for example, Robert C. Solomon's *The Passions* (Garden City, N.J.: Anchor Press/Doubleday, 1976).

20. Robert J. Sternberg, *The Triangle of Love: Intimacy, Passion, Commitment* (New York: Basic Books, 1987), pp. 3, ix.

21. I may have unconsciously borrowed the expression "appreciation-love," with a slight alteration, from C. S. Lewis, *The Four Loves* (New York: Harcourt Brace Jovanovich, 1960), pp. 25–33. Lewis's exact expression is "appreciative love." My analysis of the phenomenon, however, is substantially different from his.

22. Given the thesis that love's nature is threefold, it might be urged that love is not a single concept at all, but three concepts. No doubt it would be more exact to speak of love as a concept that embraces three subconcepts. However, to avoid the fussiness of having to distinguish between concepts and sub-concepts, both "love" and the names of each of its three principal varieties will be refered to throughout as concepts. (I am indebted to Joel Marks for pointing out the need for this discussion of whether love is one concept or three.)

23. In Ashley Montagu, ed., *The Practice of Love* (Englewood Cliffs, N.J.: Prentice-Hall, 1975), pp. 5–16 (both quotations p. 7, author's italics).

24. Ibid., p. 15.

25. M. Scott Peck, *The Road Less Traveled: A New Psychology of Love, Traditional Values and Spiritual Growth* (New York: Simon and Schuster, 1978), p. 89.

26. Nathaniel Branden, *The Psychology of Romantic Love* (New York: Bantam Books, 1981), p. 82 and passim; first quote p. 13 (author's italics); second quote, p. 92.

CHAPTER 2

1. This synonymy or near synonymy of "care" and "care-love" applies only to verb uses of "care." As a noun, "care" has a range of meanings quite its own—"worry," "anxiety," "grief," "affliction," "bother," "heed," "apprehension," "trouble," "mental pain," "close attention," and so on. "Love," when used as a noun, is not a synonym for any of these.

2. Milton Mayeroff, On Caring (New York: Harper and Row, 1971), pp. 39–40, 12.

3. Nel Noddings, Caring: A Feminine Approach to Ethics and Moral Education (Berkeley and Los Angeles: University of California Press, 1984), p. 68.

4. The fact that the union of identification lies behind care-love does not mean that care-love presupposes union-love, for the latter is not so much union itself as the desire for union. Caring presupposes union in the sense of identification with its object but does not pursue union as its goal.

5. Mayeroff, On Caring, p. 5; Noddings, Caring, pp. 24, 30 (quotation).

6. Mayeroff, On Caring, pp. 41–42 (author's italics); Noddings, Caring, p. 30.

7. Mayeroff, On Caring, p. 1.

8. Aristotle, Nicomachean Ethics 8.1156b.9–10 and 31–32.

9. Instrumental-care-love need not, in principle, be self-interested. A man might conceivably care for his mother-in-law instrumentally, as a way to care for his wife. Such non-self-interested instrumental caring is at least a logical possibility.

10. Neera Kapur Badhwar makes much the same point with respect to the love of persons. See "Friends as Ends in Themselves," in Alan Soble, ed., Eros, Agape, and Philia: Readings in the Philosophy of Love (New York: Paragon House, 1989), pp. 178–80.

11. Augustine, On Christian Doctrine, trans. D. W. Robertson, Jr. (Indianapolis: Library of Liberal Arts, 1958), III.x.16, p. 88.

12. Augustine, Contra Julianum haeresis Pelagianae defensorem libri sex, 4.iii.33, excerpted in An Augustine Synthesis, arranged by Erich Przywara (New York: Harper and Row, 1958), p. 346 (italics added); Augustine, On Christian Doctrine I.xxii.20, p. 18 (italics added).

13. Augustine, On Christian Doctrine I.xxii.21, p. 19 (long quote); Augustine, De moribus Ecclesiae catholicae et de moribus Manichaeorum libri duo, 26, cited in John Burnaby, Amor Dei: A Study of the Religion of St. Augustine (London: Hodder and Stoughton, 1938), p. 131.

14. Burnaby, Amor Dei, p. 134, citing Augustine, Sermones, 60.

15. Burnaby, Amor Dei, p. 130; Burnaby, Amor Dei, p. 121, citing Augustine, Epistolae, 155; Oliver O'Donovan, The Problem of Self-Love in St. Augustine (New Haven: Yale University Press, 1980), p. 116.

16. J. Baird Callicott, In Defense of the Land Ethic: Essays in Environmental Philosophy (Albany: State University of New York Press, 1989), p. 114.

17. Mayeroff, *On Caring*, p. 2.

18. The term "altruism" is used here to denote merely the presence of other-regarding interest. An altruistic act need not be free of self-interest; it is simply not fully reducible to it. A more thorough defense of altruism can be found in Lawrence A. Blum, *Friendship, Altruism and Morality* (London: Routledge and Kegan Paul, 1980).

19. Mayeroff, *On Caring*, pp. 47, 48 (author's italics).

20. Caesar Vallejo, "Agape," trans. John Knoepfle, in *Neruda and Vallejo: Selected Poems*, ed. Robert Bly (Boston: Beacon Press, 1971), p. 195.

21. William Shakespeare, Sonnet 116, *Shakespeare's Sonnets*, ed. Edward Bliss Reed (New Haven: Yale University Press, 1923), p. 58.

22. There may be some exceptions to this. Someone might, for example, respond to all of reality with a single, unconditional Yes, affirming everything just as it is. But probably such loves either are of short duration or are maintained only under conditions of regular spiritual practice and, as such, may not be entirely natural. Moreover, love so universal and all-embracing is more likely appreciation-love rather than care-love.

23. "A Marriage," in Robert Creeley, *The Collected Poems of Robert Creeley, 1945–1975* (Berkeley: University of California Press, 1982), p. 170.

24. The expression "neighbor love" is preferable to "agape" because, as used in the New Testament, "agape" has a wider meaning. In addition to love for the neighbor, it refers to God's love for us, our love for God, and sometimes also to a more preferential love between members of the Christian brotherhood. The word "charity" might also be used. However, since it is the cognate of *"caritas,"* the Latin translation of "agape" employed in the *Vulgate*, it is best avoided for the same reason. Nonetheless, in modern English, "charity" and "neighbor love" tend to be used interchangeably.

25. Noddings, *Caring*, pp. 18, 29, 90 (long quote).

26. Ibid., 90; Sister Agnes quoted in Desmond Doig, *Mother Teresa: Her People and Her Work* (San Francisco: Harper and Row, 1976), p. 155.

27. Mother Teresa can be seen in action in the documentary film *Mother Teresa*, directed by Ann Petrie and Jeanette Petrie (Windsor Home Entertainment Video Presentation, 1986). For a balanced biography see Anne Sebba, *Mother Teresa: Beyond the Image* (New York: Doubleday, 1997).

CHAPTER 3

1. Rainer Maria Rilke, in *Rilke on Love and Other Difficulties*, ed. and trans. John J. L. Mood (New York: W. W. Norton, 1975), pp. 27–28 (author's italics).

2. I owe the latter insight to my friend and fellow Rilke lover Rita De-Bruyne, with whom I once taught an honors course on romantic love. The relationship between Rilke's life and his views on love has been discussed recently by William Gass in his article, "Throw the Emptiness Out of Your

Arms: Rilke's Doctrine of Nonpossessive Love," in *The Philosophy of (Erotic) Love*, ed. Robert C. Solomon and Kathleen M. Higgins (Lawrence: University Press of Kansas, 1991), pp. 451–66. Then again, perhaps it was merely a requirement of Rilke's particular poetic genius that he distance himself from all intimate relations, including that with his only child.

3. Martin Heidegger, *Being and Time*, trans. John Macquarrie and Edward Robinson (New York: Harper and Row, 1962), p. 308.

4. Robert C. Solomon, *Love: Emotion, Myth and Metaphor* (New York: Anchor Press/Doubleday, 1981), and *About Love: Reinventing Romance for Our Times* (New York: Simon and Schuster, 1988). These books are sometimes exasperating because of a lack of consistency and clarity in his arguments, positions, and central concepts. It seems doubtful that a philosopher of Solomon's stature could have written these books for his fellow professionals. In the earlier work he refers to his effort as "overly playful," "irresponsible," and "not always consistent" (*Love*, p. xvii). Thus it may be inappropriate to scrutinize these works as if they were academic monographs. Nonetheless Solomon does offer a theory of love, and a theory which is both intrinsically interesting and germane to our investigation of union-love. We shall, therefore, examine his views carefully and critically.

5. Solomon, *About Love*, pp. 27 (quote), 15, 38–39; Solomon, *Love*, pp. 3–11.

6. Irving Singer, *The Modern World*, vol. 3 of *The Nature of Love* (Chicago: University of Chicago Press, 1987), p. 406; Solomon, *About Love*, pp. 64, 24.

7. Solomon, *About Love*, pp. 193, 195, 198.

8. Solomon, "The Virtue of (Erotic) Love," reprinted in Solomon and Higgins, eds., *The Philosophy of (Erotic) Love*, pp. 492–518. In this article, published the same year as *About Love*, he identifies love with the urge for shared identity and eschews the other two more problematic formulations. This work is more carefully reasoned than either of the two books cited above and contains an excellent analysis of Romantic love in the historical sense, that is, as the particular idealization of sexual love introduced into Western culture by the Romantics. Unfortunately, it is of little use in analyzing his notion of shared identity because its discussion of that concept is too brief.

9. Solomon, *About Love*, pp. 196, 201, 207 (author's italics).

10. William Shakespeare, *Romeo and Juliet*, act 2, scene 1 (ed. Richard Hosley [New Haven: Yale University Press, 1954], pp. 37–38).

11. Solomon, *About Love*, p. 251 (quote), see also p. 198, and *Love*, p. 268.

12. Ethel Spector Person, *Dreams of Love and Fateful Encounters: The Power of Romantic Passion* (New York: W. W. Norton, 1988), pp. 137–61.

13. Solomon, *About Love*, p. 65.

14. My former student Dianne Pfizenmayer first called my attention to this fact.

15. Seeing the "we" as an additional identity to the "I" is the path taken by Robert Nozick in his chapter on love in *The Examined Life: Philosophical Meditations* (New York: Simon and Schuster, 1989), pp. 68–86.

16. Solomon, *About Love*, pp. 199–200 (long quote; author's italics), 223 (author's italics).

17. Ibid., p. 224.

18. Solomon, *Love*, p. 151.

19. Singer, *Modern World*, p. 410.

20. Robert Bly, "A Third Body," in *Loving a Woman in Two Worlds* (New York: Harper and Row, 1985), p. 19.

21. Person, *Dreams of Love*, pp. 137 (author's italics), 138.

22. Ibid., pp. 146–47.

23. Ibid., p. 139.

24. J. F. M. Hunter, *Thinking about Sex and Love*, cited in Alan Soble, *The Structure of Love* (New Haven: Yale University Press, 1990), p. 178.

25. Nozick, *The Examined Life*, p. 68 (author's italics).

26. Ibid., p. 73 (author's italics).

27. Ibid., pp. 70, 71, 72, 72.

28. I am thinking of human relationships outside the family. According to a widely held spiritual view of marriage, each person's love for the divine has priority over love for the partner. Seen in this way, the couple is united not only in their love for one another but in their shared love for the divine, which, far from competing with their love for each other, anchors or grounds it.

CHAPTER 4

1. C. G. Jung, *Mysterioum Coniunctionis: An Inquiry into the Separation and Synthesis of Psychic Opposites in Alchemy*, trans. R. F. C. Hall (New York: Pantheon Books, 1963), p. 407.

2. Plato, *Symposium*, trans. Benjamin Jowett (Indianapolis: Bobbs-Merrill, 1948), 191a. I use the Jowett translation for the literary quality of these beautiful passages.

3. Ibid., 191a, 192a–93a (long quote).

4. Richard Wagner, *Tristan and Isolde*, trans. Stewart Robb (New York: E. P. Dutton, 1965), p. 93.

5. Johann Wolfgang von Goethe, "The Holy Longing," trans. Robert Bly, in *The News of the Universe: Poems of Twofold Consciousness*, ed. Robert Bly (San Francisco: Sierra Club Books, 1980), p. 70.

6. Denis de Rougemont, *Love in the Western World*, trans. Montgomery Beligion, revised and augmented edition (Princeton, N.J.: Princeton University Press, 1983), pp. 42–46.

7. Margaret S. Mahler, Fred Pine, and Anni Bergman, *The Psychological Birth of the Human Infant: Symbiosis and Individuation* (New York: Basic Books, 1975), p. 44.

8. Martin S. Bergman, *The Anatomy of Loving: The Story of Man's Quest to Know What Love Is* (New York: Columbia University Press, 1987), p. 262.

9. Harville Hendrix has written an excellent account of how adult relationships recapitulate the relationships of childhood in *Getting the Love You Want: A Guide for Couples* (New York: Henry Holt, 1988) and *Keeping the Love You Find: A Guide for Singles* (New York: Pocket Books, 1992). Despite the popular self-help titles and formats of these books, Hendrix's theory is a sophisticated account of how we select romantic partners written from the perspective of personal psychology. Nonetheless, personal psychology provides only part of the story.

10. Sigmund Freud, *Three Essays on Sexuality*, cited in Bergman, *Anatomy of Loving*, p. 159.

11. The expression is from Martin Buber, *I and Thou*, trans. Walter Kaufmann (New York: Charles Scribner's Sons, 1970), pp. 76.

12. Erich Fromm, *The Art of Loving* (New York: Harper and Row, 1956), p. 7.

13. He used the expression at a lecture delivered, I believe, at the U. N. in 1962.

14. Ibid., pp. 8, 8, 9.

15. Ibid., pp. 19–20.

16. Ibid., pp. 20–21 (author's italics).

17. See, for example, Fritjof Capra's *The Tao of Physics: An Exploration of the Parallels between Modern Physics and Eastern Mysticism*, 2nd edition (Boston: Shambhala, New Science Library, 1985), pp. 68–69; Moris Berman, *The Reenchantment of the World* (Ithaca, N.Y.: Cornell University Press, 1981), pp. 15–24.

18. Aldous Huxley, *The Perennial Philosophy* (New York: Harper and Row, 1944), p. vii.

19. Buber, *I and Thou*, pp. 76–77.

20. Ken Wilber, *Sex, Ecology, Spirituality: The Spirit of Evolution* (Boston: Shambhala, 1995), pp. 206–7 (author's italics). Much the same point is made by Mircia Eliade: "It would be a gross error to regard this supreme reintegration as a mere regression to primordial nondistrinction." *Yoga: Immortality and Freedom*, 2nd edition, trans. Willard R. Trusk (Princeton, N.J.: Princeton University Press), p. 99.

21. See Robert K. C. Forman, *The Problem of Pure Consciousness: Mysticism and Philosophy* (New York: Oxford University Press, 1990).

22. Evelyn Underhill, *Mysticism: A Study in the Nature and Development of Man's Spiritual Consciousness* (New York: E. P. Dutton, 1961), p. 89.

23. Cited in Morton Hunt, *The Natural History of Love*, revised and updated edition (New York: Anchor Books Doubleday, 1994), p. 115.

24. Dante Alighieri, "The First Canzone," chapter 19 in *Dante's Vita Nuova*, trans. Mark Musa (Bloomington: Indiana University Press, 1973), p. 33 (quotation); Maurice Valency, *In Praise of Love: An Introduction to the*

Love-Poetry of the Renaissance (New York: Octagon Books, 1975), p. 271.

25. Vladimir Solovyov, *The Meaning of Love*, trans. Jane Marshal, revisions by Thomas R. Beyer, Jr. (Great Britain: Lindisfarne Press, 1985), pp. 45, 51 (long quotation)

26. George L. Kline, "Solovyov, Vladimir Sergeyevich," in *The Encyclopedia of Philosophy*, ed. Paul Edwards (New York: Macmillan and Free Press, 1967), vol. 7, p. 492.

27. Solovyov, *Meaning of Love*, pp. 41, 42 (author's italics).

28. Solovyov, *Meaning of Love*, pp. 42 (author's italics), 43–44 (long quote; author's italics), 83.

29. Peck, *The Road Less Traveled*, pp. 92 (quote), 93. In fairness to Peck, it is not clear whether his expression "the myth of romantic love" refers to the phenomenon of romantic love itself, which he clearly holds in very low regard, or to some specific myth concerning it. He seems to begin with the latter meaning in mind, but by the end of the section appears to intend the former.

30. Francesco Alberoni, *Falling in Love*, trans. Lawrence Benuti (New York: Random House, 1983), p. 69.

31. Person, *Dreams of Love*, pp. 24–25.

32. Williams's theory of romantic love can be found in his many novels, and in his Dante studies, *The Figure of Beatrice: A Study in Dante* (New York: Noonday Press, a subsidiary of Farrar, Straus and Cudahy, 1961) and *Religion and Love in Dante* (Westminster: Dacre Press, 1941). Katharine S. Shideler sums up Williams's perspective in *The Theology of Romantic Love: A Study in the Writings of Charles Williams* (New York: Harper and Brothers, 1962).

33. Hendrix, *Getting the Love You Want*, pp. 3–85.

34. Robert A. Johnson, *We: Understanding the Psychology of Romantic Love* (New York: Harper and Row, 1983), pp. 195, 197.

35. It is technically more correct to speak of the lovers as being "in" the archetypes than the archetypes "in" the lovers.

36. One Jungian analyst who understands the role of archetypes in romantic love more in the fashion just suggested is John R. Haule, in *Divine Madness: Archetypes of Romantic Love* (Boston: Shambhala, 1990).

37. John Welwood, *The Journey of the Heart: Intimate Relationships and the Path of Love* (New York: HarperCollins, 1990), offers a nonsectarian account of how romantic love can serve spiritual love. See also Stephen Levine and Ondrea Levine, *Embracing the Beloved: Relationship as a Path of Awakening* (New York: Anchor Books, 1995), and Deepak Chopra, *The Path to Love: Renewing the Power of Spirit in Your Life* (New York: Harmony Books, 1997).

38. Paul Tillich, *The Dynamics of Faith* (New York: Harper Torchbooks, 1957), p. 42.

39. There is considerable doubt among modern New Testament scholars as to whether Paul was in fact the author of the Epistle to the Ephesians. See for example, Norman Perrin and Dennis C. Duling, *The New Testament: An Introduction*, 2nd edition (New York: Harcourt Brace Jovanovich, 1974), p.

207. The Epistle to the Ephesians certainly contrasts markedly with what we find on the same topic in 1 Corinthians 7.

40. A thorough scriptural and theological defense of such a reading can be found in Derrick Sherwin Bailey, *The Mystery of Love and Marriage: A Study in the Theology of Sexual Relation* (Westport, Conn.: Greenwood Press, 1977), pp. 43–124.

41. Buber, *I and Thou*, pt. 3. Jelaluddin Rumi, *Open Secret: Versions of Rumi*, trans. John Moyne and Coleman Barks (Putney, Vt.: Threshold Books, 1984), quatrain no. 1246.

CHAPTER 5

1. Jean Houston, *The Search for the Beloved: Journeys in Sacred Psychology* (Los Angles: Jeremy P. Tarcher, 1987), p. 134.

2. Singer, *Plato to Luther*, p. 4.

3. Singer, *Modern World*, pp. 390, 391.

4. Singer, *Plato to Luther*, p. 5 (author's italics).

5. Singer, *Modern World*, p. 391 (quote); Singer, *Plato to Luther*, pp. 3, 12 (quote).

6. Singer, *Plato to Luther*, p. 19.

7. Ibid., p. 15 (author's italics).

8. Ibid., p. 16 (author's italics).

9. Annie Dillard, *The Living* (New York: HarperCollins, 1992), p. 269.

10. Wilber, *Sex, Ecology, Spirituality*, pp. 16–21, 35–40.

11. Singer, *Plato to Luther*, p. 14.

12. Ibid., p. 21.

13. L. A. Kosman, "Platonic Love," reprinted in Soble, *Eros, Agape, and Philia*, p. 162.

14. Singer, *Plato to Luther*, p. 5; Singer, *Modern World*, p. 391 (last two quotes; author's italics).

15. Singer, *Plato to Luther*, p. 6; Singer, *Modern World*, p. 404; Irving Singer, "A Reply to My Critics and Friendly Commentators," in *The Nature and Pursuit of Love: The Philosophy of Irving Singer*, ed. David Goicoechea (Amherst, N.Y.: Prometheus Books, 1995), p. 335.

16. Singer, "A Reply to My Critics," p. 330.

17. Singer, *Plato to Luther*, p. 5; Singer, "A Reply to My Critics," pp. 391–92.

18. Nygren, Anders, *Agape and Eros*, trans. Philip S. Watson (Chicago: University of Chicago Press, 1982), pp. 146–59.

19. Singer, "A Reply to My Critics," p. 330 (author's italics).

20. Singer, *Modern World*, p. 393; Irving Singer, *The Pursuit of Love* (Baltimore: Johns Hopkins University Press, 1994), p. 108.

21. Singer, *Modern World*, pp. 391, 396.

22. The point is made again in Singer, "A Reply to My Critics," p. 325;

the same shift in emphasis continues in Singer, *Pursuit of Love*.

23. Singer, *Modern World*, p. 393.

24. Singer, *Pursuit of Love*, p. 4.

25. See ibid., p. 3, for example.

CHAPTER 6

1. Alice Walker, *The Color Purple* (New York: Washington Square Press, 1983), p. 178; Rainer Maria Rilke, *Selected Poems of Rainer Maria Rilke*, trans. Robert Bly (New York: Harper and Row, 1981), p. 207.

2. Hermann Hesse, "Concerning the Soul," in *My Belief: Essays on Life and Art*, ed. Theodore Ziolkowski, trans. Denver Lindley (New York: Farrar, Straus and Giroux, 1974), pp. 37–38.

3. Plato, *Symposium*, 211b.

4. See, for example, Gregory Vlastos, "The Individual as an Object of Love in Plato," in *Platonic Studies*, 2nd edition (Princeton, N.J.: Princeton University Press, 1981), pp. 3–42; Singer, *Plato to Luther*, pp. 84–85.

5. These are properties—sometimes called tertiary or metaphorical properties—of the music, not characteristics of the composer. Haydn's works could legitimately be described as optimistic even if biographical research should demonstrate that the composer himself was not.

6. The expression "shared history" has been widely used in recent philosophical literature on love. Unfortunately, I do not know whom to credit for using it first.

7. Nygren, *Agape and Eros*, p. 244 and passim, pp. 146–49, 218.

8. Ibid., pp. 77, 78.

9. Ibid., pp. 78, 75.

10. Neera Kapur Badhwar, "Friends as Ends in Themselves," in Soble, *Eros, Agape, and Philia*, p. 172 (both quotes).

11. Ibid. (author's italics).

CHAPTER 7

1. Hesse, "Concerning the Soul," p. 37.

2. William R. Jankowiak and Edward F. Fisher, "A Cross-Cultural Perspective on Romantic Love," *Ethnology* 31.20 (April 1992): 150 (quotation); William Jankowiak, ed., *Romantic Passion: A Universal Experience?* (New York: Columbia University Press, 1995), pp. 4–5.

3. Sydney L. W. Mellen, *The Evolution of Love* (Oxford: W. H. Freeman, 1981), pp. 136–64.

4. A summary of much of this research can be found in Diane Ackerman, *A Natural History of Love* (New York: Random House, 1994), pp. 139–74, and Anthony Walsh, *The Science of Love: Understanding Love and Its Effects on Mind and Body* (Buffalo, N.Y.: Prometheus Books, 1991).

5. William J. Goode, "The Theoretical Importance of Love," in Montagu, *The Practice of Love*, pp. 135, 125.

6. T. S. Eliot, "The Hollow Men," in *The Complete Poems and Plays, 1909–1950* (New York: Harcourt, Brace, 1930), pp. 58–59.

CHAPTER 8

1. Jill Tweedie, *In the Name of Love* (New York: Pantheon Books, 1979), p. 52 (ellipses in original).

2. Ibid., p. 54 (author's italics).

3. Germaine Greer, *The Female Eunuch* (New York: McGraw-Hill, 1970), p. 157.

4. Lewis, *Four Loves*, pp. 17–18 (de Rougemont, p. 17).

5. Ibid., pp. 19.

6. Ibid., 11–12, 19–20 (long quote).

7. Regine Pernoud, *Heloise and Abelard*, trans. Peter Wiles (New York: Stein and Day, 1973), pp. 232–33 (italics added). For our purposes, it matters not whether the historical Heloise actually wrote this and the other letters ascribed to her.

8. Barbara Stoller Miller, trans., *The Bhagavad-Gita* (New York: Bantam Books, 1986), 18.2, p. 143.

9. Lewis, *Four Loves*, pp. 19–20.

10. Greer, *The Female Eunuch*, p. 157.

11. James F. Masterson, *The Search for the Real Self: Unmasking the Personality Disorders of Our Age* (New York: Free Press, 1988), pp. 110, 122.

12. John Galsworthy, *The Forsyte Saga* (New York: Charles Scribner's Sons, 1922), pp. 259, 264.

13. Gottfried von Strassburg, *Tristan*, trans. A. T. Hatto (New York: Penguin Books, 1960), p. 195.

14. Wally Lamb, *I Know This Much Is True* (New York: HarperCollins, 1998).

15. Lao Tzu, *The Way of Lao Tzu*, trans. Wing-Tsit Chan (Indianapolis: Bobbs-Merrill, 1963), p. 97.

16. Robert Creeley, "The Wife," in Creeley, *Collected Poems of Robert Creeley*, p. 170.

EPILOGUE

1. Bhadantacariya Buddhaghosa, *The Path of Purification*, trans. Bhikkhu Nanamoli, 5th edition (Kandy, Sri Lanka: Buddhist Publication Society, 1991), IX 8, p. 289.

2. Quotations are from A. C. Graham, *Disputers of the Tao: Philosophical Argument in Ancient China* (La Salle, Ill.: Open Court, 1989), p. 41; David L. Hall and Roger T. Ames, *Thinking through Confucius* (Albany, N.Y.: State University of New York Press, 1987), p. 121.

3. Quoted in Thich Nhat Hanh, *Teachings of Love* (Berkeley, Calif.: Parallax Press, 1997), p. 1.

4. Ibid., p. 5.

5. Sharon Salzberg, *Loving Kindness: The Revolutionary Art of Happiness* (Boston: Shambhala, 1997), p. 139.

6. Nhat Hanh, *Teachings of Love*, p. 3.

7. Salzberg, *Loving Kindness*, pp. 87–88.

8. Thich Nhat Nanh, "Please Call Me by My True Names," in *Call Me by My True Names: The Collected Poems of Thich Nhat Nanh* (Berkeley: Parallax Press, 1999), pp. 72–73.

9. Quoted in Nhat Hanh, *Teachings of Love*, p. 46.

10. Buddhaghosa is cited from Harvey B. Aronson, *Love and Sympathy in Theravada Buddhism* (Delhi: Motilal Banarsidass, 1980), p. 5.

11. Salzberg, *Loving Kindness*, pp. 121, 124, 126.

12. Ibid., p. 129 (all quotations).

13. Ibid., p. 130; Sam Keen, *To Love and Be Loved* (New York: Bantam Books, 1997), pp. 42–43.

14. Aronson, *Love and Sympathy*, p. 89; Salzberg, *Loving Kindness*, pp. 138–39; Hesse, "Concerning the Soul," p. 38; Nhat Hanh, *Teachings of Love*, p. 8.

15. Kitaro Nishida, *An Inquiry into the Good*, trans. Masao Abe and Christopher Ives (New Haven: Yale University Press, 1990), pp. 174–75.

16. Salzberg, *Loving Kindness*, pp. 37–38.

Works Cited

Ackerman, Diane. *A Natural History of Love.* New York: Random House, 1994.

Alberoni, Francesco. *Falling in Love.* Translated by Lawrence Benuti. New York: Random House, 1983.

Aquinas, St. Thomas. *Summa Theologica.* Vol. 1 of *Basic Writings of Saint Thomas Aquinas,* edited by Anton C. Pegis. New York: Random House, 1945.

Aristotle. *Nicomachean Ethics.* Translated by Martin Ostwald. Indianapolis: Bobbs-Merrill, 1962.

Aronson, Harvey B. *Love and Sympathy in Theravada Buddhism.* Delhi: Motilal Banarsidass, 1980.

Augustine. *Contra Julianum haeresis Pelagianae defensorem libri sex.* Excerpted in *An Augustine Synthesis,* arranged by Erich Przywara, p. 346. New York: Harper and Row, 1958.

———. *On Christian Doctrine.* Translated by D. W. Robertson, Jr. Indianapolis: Library of Liberal Arts, 1958.

Badhwar, Neera Kapur. "Friends as Ends in Themselves." In *Eros, Agape, and Philia: Readings in the Philosophy of Love,* edited by Alan Soble, pp. 165–87. New York: Paragon House, 1989.

Bailey, Derrick Sherwin. *The Mystery of Love and Marriage: A Study of Sexual Relation.* Westport, Conn.: Greenwood Press, 1977.

Bergman, Martin S. *The Anatomy of Loving: The Story of Man's Quest to Know What Love Is.* New York: Columbia University Press, 1987.

Berman, Moris. *The Reenchantment of the World.* Ithaca, N.Y.: Cornell University Press, 1981.

Blum, Lawrence A. *Friendship, Altruism and Morality.* London: Routledge and Kegan Paul, 1980.

Bly, Robert. *Loving a Woman in Two Worlds.* New York: Harper and Row, 1985.

Branden, Nathaniel. *The Psychology of Romantic Love*. New York: Bantam Books, 1981.

Buber, Martin. *Between Man and Man*. Boston: Beacon Press, 1955.

Buber, Martin. *I and Thou*. Translated by Walter Kaufmann. New York: Charles Scribner's Sons, 1970.

Buddhaghosa, Bhadantacariya. *The Path of Purification*. Translated by Bhikkhu Ñānamoli. 5th edition. Kandy, Sri Lanka: Buddhist Publication Society, 1991.

Burnaby, John. *Amor Dei: A Study of the Religion of St. Augustine*. London: Hodder and Stoughton, 1938.

Callicott, J. Baird. *In Defense of the Land Ethic: Essays in Environmental Philosophy*. Albany: State University of New York Press, 1989.

Capra, Fritjof. *The Tao of Physics: An Exploration of the Parallels between Modern Physics and Eastern Mysticism*. 2nd edition. Boston: Shambhala, New Science Library, 1985.

Chopra, Deepak. *The Path to Love: Renewing the Power of Spirit in Your Life*. New York: Harmony Books, 1997.

Creeley, Robert. *The Collected Poems of Robert Creeley, 1945–1975*. Berkeley: Univesity of California Press, 1982

Dante Alighieri. *Dante's Vita Nuova*. Translated by Mark Musa. Bloomington: Indiana University Press, 1973.

Dillard, Annie. *The Living*. New York: HarperCollins, 1992.

Doig, Desmond. *Mother Teresa: Her People and Her Work*. San Francisco: Harper and Row, 1976.

Eliade, Mircia. *Yoga: Immortality and Freedom*. 2nd edition. Translated by Willard R. Trask. Princeton, N.J.: Princeton University Press, 1969.

Eliot, T. S. *The Complete Poems and Plays, 1909–1950*. New York: Harcourt, Brace, 1930.

Forman, Robert K. C. *The Problem of Pure Consciousness: Mysticism and Philosophy*. New York: Oxford University Press, 1990.

Fromm, Erich. *The Art of Loving*. New York: Harper and Row, 1956.

Galsworthy, John. *The Forsyte Saga*. New York: Charles Scribner's Sons, 1922.

Gass, William. "Throw the Emptiness Out of Your Arms: Rilke's Doctrine of Nonpossessive Love." In *The Philosophy of (Erotic) Love*, edited by Robert C. Solomon and Kathleen M. Higgins, pp. 451–66. Lawrence: University of Kansas Press, 1991.

Goethe, Johann Wolfgang von. "The Holy Longing." Translated by Robert Bly. In *The News of the Universe: Poems of Twofold Consciousness*, edited by Robert Bly, p. 70. San Francisco: Sierra Club Books, 1980.

Goode, William J. "The Theoretical Importance of Love." In *The Practice of Love*, edited by Ashley Montagu, pp. 120–35. Englewood Cliffs, N.J.: Prentice-Hall, 1975.

Graham, A. C. *Disputers of the Tao: Philosophical Argument in Ancient China*. La Salle, Ill.: Open Court, 1989.

Greer, Germaine. *The Female Eunuch.* New York: McGraw-Hill, 1970.

Hall, David L., and Roger T. Ames. *Thinking through Confucius.* Albany, N.Y.: State University of New York Press, 1987.

Haule, John R. *Divine Madness: Archetypes of Romantic Love.* Boston: Shambhala, 1990.

Heidegger, Martin. *Being and Time.* Translated by John Macquarrie and Edward Robinson. New York: Harper & Row, 1962.

Hendrix, Harville. *Getting the Love You Want: A Guide for Couples.* New York: Henry Holt, 1988.

————. *Keeping the Love You Find: A Guide for Singles.* New York: Pocket Books, 1992.

Hesse, Hermann. "Concerning the Soul." In *My Belief: Essays on Life and Art,* edited by Theodore Ziolkowski, translated by Denver Lindley, pp. 37–45. New York: Farrar, Straus and Giroux, 1974.

Houston, Jean. *The Search for the Beloved: Journeys in Sacred Psychology.* Los Angles: Jeremy P. Tarcher, 1987.

Huxley, Aldous. *The Perennial Philosophy.* New York: Harper and Row, 1944.

Jankowiak, William, ed. "Editor's introduction." In *Romantic Passion: A Universal Experience?* pp. 1–19. New York: Columbia University Press, 1995.

Jankowiak, William R., and Edward F. Fisher. "A Cross-Cultural Perspective on Romantic Love." *Ethnology* 31.20 (April 1992): 149–55.

Johnson, Robert A. *We: Understanding the Psychology of Romantic Love.* New York: Harper and Row, 1983.

Jung, C. G. *Mysterioum Coniunctionis: An Inquiry into the Separation and Synthesis of Psychic Opposites in Alchemy.* Translated by R. F. C. Hall. New York: Pantheon Books, 1963.

Kant, Immanuel. *Critique of Practical Reason.* Translated by Lewis White Beck. New York: Library of Liberal Arts, 1956.

————. *The Doctrine of Virtue.* Part 2 of *The Metaphysics of Morals,* translated by Mary J. Gregor. New York: Harper Torchbooks, 1964.

————. *Foundations of the Metaphysics of Morals.* Translated by Lewis White Beck. New York: Library of Liberal Arts, 1959.

Keen, Sam. *To Love and Be Loved.* New York: Bantam Books, 1997.

Kline, George L. "Solovyov, Vladimir Sergeyevich." In *The Encyclopedia of Philosophy,* edited by Paul Edwards, vol. 7, pp. 491–93. New York: Macmillan and Free Press, 1967.

Kosman, L. A. "Platonic Love." In *Eros, Agape, and Philia: Readings in the Philosophy of Love,* edited by Alan Soble. New York: Paragon House, 1989.

Lamb, Wally. *I Know This Much Is True.* New York: HarperCollins, 1998.

Lao Tzu. *The Way of Lao Tzu.* Translated by Wing-Tsit Chan. Indianapolis: Bobbs-Merrill, 1963.

Levine, Stephen, and Ondrea Levine. *Embracing the Beloved: Relationship as a Path of Awakening.* New York: Anchor Books, 1995.

Lewis, C. S. *The Four Loves*. New York: Harcourt Brace Jovanovich, 1960.

Mahler, Margaret S., Fred Pine, and Anni Bergman. *The Psychological Birth of the Human Infant: Symbiosis and Individuation*. New York: Basic Books, 1975.

Masterson, James F. *The Search for the Real Self: Unmasking the Personality Disorders of Our Age*. New York: Free Press, 1988.

Mayeroff, Milton. *On Caring*. New York: Harper and Row, 1971.

Mellen, Sydney L. W. *The Evolution of Love*. Oxford: W. H. Freeman, 1981.

Miller, Barbara Stoller, trans. *The Bhagavad-Gita*. New York: Bantam Books, 1986.

Montagu, Ashley. "A Scientist Looks at Love." In *The Practice of Love*, edited by Ashley Montagu. Englewood Cliffs, N.J.: Prentice-Hall, 1975.

Neruda, Pablo. "Agape." Translated by John Knoepfle. In *Neruda and Vallejo: Selected Poems*, edited by Robert Bly, p. 195. Boston: Beacon Press, 1971.

The New English Bible. Oxford: Oxford University Press, 1961.

Nhat Hanh, Thich. *Call Me by My True Names: The Collected Poems of Thich Nhat Hanh*. Berkeley, Calif.: Parallax Press, 1999.

———. *Teachings of Love*. Berkeley, Calif.: Parallax Press, 1997.

Nishida, Kitaro. *An Inquiry into the Good*. Translated by Masao Abe and Christopher Ives. New Haven: Yale University Press, 1990.

Noddings, Nel. *Caring: A Feminine Approach to Ethics and Moral Education*. Berkeley and Los Angeles: University of California Press, 1984.

Nozick, Robert. *The Examined Life: Philosophical Meditations*. New York: Simon and Schuster, 1989.

Nygren, Anders. *Agape and Eros*. Translated by Philip S. Watson. Chicago: University of Chicago Press, 1982.

O'Donovan, Oliver. *The Problem of Self-Love in St. Augustine*. New Haven: Yale University Press, 1980.

Outka, Gene. *Agape: An Ethical Analysis*. New Haven: Yale University Press, 1972.

Peck, M. Scott. *The Road Less Traveled: A New Psychology of Love, Traditional Values and Spiritual Growth*. New York: Simon and Schuster, 1978.

Peele, Stanton. *Love and Addiction*. New York: Signet Books, 1975.

Pernoud, Regine. *Heloise and Abelard*. Translated by Peter Wiles. New York: Stein and Day, 1973.

Perrin, Norman, and Dennis C. Duling. *The New Testament: An Introduction*. 2nd edition. New York: Harcourt Brace Jovanovich, 1974.

Person, Ethel Spector. *Dreams of Love and Fateful Encounters: The Power of Romantic Passion*. New York: W. W. Norton, 1988.

Petrie, Ann, and Jeanette Petrie, directors. *Mother Teresa*. Windsor Home Entertainment Video Presentation, 1986.

Plato. *Symposium*. Translated by Benjamin Jowett. Indianapolis: Bobbs-Merrill, 1948.

Radice, Betty, trans. *The Letters of Abelard and Heloise*. New York: Penguin Books, 1974.

Rilke, Rainer Maria. *Rilke on Love and Other Difficulties*. Edited and translated by John J. L. Mood. New York: W. W. Norton, 1975.

———. *Selected Poems of Rainer Maria Rilke*. Translated by Robert Bly. New York: Harper and Row, 1981.

Rougemont, Denis de. *Love in the Western World*. Translated by Montgomery Beligion. Revised, augmented edition. Princeton, N.J.: Princeton University Press, 1983.

Rumi, Jelaluddin. *Open Secret: Versions of Rumi*. Translated by John Moyne and Coleman Barks. Putney, Vt.: Threshold Books, 1984.

Salzberg, Sharon. *Loving Kindness: The Revolutionary Art of Happiness*. Boston: Shambhala, 1997.

Sebba, Anne. *Mother Teresa: Beyond the Image*. Newport: Doubleday, 1997.

Shakespeare, William. *Romeo and Juliet*. Revised edition. Edited by Richard Hosley. New Haven: Yale University Press, 1954.

———. *Shakespeare's Sonnets*. Edited by Edward Bliss Reed. New Haven: Yale University Press, 1923.

Shideler, Katharine S. *The Theology of Romantic Love: A Study in the Writings of Charles Williams*. New York: Harper and Brothers, 1962.

Singer, Irving. *The Modern World*. Vol. 3 of *The Nature of Love*. Chicago: University of Chicago Press, 1987.

———. *Plato to Luther*. Vol. 1 of *The Nature of Love*. 2nd edition. Chicago: University of Chicago Press, 1984.

———. *The Pursuit of Love*. Baltimore: Johns Hopkins University Press, 1994.

———. "A Reply to My Critics and Friendly Commentators." In *The Nature and Pursuit of Love: The Philosophy of Irving Singer*, edited by David Goicoechea. Amherst, N.Y.: Prometheus Books, 1995.

Soble, Alan. *The Structure of Love*. New Haven: Yale University Press, 1990.

Solomon, Robert C. *About Love: Reinventing Romance for Our Times*. New York: Simon and Schuster, 1988.

———. *Love: Emotion, Myth and Metaphor*. New York: Anchor Press/Doubleday, 1981.

———. *The Passions*. Garden City, N.J.: Anchor Press/Doubleday, 1976.

———. "The Virtue of (Erotic) Love." In *The Philosophy of (Erotic) Love*, edited by Robert C. Solomon and Kathleen M. Higgins, pp. 492–518. Lawrence: University Press of Kansas, 1991.

Solovyov, Vladimir. *The Meaning of Love*. Translated by Jane Marshal with substantial revisions by Thomas R. Beyer, Jr. Great Britain: Lindisfarne Press, 1985.

Sternberg, Robert J. *The Triangle of Love: Intimacy, Passion, Commitment*. New York: Basic Books, 1987.

Strassburg, Gottfried von. *Tristan*. Translated by A. T. Hatto. New York: Penguin Books, 1960.

Tillich, Paul. *The Dynamics of Faith.* New York: Harper Torchbooks, 1957.

Tweedie, Jill. *In the Name of Love.* New York: Pantheon Books, 1979.

Underhill, Evelyn. *Mysticism: A Study in the Nature and Development of Man's Spiritual Consciousness.* New York: E. P. Dutton, 1961.

Valency, Maurice. *In Praise of Love: An Introduction to the Love-Poetry of the Renaissance.* New York: Octagon Books, 1975.

Vlastos, Gregory. "The Individual as an Object of Love in Plato." In *Platonic Studies,* pp. 3–42. 2nd edition. Princeton, N.J.: Princeton University Press, 1981.

Wagner, Richard. *Tristan and Isolde.* Translated by Stewart Robb. New York: E. P. Dutton, 1965.

Walker, Alice. *The Color Purple.* New York: Washington Square Press, 1983.

Walsh, Anthony. *The Science of Love: Understanding Love and Its Effects on Mind and Body.* Buffalo, N.Y.: Prometheus Books, 1991.

Welwood, John. *The Journey of the Heart: Intimate Relationships and the Path of Love.* New York: HarperCollins, 1990.

Wilber, Ken. *Sex, Ecology, Spirituality: The Spirit of Evolution.* Boston: Shambhala, 1995.

Williams, Charles. *The Figure of Beatrice: A Study in Dante.* New York: Noonday Press, 1961.

———. *Religion and Love in Dante.* Westminster: Dacre Press, 1941.

Index